Hacking Capitalism

Routledge Research in Information Technology and Society

Hacking Capitalism

The Free and Open Source Software Movement

Johan Söderberg

Routledge
Taylor & Francis Group
New York   London

First published 2008
by Routledge
270 Madison Ave, New York, NY 10016

Simultaneously published in the UK
by Routledge
2 Park Square, Milton Park, Abingdon, Oxon OX14 4RN

Routledge is an imprint of the Taylor & Francis Group, an informa business

© 2008 Taylor & Francis

Typeset in 10 point Sabon by IBT Global.
Printed and bound in the United States of America on acid-free paper by IBT Global.

Library of Congress Cataloging in Publication Data
Söderberg, Johan, 1976-
Hacking capitalism : the free and open source software movement / Johan Söderberg.
p. cm. — (Routledge research in information technology and society ; 8)
Includes bibliographical references and index.
ISBN 978-0-415-95543-0 (hardback : alk. paper)
1. Open source software. 2. Computer software—Development—Social aspects.
I. Title.
QA76.76.S46S63 2007

005.3—dc22   2007018756

ISBN10: 0-415-95543-2 (hbk)
ISBN10: 0-203-93785-6 (ebk)

ISBN13: 978-0-415-95543-0 (hbk)
ISBN13: 978-0-203-93785-3 (ebk)

Contents

Acknowledgments

Quite a number of people have helped me in making this book. I would especially like to thank George Dafermos and Johan Lindgren who have supported me throughout the five years that I have been working on the project. I'm also indebted to Jenny Fornell and Mark Elam for extensive and constructive engagement with the manuscript. Other key contributions have been made by Stefan Merten, Alan Toner, Roul Victor, Graham Seaman, Olle Lindell, Tove Karlsson, Mathias Klang and Bo Göransson, and many more people, to whom I owe a great deal for various reasons. The book is dedicated to all of you out there who make something new and interesting with it.

Introduction

The rise of computing, like so many other things in the modern world, could arguably be dated to the aftermath of the French Revolution. The embryo of software programs is a system of perforated cards used in the Jacquard loom and first exhibited in 1801. Joseph-Marie Jacquard's device was the culmination of a series of inventions made during the course of the eighteenth century in the silk-weaving district of Lyon. The principal idea which he borrowed from earlier designs was the use of perforated cards to steer the loom. The movements of the machinery pushed the cards against a set of rods. If a card was pierced the rod could pass through the hole. Thus a thread in the loom was lifted which allowed the shuttle to slip under the thread. If there was no hole in the card, conversely, the rod bounced back and the thread stayed down. The presence or absence of a hole could be said to represent the binary 'one' and 'zero' of the modern computer. In this way, complex textile patterns were stored in stacks of perforated cards.[1] Up until then it had required great skill of the weaver to produce luxury fabric. Not only did the weavers stand to lose their mastery in the craft, the Jacquard loom could be operated by a single weaver without the help from a drawgirl. The prospect of getting rid of the drawgirl was a strong inducement to master weavers for supporting innovations in the field.[2] Hardly any family in the city of Lyon was unaffected by the invention. The weavers responded promptly by wrecking the machinery. They discovered that by throwing their wooden shoes into the loom the mechanics could grind to a halt. We might elect to call it the first Denial-of-Service attack in history.[3] Hence, the birth of sabotage was coincident with the first computerisation of a workplace.

Throughout the nineteenth century, the textile industry was a major theatre for labour conflicts over technological development. The most famous of these clashes, the Luddite uprising, consisted of combers, weavers, and artisans in the wool and cotton districts of central England. At the time of their rebellion, culminating in 1811–1813, the Jacquard loom had not yet been diffused to Great Britain.[4] Their attacks were mainly directed against the power loom and related, organisational changes in the trade. Luddites conducted nightly raids to smash woollen mills and weaving frames and their operations were commanded by the fictive 'general Ludd'. The English crown had to deploy 14,400 soldiers in the region to crush the nightly insurgencies. Quite remarkably, more English soldiers were mobilised against the Luddites than had been sent to Portugal four years earlier to face Napoleon's army.[5] Still, given the resources and logistics commanded by the state and the capitalists, the workers had very limited chances of stalling the emerging capitalist system. A crucial weakness of the Luddites was that they lacked the means to develop a positive technology of their own. They could only rely on their mastery of old technologies against the innovations and the scaled-up economy imposed by capital. Thus their struggle against capitalist restructuring acquired a quixotic flavour that has today become the meaning of the word 'luddite'.[6]

Given the technophobia commonly associated with "Luddism", it is not clear that Luddites would be the ancestors of techno-savvy hackers. Nevertheless, what they have in common is that they are both caught up in the web of the same social forces and are fighting on the same contested terrain, the terrain of technological development. The main difference between Luddites and hackers is that the latter have a technology of their own to draw upon. The universally applicable computer run on free software and connected to an open network, all of it achievements continuously fought for by the hacker movement, have in some respects levelled the playing field. Through the global communication network, hackers are matching the coordinating and logistic capabilities of state and capital. The conviviality of free software tools made by hackers is not accidental. It boils down to their alternative model for organising labour relations. The novel approach to arranging labour power is the chief accomplishment of the Free and Open Source Software (FOSS) movement. In hacking, a new subjectivity is taking shape around a voluntarily-entered, collective labour activity. When hackers are asked what motivates them to write free code or crack computer systems their answers are many and diverse. A recurrent theme, however, is the thrill they get from doing it.[7]

The notion of hackers becoming revolutionaries just for fun would have appealed to the eighteenth century poet Friedrich Schiller. Disappointed by the failure of the French Revolution, he sat down to ponder over how to make it work better the next time. Friedrich Schiller saw the 'aesthetic play-drive' as the primary force which could foster a more wholesome human being, whose maturing would also create and be able to sustain a post-revolutionary aesthetic state. Schiller meant that the aesthetic education of man was necessary to heal the rift within man caused by specialisation: "[. . .] If man is ever to solve the problem of politics in practice he will have to approach it through the problem of the aesthetic, because it is only through Beauty that man makes his way to Freedom."[8] Both adherers and critics of Schiller have pigeonholed him in the tradition of romanticism. Marxist scholars have followed Marx's lead and passed over Schiller's work as a footnote in German, idealist philosophy, with the notable exception of Herbert Marcuse. He declared his indebtedness to Schiller for his own life-long investigation into the liberating potential of aesthetics and play. Marcuse insisted on play as a constitutive practice on a parity with labour. The idea that play can be juxtaposed to labour invites us to reassess the legacy of Friedrich Schiller as a political theorist. His philosophy must be reclaimed from the fine art scene and high-browed poetry. It would do Schiller more justice if his words were applied to the politics that flow from the 'beauty of the baud' and the play with source code in the computer underground. Hackers are picking up the war cry of the rave movement: 'we make joy a crime against the state'. This strategy will be discussed under the label 'play struggle' and it is the main topic of the book. The term 'play struggle' is meant to highlight its closeness to labour struggle. Similar to labour in that it is a productive engagement with the world, play differs in that it is freely chosen and marked by a high degree of self-determination among the players. At its heart, the politics of play struggle consist in the distance it places between doing and the wage relation. Play is a showcase of how labour self-organises its constituent power outside the confines of market exchanges.

It is more than a little ironic, or perhaps, highly consistent with the dialectic dramaturgy of our tale, that this potential first arises in the field of computers—historically speaking the very antithesis of labour autonomy. A common thread runs through the perforated cards devised by Joseph-Marie Jacquard to deprive weavers of their craft skills, and the writings of Charles Babbage, the distinguished forerunner of modern computer science. He envisioned the world's first computer, the Difference Engine, and incorporated Jacquard's punched card system in his second attempt to build a computer, the Analytical Engine. These machines were intended to replace the personnel, at the time known as 'computers', who were then employed to calculate mathematical tables. In addition to figuring out the principles of computing, Charles Babbage was also a pioneer in writing management literature. In *On the Economy of Machinery and Manufactures*, published in 1832, he advised factory owners how to break up the labour process into simple tasks that could be operated by workers with the least possible skills. His deep understanding of technology did not fail him when assessing the expediency of machinery on the factory shop-floor: "One great advantage which we may derive from machinery is from the check which it affords against the inattention, the idleness, or the dishonesty of human agents."[9] Charles Babbage's words inadvertently point to the antagonistic relation between labour and capital that computing has grown out of. The computer makes the 'machinery check' against human agents surgical in its precision. Furthermore, software-mediated machinery checks are now being exported from the factory to the whole of society. Through so-called Digital Rights Management (DRM) technology, the behaviour of workers, consumers, and citizens are increasingly regulated by software code. And yet, human agents persist in haunting the computerised network—the spectre of hacking. Karl

Marx made a well-known allegory between class struggle and the mole. It disappears beneath the earth for long periods of time only to reappear again at an unexpected time and place. Capital's strategy to subdue labour conflicts with the help of computers has merely resulted in the mole respawning on the Internet. Charles Babbage's endorsement of machinery as an instrument of control is diametrically opposed to how a hacker from the Hacksec group assesses the great advantage which we may derive from technology: "So that is the spirit, to be able to take these components, to put together the technology that was the domain of governments and let the average person figure out how to use it. That is the promise of technology."[10]

The promise of hacking is that, by making computer technology accessible to non-professionals, it undermines the social division of labour as the regulating principle for technological development. In plain language; corporate and government institutions have lost their monopoly over research and development. Concrete political results follow when decisions over technology are spread to the crowd. The mass defection from the intellectual property regime in filesharing networks, the challenge posed by the free operating system GNU/Linux to Microsoft's dominance over the computer desktop, and the circumvention of state censorship and surveillance on the Internet, all hinges on that the tools and skills for writing software code are made public by hackers. This emancipatory promise contradicts the association regularly made between cyber-politics and high-tech libertarianism. Occasionally, the potential of hacking for progressive and radical change has been acknowledged by public commentators. Readers of *New York Times* were in 2000 confronted with the proclamation that the communist republic now existed on the Internet. The journalist Andrew Sullivan made the point that dot-communism had sprung up in the heartland of the most advanced capitalist country of our time, America, just as Karl Marx had predicted.[11] Similar ideas have been voiced by the Slovenian philosopher Slavoj Zizek. In a paraphrase of Vladimir Lenin's famous endorsement of electricity, Zizek exclaimed in a tongue-in-cheek way that: "socialism = free access to the Internet + power to the soviets".[12] Sporadic allusions to the Communist Manifesto are frequent within the computer underground. The most renowned insider drawing parallels between Marx and the hacker movement is Eben Moglen. As the *pro bono* general counsellor for the *Free Software Foundation*, an influential organisation of hackers, Eben Moglen is well accustomed with the practice of hacking. He is convinced that capitalism will be brought to an end by a tide out of which hacking is just the first wave.[13]

Concurrently, a range of antagonists to the FOSS movement have accused GNU/Linux and alternative licensing schemes for being un-American, subversive, and cancerous. Bill Gates caused a stir when he declared that the people behind FOSS and Creative Commons licenses are "new modern-day sort of communists".[14] Even as multinational corporations move in to invest in hacker projects, they do so while adding to the rebellious gloss.

For example, when IBM vowed to spend one billion dollars on FOSS development, they marketed their engagement in a public campaign under the slogan: "Peace, Love, and Linux".[15] In this case, as in many others, the revolutionary vocabulary is merely an eye-catching stunt. Opponents to the FOSS movement apply the same rhetoric to brand free software as Stalinist. No deeper understanding can be expected to come out of either endeavour. But there are also serious attempts at using critical theory to analyse the emergence of free software. The *Oekonux* project based in Germany, the Dutch group behind the *Nettime* discussion list, the predominantly Spanish-speaking initiative by the name *Hipatia*, and hack-labs in Italy and South-America, are examples of such outposts of reflection taking place inside the hacker movement. In the traditional left and in academia, however, indifference and suspicion has been the predominant attitude towards the subject for a long time.[16] Throughout the 1980s and 1990s, Marxist scholars were preoccupied with demystifying the hype and vulgarities of post-industrial ideology along with the many unwarranted hopes attached to information technology and the Internet. Progressive academics are concerned about electronic surveillance, intensified deskilling of workers due to microprocessors, big business lobbying for global enforcement of intellectual property monopolies, and the Goliath-scale acquisitions by media corporations, all trends that seem to run in consistency with Internet's roots in Pentagon's nuclear warfare strategies.[17]

Though these perils are very real, this book will investigate capital's bid to commodify information from a different angle altogether. The intellectual property regime should be read out as a 'negative shape' in the struggle of hackers. Hacking is the prism through which the book moves outwards to look at intellectual property law, computing, the Internet, and networked capitalism in general. It is the restructuring of capitalism and the possibilities of resisting it that is at the heart of our discussion. The critique is made from a general Marxist theoretical viewpoint. Marxism, however, is as multifaceted as the many topics covered in the book. In order to unravel hacking, we have to cross through innumerable controversies, positions and hypothesises, taking issue with camps within the hacker movement, reformist intellectual property critics, mainstream economic theory, as well as different schools within the Marxist discipline. This is reflected in the style of writing. The argument in the book progresses by a method of triangulation, closing in on the subject from several different angles at once. Few self-described hackers will recognise themselves in the result. Were we to judge the politics of hacking by an opinion poll among the members of the hacker movement, we might have concluded that hacking is predominantly apolitical, and possibly with a bent towards liberal, voluntarist ideology. Appearance to the contrary, however, this book is not a historical nor an anthropological account of the FOSS community. What concerns us is not 'hackers as a noun' but 'hacking as a verb'. Hacking is emancipatory to the extent that it opens up the practice of intervening in computer technology to a non-denumerable mass of people. In other words, its politics consist in that decisions about technological development escape from being confined to either professions or/and subcultures. This potential of hacking is set back not only by intellectual property law, knowledge monopolies, and black box designs, but also by identities excluding outsiders. The hacker movement is of interest in so far as it helps us to understand the practice of hacking. Our ambition is not, though, to explain the FOSS movement with Marxist theory, but to take hacking as a departing point when reviewing Marxist theory in relation to networked capitalism.

The controversy that has captivated Marxist scholarship in recent years is the standoff between followers of *Empire*, the post-modern, anti-capitalist best-seller by Michael Hardt and Antonio Negri, and traditionally oriented Marxists.[18] At stake is the question of how to revise Marxism and bring it back to the centre of public debate and scholarly thinking. It is a theme that will run in parallel throughout the book. The struggle of hackers provides a good reference point for casting new light on theoretical positions on labour, struggle, and technology. Some characteristics of the hacker movement are at odds with assumptions held in classic Marxism. The failure of hackers to conform to established classifications has surely contributed to their invisibility in labour theory up till now. The ideas advanced by Hardt and Negri, and, more generally, by the autonomist Marxist tradition to which they belong, are at times more successful in explaining the conflicts in the computer underground. In particular, FOSS developers challenge our concept of the nature of labour and the composition of the working class. A key note in this book, recurrent in the writings of many autonomous Marxists, is that the production process has left the direct site of production. There are no clear boundaries any longer between work time and leisure time, between the inside and outside of the factory, and between waged and volunteer labour. The FOSS development model is a parade example of how the labour process has been diffused to the whole of society. One consequence is that the subjective experience of the antagonist relation is muddled. Day-to-day events do not immediately translate into a sharp, bi-polar opposition between employer and employee. A programmer might freelance for a multinational company three days a week, spend two days as an entrepreneur of a FOSS start-up venture, and in the meantime he will be a user of software applications, all of which are activities that feed into the capitalist production apparatus. Given this diversity of labour, Antonio Negri's longstanding ambition to open up the category of the working class is a valid project. In the best case scenario, it might prevent us from foreclosing emerging, unfamiliar sites of exploitation and struggle. The latest attempt by him and Michael Hardt in redefining the proletariat is the notion of the multitude. They give priority to the multitude as an agent of change, a position otherwise held by the working class in Marxist theory. One complaint about *Empire* raised by its many critics is the failure of Hardt and Negri to explain who the 'multitude' really is. No satisfactory answer has been given by the two authors. For our purpose of analysing the hacker movement, we will instead borrow an idea Negri drafted during his years in prison. Back then he suggested that a 'social worker' had emerged in conjunction with a labour process dispersed to the whole of society. The social worker replaced the 'mass worker' of the Fordist factory as the dominant composition of the working class.[19] The concept of the social worker is preferable to the term multitude since it puts emphasis on the continuity with earlier forms of class struggle and industrial conflicts.

Another premise that the reader might recognise as an influence from autonomous Marxism is the stress placed on class struggle. This is particularly forthcoming in regard to a major sticking point in a book about hacking and information systems, namely; how to understand the role of technological development. Antonio Negri is representative of his tradition when he declares that innovations are capital's way of coping with working class resistance. It is a counter-intuitive thought that takes some time to get used to. Even so, the direction of causality proposed by Negri can be reasonably substantiated in the case of the computer underground. For instance, the architecture of the personal computer was more or less forced upon IBM by hobbyist computer enthusiasts. Putting emphasis on class struggle is an important corrective to the dejected image of capitalism as an overbearing juggernaut. This must not swing to the other extreme, however, where the 'pessimism of the will' is contrasted with an 'optimism of the intellect'. Negri sometimes lapses into wishful thinking and this is even more the case with John Holloway and the branch of Open Marxism to which he belongs. Though Holloway's influence on this study should be easily recognised, the book takes issue with his refusal to concede any ground to structural explanations. Thus the historical specificity of capitalism is lost, together with any direction of how to resist it.[20] Both Holloway and Negri are at pains to restore hope in anti-capitalist struggle but do so only by confining themselves to a very high level of abstraction. Once we take a concrete movement as the stepping stone for our speculations we can no longer disregard the limitations that intervene and co-produce their struggle. Returning to the example above, the dream of hobbyist computer enthusiasts to democratise the computer was realised at the price of an expanded market in consumer electronics. In the end, IBM benefited greatly from selling personal computers. It is hard to think that hardware hackers could have achieved their dream in any other way. Karl Marx struck a balance between agency and structure in an unsurpassable passage when he stated that men make their own history, but not under conditions of their own choosing.

The first chapter starts out with providing a background dossier on the struggle of hackers. This is necessary since the public only has previous knowledge of hackers from the biased reporting in mainstream media. But it would be foolish to try to sum up in print a field which changes so fast. The aim is therefore not to 'provide the dots' but to 'draw the lines'. Those lines run alongside two hundred years of labour struggle. With this perspective, the story of the hacker movement comes out very differently from how voices within the FOSS community present themselves. In particular, we must be more provisional when assessing the outcome of their endeavours. FOSS licenses might strengthen the position of labour by fostering open standards and free access to software tools. Capital's strategy of Taylorism is set back by such computer architecture. It is equally possible, however, that alternative development models involving volunteer labour are in alignment with a restructured, post-Fordist production process. An unfortunate side effect of free and open licenses might then be intensified exploitation of waged and voluntary labour. Some clues can be found by analysing FOSS business models with Marxist theory.

In the next chapter, the focus on the hacker movement is broadened, both theoretically and historically. Notions about the information age, which many hackers tend to draw from when conceptualising Internet-related issues, are contrasted with Marxist theory. It is argued that post-Fordist restructuring of the labour market provides a better backdrop against which we can assess the role of computer networks and digitalisation. This perspective calls into question many of the assumptions held in the computer underground, for instance, the willingness to attribute historical change to technology and the unique properties ascribed to information. Against those beliefs, it is contended that digitalisation originates in the antagonistic relation between labour and capital. Infinite reproducibility of digital information means the same thing as infinitely redundant labour. With a simple 'copy-and-paste', a given amount of objectified labour is instantly duplicated. Marxist theory suggests that this extreme form of automation in the computer sector forces capital to exploit living labour elsewhere in the economy. In the chapter it is proposed that the users have become a major source of surplus labour for capital. The enrolment of FOSS communities by corporations is part of a more general pattern in post-Fordist capitalism where audiences and users are 'put to work'.

The third chapter is concerned with the commodification of information, and, more to the point, the commodification of the labourers producing information. In the final analysis it is the freedom of living labour, not the freedom of information, which is our concern. Commodification of labour occurs when a subjectivity of individual authorship is fixated over the labour process. In his function as an author the individual puts his efforts into producing commodities for a market. But the fixation of individual authorship is constantly challenged. In mainstream media the violations against intellectual property on the Internet are typically framed as a consumer revolt. With this interpretation the main issue becomes the price of information content. We will argue that the surge of filesharing networks is part of a more radical upheaval. Defiance against copyright law, the advancement of an open technological platform, and the assertion of the right to share information freely, are rejections of the commodity form as such. The individual author is under threat to be dissolved into the anonymous, ambulant, and playful authorship of user collectives.

Chapter four moves on to look at hacking from the perspective of consumption and satisfaction of needs. The hacker movement, like other subcultures, is intimately related to the surge of a consumer-driven capitalism. It is argued that, on one hand, the provision of material needs has enabled people to engage in hacking, and, on the other hand, people are motivated to do so because of the dearth of non-material needs in consumer society. Boredom with commodity relations, both in work and in consumption, is the driving force. It is boredom that points beyond the endless game of conspicuous and semiotic consumption. A categorical renunciation of consumer society will not do, however, since the resistance draws its resources from the same society. Without markets in consumer electronics there would not be a hacker movement. Parallels can be drawn between hacking and the subversion of commercial messages and goods by consumers. Studies of consumer resistance are often associated with the tradition of cultural studies. Labour theoreticians have reproached the cultural studies' discipline for making too much out of the rebellion by consumers. They rightly insist that a serious challenge against capitalism can only be mounted from inside production. Our argument here is that interesting things start to happen when consumer goods are taken by users as the departing point of a new cycle of production. Crucially, this cycle of consumption-production is disjointed from capitalist circulation. User-centred production models stand a good chance of outdoing markets in the provision of social needs. The reason is simple; it was the failure of markets in satisfying those needs that motivated users to side-step market relations in the first place.

Thus we are led over to the topic of the fifth chapter, production. The case is made that the success of the FOSS development model over proprietary software development is an important cursor. It tells us about the inadequacy of capitalist relations in organising labour in the information sector. The justifications for property-based research find little support in economic history, it is contradicted by empirical data, and it cannot even be convincingly argued in theory. The shortcomings of the proprietary development model translate into advantages for user-centred innovation models based on less strict license schemes. A paradoxical series of events have brought about user empowerment. We trace it to the termination of craft skills inside the capitalist production process. Deskilling of employees has come full circle with the reskilling of non-employees. Tools and skills are cheapened and spread from the capitalist production site to the whole of society. Arguably, the means of production are being re-appropriated by the proletariat in this way. It should be kept in mind, however, that user-centred innovation models are enrolled in capital's valorisation process. Capital might have lost its monopoly over the means of software production, but it has other methods to discipline the 'user force'. It can rely on its control over circulation, and, if worst comes to the worst, fall back on the state.

The sixth chapter approaches hacking from the perspective of circulation. Our discussion connects back to the century-old dispute between market liberals and state socialists on the most efficient method for distributing resources in society. The advent of filesharing networks has actualised the question if there could be a third way of allocating information resources, different from both markets in information and state planning. That model might be called an information commons, or, what amounts to the same thing, a high-tech, anarchistic gift economy. Hackers have borrowed the concept of a gift economy from anthropology in order to describe the economic activities in the computer underground. It goes without saying that gift economies in tribal societies and the giving of information on the Internet are essentially different. On closer inspection, we will find that filesharing networks are hybrids that combine the impersonality of market exchange with the non-coerciveness of gift giving. It is thus we can envision a third method for allocating resources that lies beyond both markets and planning.

The final chapter returns to the core argument of the book, that hacking is a showcase of play struggle. This struggle is at its heart a reaction against alienation. However, the resistance of hackers looks nothing like the kind of struggle we know from industrial conflicts. Instead of confronting the wage relation heads on, in strikes, sabotages etc., it attacks alienated labour by circumventing it. A different labour relation is being invented in the play of FOSS developers. The utopian hopes of Friedrich Schiller and Herbert Marcuse are accentuated with the current development in the computer underground. The chapter reviews scholarly definitions of play, and calls attention to ludic forms of resistance against the factory discipline previously in history. The triviality commonly associated with play is owing to the fact that the activity is non-instrumental. In contrast, the development of technology is archetypical of instrumentality. The hacker movement has submitted the development of computer technology under a model determined by the play-drive. That can hardly be called trivial.

1 A Background of the Hacker Movement

THE HISTORY OF INTERNET

One could argue that cyberspace emerged in 1876 with the telephone. The Internet, as we presently know it, is commonly thought of as the merger of telephony and computers. Leading on from the Internet's heritage in telephony, Bruce Sterling light-heartedly proclaims that the first hackers were the boys employed as switchboard operators by the telephone companies. The boys played pranks while connecting customers and they were soon replaced with more reliable, female personnel.[1] This historical anecdote is in accordance with the portrayal of hacking as it comes across in mainstream media. Hacking is regularly reduced to an apolitical stunt of male, juvenile mischievousness, and, ultimately, it is framed as a control issue. In order to emphasise the political dimension of hacking, it is apt to outline a different 'mythical past' of hackers. This story too begins with the invention of the telephone. Graham Bell was not only a prominent inventor but also a forerunner in exercising his patent rights. The business model which his family built up around the patent was no less prophetic. Telephones were leased rather than sold to customers and the monopoly service was provided through a network of franchised subsidiaries. All in all, Graham Bell established one of the most controversial and longstanding monopolies in American twentieth century corporate history. When the communication infrastructure was built, the Bell Telephone Company concentrated on catering to urban dwellers while rural areas fell by the wayside. The telephone had its biggest impact on life in the countryside but it was not profitable for companies to connect distant farmhouses. Long before Bell's patent had expired, farmers began to construct their own telephone lines, sometimes using fence wire to pass the signal from one farm to the next. The movement spread rapidly in rural areas. The first telephone census made in 1902 counted more than 6000 small farmer lines and cooperatives. Over the years, the farmer lines were incorporated into the national dialling system.[2] The most direct parallel to those farmers today are community activists establishing gratis, wireless Internet access in their neighbourhoods. The farmers and hackers both demonstrate the ingeniousness of living labour, to route around constraints and to appropriate tools (even when it takes fence wire) for its own purposes. This interpretation is rather consistent with the original meaning of the term *hacking*. The word was first used by computer scientists in the 1950s to express approval of an ingenious and playful solution to a technical problem. These privileged few enjoyed a great amount of autonomy to do research and 'hack' while having access to very expensive equipment. After the end of the cold war, when computer equipment got cheaper while researchers lost some of their former autonomy, the joy of playing with computers was picked up by groups outside the institutions, by people calling themselves hackers. Though this book is mainly about the latter group, the story begins in the science laboratory. Readers that are familiar with the background of the Internet can skip ahead to the next heading.

If any time and place could be pinpointed as the springboard for the merger of computing and telephony, later to become the Internet, John Naughton suggests that it was the thriving experimental milieu at Massachusetts Institute of Technology (MIT) before and around the two World Wars.[3] When Vannevar Bush completed the first *Differential Analyser* in 1928, it was a massive compartment of gears and pressure cylinders. The machine was used for advanced equations in engineering projects and for calculating ballistic trajectories for the military. To build such a computer represented a huge investment affordable only to the biggest institutions. Despite the immense costs, the computer could only perform a limited set of operations and each calculation had to be hardwired into the machine. To give a significantly different instruction, or to correct a bug, meant to physically replace hardware components. The cost efficiency of computing resources would be vastly improved if computers were made more flexible. This required an architecture where the physical components were given an open-ended function so that more instructions could be provided in software code. Norbert Wiener, the founder of cybernetics, sketched on such a digital computer and his ideas were implemented towards the end of the Second World War. MIT scientists hoped for a deepened symbiosis between man and machine. By shortening the feedback loops between the computer and the user, they envisioned a computer that would function as a complement to the human brain. The computer could take care of intricate and monotonous calculations and leave the humans free to engage in innovative and associative exploration. This dream was held back by the computer design of the time. Batch-run computers were provided with a set of instructions which had to be completed in advance. The computer processed the instructions in one chunk without allowing for any human interruptions. If something went wrong the researcher had no choice but to rewrite the program and start all over from square one.

A solution to this awkwardness was found in an alternative design, time-sharing computers. The selling case for time-sharing computers was that several users could share the capacity of a single computer. It saved a very expensive resource, computer calculation time. Later on, the principle of time-sharing was extended beyond the confines of the computer box. It was extended from a number of users in one place sharing a single computer to many users in a wide area pooling and sharing their combined computer resources. This idea occurred to Bob Taylor who presided over Advanced Research Projects Agency (ARPA). The organisation had been set up in the aftermath of the launch of Sputnik. It was part of American policy to catch up with the Soviet Union in the race for technological supremacy. Bob Taylor realised that ARPA was in possession of a cacophony of computer terminals unable to exchange information with each other and that internal communication would be alleviated if these computers were linked together. His ambitious plan was stalled by the fact that the terminals had not been manufactured with the intent to speak to one another. Furthermore, the complexity of the system would grow exponentially with every new computer added to the cluster. To overcome these two problems, of incompatibility and complexity, ARPA researchers placed nodes in-between the terminals. The nodes consisted of small computers that served as network administrators, receiving and sending data, checking for errors and verifying that messages arrived at prescribed destinations. The nodes bridged the incompatibilities of end-user terminals in a decentralised fashion. By dispersing the intelligence to the edges of the network, rather than collecting information on the whole system in a server and guiding every intricate detail of the network from this centre, the problem of complexity was somewhat reduced. This end-to-end solution still remains basic to the architecture of the Internet.

The common notion that Internet originates in Pentagon is partly misleading. It is correct, though, that a theory on a networked mode of communication had been devised previously to ARPA's undertaking in an organisation affiliated with Pentagon. The individual behind this feat was Paul Baran and his employer was Research ANd Development (RAND).[4] Nuclear holocaust was the policy area of RAND's strategists. A major concern of theirs was the game-benefits of a nuclear first strike. A first strike, or an accident for that matter, could sever the connections running between the headquarters and the missile silos. The mere possibility of such an outcome created uncertainties and jeopardised the MAD (Mutual Assured Destruction) doctrine. A resilient communication system was therefore crucial to guarantee retaliation capacity. Vulnerability was located at the single line which carried the message: 'fire', or: 'hold fire'. Hence, the model envisioned by Paul Baran distanced itself as far as possible from a centralised communication infrastructure. In a network all the nodes are linked with their neighbours and there are several possible routes connecting any two destinations. Baran had the plan sketched out in 1962 but he ran into opposition from the phone company. AT&T was entrenched in analogue telecommunication technology and obstructed to build the infrastructure that Baran's system required. In analogue communication systems the sound waves are faithfully reproduced in a single stream running through the phone line. In a digital communication system, in contrast, the signal is translated into ones and zeroes and sent as a number of information packages. Once the data arrives at the destination, the packages are reassembled and put together so that it appears to the receiver as a continuous stream of sound. Baran's idea demanded a digital communication system where the signal was divided up in information packages and each package could decide individually for the best route to travel. If a channel was blocked the package could take a different route. Because of the resistance from AT&T, Paul Baran's plans were left in a drawer and he did not learn about the work in ARPA until much later.[5]

Towards the end of the 1960s, ARPA built the first computer-to-computer connection and named it ARPANET. It linked together a small selection of universities and military bases. For a long time it remained an exclusive system confined to the top academic and military echelons. Over the years, however, other networks began to crop up in the US and elsewhere. The Télétel service in France is the most well-known example, though less successful trials were made in England and Germany too. It was implemented by the French telephone company in 1982 after many years of testing. The terminals, known as Minitel, were handed out for free with the intention that they would replace the need for printed white page directories. Instead the users quickly found out how to communicate with each other through their Minitels. Most of the traffic was driven by conversations between users and by erotic bill boards, so called 'messageries roses'.[6] The Internet, the network of networks, took shape as these diverging net-clusters were joined together. To cope with a growing diversity of standards, Robert Kahn and Vint Cerf designed a system of gateways in the mid 1970s. The Transmission-Control-Protocol (TCP) and Internet Protocol (IP) links together and carries the traffic over the many networks of Internet.

The increased flexibility of computer hardware has allowed important advances in the utilisation of computers to be made solely on the level of software code. This in turn implies lower costs to innovate and thus less dependency on government or business support. UNIX is a landmark in the history of software development but it is also archetypical in that it partially emerged to the side of institutions.[7] The two enthusiasts responsible for UNIX, Ken Thompson and Dennis Ritchie, had been working on an operating system for Bell Laboratory, a subsidiary of AT&T, for some time. They had become disheartened and started their own, small-scale experiment to build an operating system. The hobby project was taken up in part to the side of, in part under the wings of, the American telephone company. UNIX rapidly grew in popularity and became so widely used by AT&T staff that the company eventually endorsed it. Moreover, it also became known among users outside the phone company. An anti-trust settlement in 1956 against AT&T was of utmost significance for the success of UNIX. As part of the settlement the phone company agreed not to enter the computer business. The AT&T was thus barred from selling UNIX or charging a higher tariff against computer transmissions running on its phone lines. Consequently, UNIX could be freely distributed and became widely popular in universities and in the private sector. John Naughton's explanation for the success of the operating system is instructive: "The main reason was that it was the only powerful operating system which could run on the kinds of inexpensive minicomputers university departments could afford. Because the source code was included, *and the AT&T licence included the right to alter the source and share changes with other licensees,* academics could tamper with it at will, tailoring it to the peculiar requirements of their sites."[8] It is logical that UNIX was designed to run on relatively inexpensive computers, since for most part it was developed on such computers by users with limited access to large-scale facilities. The same pattern is repeated once again when AT&T's original UNIX program metamorphoses into versions of BSD UNIX, and later inspires GNU/Linux. This time around the code was written on computers that were just-about affordable to individuals. Using personal computers to write software must have felt like an impediment at the time. And yet the accessibility of small computers was the key factor for the eventual success of operating systems like BSD UNIX and GNU/Linux. The point should be stressed since it highlights two important lessons. First, the success of this technology often stands in inversed relationship to the size of fixed capital (i.e. machinery and facilities) that is invested in it. Second, as a consequence, much computer technology has been advanced by enthusiasts who were, at least partially, independent of institutions and corporations. Users joined forces in a collaborative effort to improve UNIX, fix bugs, and make extensions, and to share the result with each other. The environment of sharing and mutual support was spurred in the early 1980s, thanks to the invention of a protocol for UNIX computers to share files with each other through the phone line. It facilitated community building and fostered values that foreboded later developments. With the option to connect computers over the telephone infrastructure, a cheaper and more accessible communication channel than ARPANET had been created. The stage was set for hackers to enter.

THE HISTORY OF THE COMPUTER UNDERGROUND

It is one of history's ironies that the roots of the Internet can be traced to two sources, U.S. Cold War institutions and the anti-war movement. The hacker community grew out of American universities in the 1960s. Bruce Sterling attributes the potent ideological hotbed of the computer underground to a side effect of the Vietnam War. Many youngsters then chose to enter college studies to avoid being sent into battle. Disposition for civil disobedience was reinforced by the communicating vessels between university drop-outs, peace activists, and hippies. The radicalism of students mixed with the academic cudos of researchers.[9] In the following decade, the mixture of hippie lifestyle and technological know-how was adopted by so-called Phone Phreaks, a subculture specialised in tapping phone lines and high-tech petty theft. Political self-awareness within the movement was propagated in the pioneer newsletter, *Youth International Party Line*. It was edited by Abbie Hoffman who started it in 1971. He saw the liberation of the means of communication as the first step towards a mass revolt. Two years later the newsletter was superseded by the *Technological American Party*. The new publication jettisoned most of the political ambitions of its predecessor and concentrated on circulating technical know-how. The forking of the fanzine epitomises two polarities within the movement, still in force today. On one side are activists motivated by ideology and on the other side are 'techies' who find satisfaction in mastering technology. Some techies have come to look unkindly upon the efforts by activists to politicise the movement. Techies tend to perceive 'hacktivists' as latecomers and outsiders claiming the hobby for their own purposes. The truth of the matter is that the sub-culture has always been deeply rooted in both traditions. Indeed, the hacker movement was more or less forked out of the New Left.[10] De-politicisation came later, mirroring general trends in society. In the aftermath of the clashes of 1968, the line of thought within the hippie and environmentalist move-ments changed. Rather than engaging in head-on confrontations with the system and the police, hopes were placed in the building of an alternative system. The leading thought was to develop small-is-beautiful, bottom-up, and decentralised technology. The personal computer fits into this picture. A central figure in advocating such an approach, with a foothold both in the environment movement and the embryonic hacker movement, was Stew-art Brand, publisher of the *Whole Earth Catalog*. Another key name in the philosophy of 'appropriate technology' was the industrial designer Victor Papanek. They denounced mass production in the same breath as they pro-vided blueprints for Do-It-Yourself technologies. The leading thought was that a 'better mousetrap' would win out against faulty industrial products on the merits of its technical qualities. Hackers show no less confidence in the superiority of Free/Open Source Software (FOSS) code and are assured of their victory over flawed, proprietary code. The historian of technology Langdon Winner was more sceptical when he wrote a few years after the Reagan administration had quenched the high spirit of 'appropriate tech-nology' campaigners.[11] The ease by which the government purged the pro-grams for appropriate technology is a sobering lesson of the raw power of the state. Winner complained that the thrust of the hippie and environ-mental movement had quickly been deflected inwards, into consumption of bohemian lifestyles and mysticism. His pessimistic account of the events is understandable but must be amended by the fact that he was unaware of the sprouting activity of phone phreaks and hackers at the time he wrote. The ideals of the appropriate technology movement jumped ship and thrived long after the zenith of the hippies and the environmentalists. This could be a precious reminder in a possible future when the hacker movement has faded and its heirs have not yet announced themselves. But it is also possible that the hacker movement proves itself to be more resilient than the New Left. A principal difference, though not the only one, is the motivational force behind hacking. The advocates of appropriate technology were led to experiment with Do-It-Yourself techniques as a deduction of their politics. Hackers, on the other hand, write code primarily for the sake of it, and politics flows from this playfulness.

Steven Levy writes about the hardware hackers gathering at the *Homebrew Computer Club* in the mid 1970s. His retrospect gives an account of the two, partially coinciding, partially inconsistent, sentiments expressed by the people involved. They were drawn together by the excitement of tinkering with electronics. Even so, the pleasure they experienced from hacking was tied up with a political vision and messianic hopes. By constructing a cheap and available computer able to 'run on the kitchen table', they set out to liberate computing from elite universities and from corporate and military headquarters. But persons with overtly political motives found themselves out of place. The initiator of the *Homebrew Computer Club*, Fred Moore, eventually dropped out, expressing disappointment with the lack of political awareness among club members. Reflecting on his departure, the activist and long-time moderator of the *Homebrew Computer Club*, Lee Felsenstein, suggested that Fred Moore got his politics wrong. The politics of the *Homebrew Computer Club* was the "propaganda of the deed" rather than "gestures of protest".[12] Indeed, what the hardware hackers accomplished from playing with electronic junk is impressive. The microprocessor had recently been invented by Intel and the company expected the item to be used in things like traffic light controllers. Hardware hackers thought differently. They combined Intel's microprocessor with spare parts and built small computers. Ed Robert's *Altair* marked a watershed in 1975. *Altair* was not the first hacker computer but it was the first computer built for small-scale sale that enjoyed some commercial success. Robert's market consisted exclusively of other hackers and radio amateurs. The purchaser had to assemble the parts painstakingly by himself. If the customer endured, he was rewarded with a completely useless gadget.[13] But within the cooperative milieu of the *Homebrew Computer Club*, improvements were rapidly made and many more prototypes followed. One model was *Apple*. It departed from the earlier designs in that it was somewhat user-friendly and had functions beyond just being a computer. Apple was a decisive step towards creating a consumer market larger than the cabal of hardware hackers. As demand for computers picked up, venture capitalists began to pay attention to the home computer market. The establishment of a proper industry for small computers was crowned by IBM's decision in 1981 to launch the *Personal Computer* (PC). It is true that the burgeoning economic opportunity in home computers led to a decline of idealism among the members of the *Homebrew Computer Club*. We are, however, equally justified to say that community norms disintegrated in response to the fulfilment of the original aims of the club. Hardware hackers succeeded in democratising computer resources. Up till that point, decision-making over computers had been concentrated in the hands of a few privileged, white-coated engineers who were in charge of mainframe computers. Workers detested these mechanical monsters and hackers hated them for much the same reason, mainframe computers were the embodiment of 'office despotism' in the 1960s and 1970s. By channelling their play-drive into computer building, hardware hackers forced the industry to embrace their dream of decentralised computing.

Techies are therefore right in insisting on the centrality of play over ideological zealousness. It is play (desire) which sets the hacker movement apart from the 'gestures of protest' of more traditional political organisations. The problem with an apolitical standpoint is rather that it does not stay clear of politics. When class consciousness has been evacuated, the void is colonised by right-wing, commonsensical ideology. Editorials in later issues of the *Technological American Party* expressed a strong libertarian conviction, a tradition which has been upheld by *Wired Magazine*. To get the blend of politics and pleasure right is a tightrope to walk. History indicates, however, that radicals can trust the outside world to intervene. The pure joy derived from comprehending and building systems is political in itself in a class society were power relations are mediated through black box designs. At its heart, hacking is a gut reaction against capital's strategy of taylorism. Even libertarian hackers inevitably partake in challenging capital's monopoly over technological development. That is not to say that political awareness is irrelevant. The point is rather that play triggers repercussion, and repercussion against play guarantees that class consciousness is passed on from generation to generation. This dynamic can be illustrated with the standpoint that information should be freely shared. The left, the right, and the supposedly apolitical, all rally behind this belief. Their demand boils down to something more than an opinion. As a matter of self-preservation, hackers cannot help but to work towards free information flows. Free access to software tools is a prerequisite for the existence of a hacker community. While the norm of sharing was a given in the academic setting of the 1950s and the 1960s, it is out-of-step with the growing market value of information today. It is unavoidable that this conviction will set the hacker movement on collision course with the establishment.

Two enclosures of software code at the beginning of the 1980s heralded the soaring economic and political stakes in information. It is telling that IBM, currently a close ally of the Open Source movement, was the chief propagator for enclosing software behind copyright law.[14] Japan's Ministry of International Trade and Industry (MITI) promoted in the early 1980s a *sui generis* intellectual property law on software. The suggested law provided 15 years of protection and provisioned compulsory licensing of software. A similar draft surfaced in the World Intellectual Property Organisation (WIPO) at the time. IBM was agonised by these proposals. Assisted by U.S. trade officials and supported by governments in Europe, IBM managed to submit software under the stricter terms of copyright law.[15] IBM's new-found romance with the Free and Open Source Software movement, which is for sure to be a short-lived one, is a consequence of its strategy in the 1980s backfiring. Microsoft got the upper hand over IBM from the introduction of strong software licenses. At about the same time, in 1982, AT&T was relieved from the anti-trust ruling, which had prevented the company from entering the computer business. The company soon began to enforce own-ership rights over UNIX. By then the operating system had been extended and rewritten many times over by students, scientists and enthusiasts col-laborating across institutions and corporations. The attempt by AT&T to privatise UNIX qualifies as one of the most notorious enclosures saluting the dawn of the 'information age'. It had a resolute impact on the collec-tive mindset of the programmers' community and fuelled their scepticism towards big corporations and the intellectual property regime. AT&T's bid to own UNIX demonstrated that copyright can be used to rob authors of their work, the very opposite of the ideological justification for the law. Hackers thus realised that the collective authorship of software develop-ers has to be shielded from the legal powers instituted in a single party by copyright law.

THE BIRTH OF THE GENERAL PUBLIC LICENSE

The politics of the hacker movement gravitate around the issue of public access to source code. Source code provides a list of instructions that can conveniently be read and modified by an engineer. Software released under Free and Open Source Software (FOSS) licenses are required to be published together with the source code. In proprietary software the source code is hidden away as unintelligible binary code. Binary code is the list of instruc-tions, represented as lines of ones and zeroes, as it is read and executed by the computer.[16] In addition to the technical obstacles, copyright law forbids users to read the code of proprietary software.

The most explicit vision of how public access to source code relates to social change is voiced by the Free Software Foundation. It was initiated by Richard Stallman as a response to the commercialisation of his own field of work.[17] The foundation has set itself the task of liberating computers from proprietary software code. To realise the dream of a computer run entirely on free code, the Free Software Foundation has since the mid 1980s produced non-proprietary software applications. The name of the software published by the foundation, 'GNU' is an acronym that stands for 'Gnu is Not Unix'. In addition to publishing GNU applications, the Free Software Foundation is the maintainer of the most widely used license in the com-puter underground, the General Public License (GPL).

The need for legal protection of shared work has been learned the hard way by hackers. Richard Stallman made the discovery when he was working with GNU Emacs, an application for editing source code. An Emac for UNIX had previously been written by another programmer, James Gosling. Initially, Gosling distributed his source code for free of charge and without restrictions. Richard Stallman incorporated bits of James Gosling's work into GNU Emacs. Later, James Gosling changed his mind and sold his copyright to UniPress. The company went after Richard Stallman and told him not to use the source code that was now had become theirs. That experience contributed to the creation of the General Public License. The nick-name for GPL is telling; '*Copyleft—All Rights Reversed*'. In Richard Stallman's own words: "Copyleft uses copyright law, but flips it over to serve the opposite purpose: instead of a means of privatising software, it becomes a means of keeping software free."[18]

Copyright automatically befalls the creator of a literary work. The author has the right to specify the terms under which her creation may be used. The copyright holder is nominally entitled to have her request enforced in court. The General Public License makes use of this flexibility in the law. It lists a number of conditions that protect the freedom of users. As long as these conditions are respected, anyone may access the program without asking for permission.[19] If a user violates the GPL agreement the freedoms granted by the license is voided and normal copyright law kicks in. Paradoxically, it is the copyright law that puts teeth in the free license. The General Public License is a free license in four regards. The user has the right to run a program for any purpose. He is allowed to study how a program works. It is up to him to distribute the program as he sees fit. And the user is free to alter the program and publish the modified version. It is a common misunderstanding that the General Public License forbids commercialism. On the contrary, it guarantees the freedom to use a program for any purpose, including commercial uses. In practice, however, the option to sell a copy is constrained by the same freedom of everyone else to give copies away for free. The GPL is not as innocent as many of its advocates make it out to be. As will be argued from a more theoretical angle in later chapters, the GPL directly intervenes in how private property works. Free licenses protect the collective efforts of an anonymous mass of developers from individual property grabs. Under the GPL, the creator inverts the individualising force of copyright by denouncing his individual rights and has these returned back to him as a collective right. He enjoys the collective right not to be excluded from a shared body of work. Private property, on the other hand, is nothing but the right of a single party to exclude all others. A fringe within the hacker movement, whose rejection of copyright law is absolute; objects to FOSS licenses for making concessions to the law. In general, those hackers who define themselves as free software developers tend to be more ambivalent towards copyright law. While politically minded filesharers and activists wish to abolish copyright altogether, such a move could actually be harmful to FOSS development. Nothing would then prevent companies from incorporating free source code into closed software lineages. Hackers could not do the same to companies since closed software is delivered as binary code. As a result, FOSS development would fall behind in the race for the technological edge. Radical critics thus end up in the company of those pro-business advocates who campaign for license schemes that facilitate the private appropriation of software commons. One provision in GPL states that the license must be passed on to derivative copies. In order to include a line of GPL in a software application, the entirety of that program must be licensed under GPL. Adversaries have labelled this characteristic as 'viral'. This so-called viral feature is designed to prevent the opposite, i.e. that strings of GPL code is subdued under proprietary licenses.[20]

At this point it is justified to ask: why would a company bother to abide to the terms of copyleft? And would a court care to enforce the Do-It-Yourself-licence? Ira Heffan tries to answer the question if the GPL would stand in court by comparing copyleft with shrinkwrap licenses. Shrinkwrap licenses were introduced by companies who sought a convenient way to define user rights of retail customers. The name 'shrinkwrap license' owes to the shrink-wrap plastic that surrounded boxes with computer disks. The terms of the license were visible through the plastic and the customer demonstrated her approval of the terms by breaking the seal. By extension, it is considered to be an equivalent 'demonstration of consent' when a user decides to open a software application after the terms have been displayed on the screen, a so-called 'clickwrap license'. Shrinkwrap license agreements claim protection under both contract law and copyright law. The restrictions to use that are specified in shrinkwrap licenses are no different in principle from those made in the GPL. Since shrinkwrap licenses have been acknowledged in courts, Heffran reasons the GPL is protected on the same merits.[21] The resilience of the GPL is indicated by the fact that the license is mostly respected despite legal uncertainties. Indeed, the legal deterrent is secondary to other considerations in support of GPL. Companies tempted to abuse the free license know that such a move would dishearten key employees. Of greater significance, companies recognise that it is often in their long-term interest to keep FOSS development free. It is preferable to managers that the code stays in an information commons rather than to risk that the software is monopolised by a competitor. Furthermore, the move to enclose a software development project is also a stoppage. In other words, it is to cut oneself off from a development flow that runs fastest in the open. In the long run, a firm could suffer more from losing out on the continuous improvements made by the community of developers, than could be gained in the short run from breaking the GPL agreement. It is in this way that Linus Torvalds, the originator of the Linux kernel, explains widespread compliance with GPL: "Somebody might [ignore the GPL] for awhile, but it is the people who actually honour the copyright, who feed back their changes to the kernel and have it improved, who are going to leg up. They'll be part of the process of upgrading the kernel. By contrast, people who don't honour the GPL will not be able to take advantage of the upgrades, and their customers will leave them." (*Torvalds*, 96–97) On the other hand, companies risk little and can maximise their immediate gains from secretly including GPL source code in their commercial development projects. Two major difficulties arise when attempting to uphold the GPL license. First, the violation must be detected. This can be tricky if the GPL code is sunken into a larger chunk of copyrighted, binary code. Second, the entitlement to assign and then enforce copyleft resides not with the Free Software Foundation. It stays with the original author of the violated code which can be a complication. Fear of an unfavourable court ruling has cautioned the Free Software Foundation in its confrontations with offenders. Negotiations and out-of-court settlements have usually followed when a firm was caught cheating. Even if negotiations end successfully with the firm eventually releasing the source code and pledging to respect GPL in the future, several months have passed and the commercial value of the software might already have been exploited. Thus, firms have an incentive to play a game of hiding its violation, and when discovered, delay settlement till the software has gone out-of-date. A free software development team in Germany working on a sub development project for GNU/Linux, decided to pursue violations all the way to court. In April 14th, 2004, a Munich district court granted the team a preliminary injunction against Sitecom Germany GmbH. Sitecom was banned from shipping their product unless the company agreed to comply with all obligations made in the GPL.[22]

Though the GPL seems to hold water when tried in the juridical system, new legal inventions are affecting the appliance of copyright. The expansion of patent rights to cover information processes has caused a stir in the free software movement. Previously, software has been protected as an artistic work under copyright law. In the US and Japan, patents on software have existed for a long time but it is now becoming a common practice among companies to enforce them. In EU a struggle has been ongoing for years over the introduction of European software patents. Software patents pose a threat to GPL because companies can follow copyright law and abide to the terms specified in the free license, while restricting access to the source code through patent law. While submitting to the letter of GPL the spirit is abused. Much the same can be done through Digital Rights Management technology. If a free software application is locked up behind a hardware design, having access to the source code and the manuals wont do users any good. The Free Software Foundation hopes to battle these developments in a third version of the GPL by adding conditions against software patents and Digital Rights Management technology. The updated version was released in 2007. However, the decision to adopt the changes suggested by the Free Software Foundation rests with stakeholders in the community. Many of them have objected that the new GPL is too restrictive and that the license will lose in relevance because of this. At the time of writing these issues are still under discussion.

THE HISTORY OF GNU/LINUX

In order to realise the dream of a computer run entirely on free software, the Free Software Foundation has produced a great deal of GNU software tools over the years. However, one crucial part kept missing out, the kernel. The kernel is the heart of an operating system and works like a bridge between the software and the hardware on a computer. Linus Torvalds filled the gap when he initiated the Linux project.[23] In 1991 Torvalds was studying computer science at Helsinki University, Finland. He got inspiration from another operating system, Minix, which had been written by Andrew Tanenbaum as an educational device. Where UNIX was made to be run on state-of-the-art machines owned by university departments, Minix was designed for personal computers, expensive but affordable to (middle class, western) individuals. Minix was shipped with its source code but had a restrictive license that limited the options to tamper with the program. Linus Torvalds studied the design of Minix and constructed his own kernel from scratch. Linux and Minix briefly competed for the hearts and minds of a small community of developers. The eventual triumph of Linux over Minix is explained by Linus Torvalds in part by technical niceties. However, he also admits to some technical weaknesses of Linux compared to the competitor. (*Torvalds*) In the end, the success of Linux over Minix owes not to technical but to social factors. The restrictive licence of Minix prevented users from improving the software. Andrew Tanenbaum's main concern was to keep Minix accessible and easy for students to learn from. Extending the program with more features would, from this perspective, just complicate matters. Linus Torvalds, in contrast, had made the decision from early on to license his work under the GPL license. Hence, everyone could rest assured that the Linux kernel would stay open for users.[24] The breakthrough for GNU/Linux came a few years down the road, again boiling down not to technical superiority, but to social relations of property and licensing.

When the telephone company AT&T begun to exercise ownership rights over the UNIX operating system, researchers at Berkeley University were enraged. They had contributed as much to the development of UNIX as the employees at AT&T had. Abandoning their long-time project was not an option. Instead of starting up anew from square one, like Richard Stallman and Linus Torvalds, they painstakingly removed the lines of UNIX code which had originated in AT&T. New lines were written to replace the old ones claimed by the telephone company. The result was named Network Release 1 and later Network Release 2. Berkeley sold the product while allowing the purchaser to do whatever he pleased with the software. Over the years the project forked into three versions; NetBSD, FreeBSD and OpenBSD. Many experienced co-developers were working on these releases at the time when Linus Torvalds, single-handedly, started up his garage project. From the outset, the scales weighted heavily in favour of any of the BSD UNIX projects. The promising future of BSD Unix came to a halt in a single blow. AT&T took notice of a company marketing a version of Network Release 2. AT&T sued Berkeley for infringement, since the university had licensed the product to the company. The case was brought up to trial in 1992. When the court case was settled eighteen months later, AT&T had to give up its claims over BSD UNIX. But the damage had already been done. Programmers shunned away from BSD UNIX during the court trial since they feared that their work might end up with AT&T. Suddenly, the Linux development team was flooded with programmers from across the Atlantic.

A lesson from the Linux tale is that the success of one forked project over another does not owe exclusively to its technical features. The history of technology is full of examples of inferior products surpassing more advanced competitors on the market. The schoolbook example is the battle between Betamax and VHS over the industrial standard in video cassette recording. Though the technological excellence of Betamax is widely recognised, VHS won out since the producer, JVC, could muscle the most support from content providers (Hollywood) and instil confidence among retailers and consumers. In short, it was the strength of one capital over another to tie strategic allegiances with other capitalists and to invest in marketing, which proved decisive for the outcome. The performance of the device itself was only of secondary importance. The novelty with free and open source software development is that the social factors determining the success of a fork are reversed. GNU/Linux won out over Minix and BSD Unix not because it was backed by the highest concentration of capital, but to the contrary, because under the GPL it had the *purest absence of private property relations*. This is true also when FOSS comes up against proprietary software. GNU/Linux is but one out of many successful FOSS development projects.

THE SUCCESS OF THE FREE AND OPEN SOURCE SOFTWARE MOVEMENT

A measure of the strength of the FOSS development model is given by the extent to which free software outdoes proprietary software in the marketplace. In this regard GNU/Linux has only been moderately successful. Although popular in academic settings and among corporate clients, very few ordinary users have switched to the free operating system. It is hard to reach end users since they value familiarity with the graphical interface higher than the technical performance of the program. Those FOSS applications that target administrative and specialised functions have therefore enjoyed the greatest diffusion. Apache is a software program for running web servers. As of January 2006 it held 70% of the market. The largest commercial competitor, Microsoft, had only 20% of the market. Other competitors were next to eradicated. A major boost for Apache came when IBM gave up its own in-house development project and endorsed the free server program instead.[25] Berkeley Internet Name Domain (BIND) is another software application that has become a standard in its niche. It translates domain names into IP-numbers. No less remarkable is the success of Sendmail. Though most ordinary computer users have never encountered it directly, Sendmail has for many years been the most commonly used program for managing e-mail traffic. The success-story of projects developed in the spirit of the FOSS model could also extend to the World Wide Web (www). Technically speaking www is not a software application but a protocol for websites and hyperlinks that makes it more convenient to navigate through the Internet. The idea of www first occurred to Tim Bernes-Lee when he was an employee at Conseil Européen pour la Recherche Nucléaire (CERN), a research centre for particle physics near Geneva. In the early 1990s the www was up-front against a rivalling system called Gopher. That system faced a swift end after the University of Minnesota, from where it had originated, announced their intent to charge a license fee for it. Even though the ownership claim was only partial and it was never fully implemented, the threat was enough to scare away users and developers. To be 'Gopherised' became a term describing the process when a software development project hits an evolutionary dead-end due to attempts by one part to enclose it. After the Gopher incident, CERN declared that the institute refrained from any claims of ownership over www in the future.[26]

Many attempts have been made to explain why the development model of hackers works so well, both by the people directly involved in it and more recently by social scientists. One of the most vocal insiders theorising about the hacker movement is Eric Raymond. In an influential article, *The Cathedral and the Bazaar,* he compares two opposing styles of software development. He contrasts the Cathedral model of conventional, centralised development with the Bazaar model of accessible, open development. The recurring reference of a software application built as a cathedral is Microsoft's Windows. However, FOSS projects that are written by a tightly knit group of developers who rarely accept contributions from outsiders also qualify as cathedrals. According to Raymond, Linux was the first large-scale project that demonstrated the efficiency of the opposite approach, the Bazaar model. In this model, anyone with Internet access and programming skills can partake in the development process. Thus, a zero-budget, bazaar FOSS project often involves more working hours from skilled programmers than the biggest corporation can possibly afford.[27] The large number of beta-testers and co-developers is a major advantage because it critically speeds up the time of identifying and fixing bugs in the program. To fully utilise the feedback cycle from users, bazaar-developments are released frequently, in extreme cases with one new version every day, and improvements are made continuously. In contrast, upgrades of cathedral-style software must undergo a long period of testing to ensure that all bugs are removed before the program can be shipped to the market. In the long run bazaar-styled FOSS projects will triumph, Raymond attests, and puts it in a sentence reminiscent of old-school historical materialism:[28] "[. . .] because the commercial world cannot win an evolutionary arms race with open-source communities that can put orders of magnitude more skilled time into a problem."[29] Without doubt, Eric Raymond is a partisan observer, but his claims are echoed by his nemesis. In an internal memo, Microsoft assessed the threat to the company posed by the FOSS movement. The text leaked into the hands of Eric Raymond and was posted on the Internet in Halloween 1998. Subsequently the text is known as the Halloween document.[30] Just like Eric Raymond, the authors of the Halloween document pay tribute to the bigger battery of free labour that can be deployed in a FOSS development project and its ability to harvest the collective intelligence of users.

Linus Torvald's have offered his own explanation to the GNU/Linux phenomenon. The competitive edge of free software over proprietary software owes to the higher motivation of its authors. Speaking at a Linux User Group meeting in San Francisco, he stated: "Those other operating systems aren't bad because of [technical detail] A or technical detail B. Those systems are bad because the people don't care"[31] Linus Torvald avoids reflecting over how the lack of motivation among hired programmers hangs together with the labour relations under which they work.[32] It is not the individuals working as programmers that are the weak link in the proprietary development model. The weakness consists in that when they write software applications for a consumer market, production for use is subjugated under production for exchange. To a hired programmer, the code he is writing is a means to get a pay check at the end of the month. Any shortcut when getting to the end of the month will do. For a hacker, on the other hand, writing code is an end in itself. He will always pay full attention to his endeavour, or else he will be doing something else. It is hard for companies to compete with that kind of commitment.

Yet another take on the matter is offered by Robert Young, chairman of the free software company Red Hat. According to him the success of free software can be explained by the absence of warring intellectual property claims. In property-based research, discoveries are kept secret and inaccessible to others. This creates an overall tendency for proprietary software to break up in separate strains and it prevents sequential development. In free software development the pressure is reversed. If one distributor of GNU/Linux adopts an innovation that becomes popular, the other vendors will immediately adopt it too. Everyone has equal access to the source code and is permitted to use it. Innovations are speeded up since people can build on the discoveries of others. By removing intellectual property barriers there is an overall convergence towards a common standard.[33] Robert Young's case against proprietary software gains weight due to the growing importance of standards in the computer market. The two economists Carl Shapiro and Hal Varian points at the computer market as a showcase of what they call a 'network industry'.[34] In network industries, single products function as parts of a larger system made up of many other products.

The components tend to be produced by several competing manufacturers. Interoperability becomes as important to the customer as the price and quality of the individual product. Users desire compatibility, not excludability. In fast moving high-tech markets, customers and suppliers are wary of the risk of investing money and know-how in a product that might soon be obsolete. Historically, the size of capital has been the best insurance that a company's product will stay in service for a long time. But irrespectively of the strength of the firm, bankruptcy, hostile acquisition, or changes of corporate policy is always a possibility. Software applications with rights holders are in jeopardy of being turned into evolutionary dead-ends. Customers will then be unable to get hold of updated versions that are compatible with the latest utilities. Users of GPL software, in contrast, are guaranteed the freedom to adapt the code for as long as they need it. Hence, the absence of capital, instead of the size of capital, provides the best insurance that a product will stay relevant to users in the future.

The three accounts given above to explain the success of the FOSS development model differ only on a superficial level. They have in common that they testify to *the inadequacy of capitalist relations in organising labour* in the information sector. The productivity of free software development stands in an inverted relation to the jungle of property claims that impede proprietary software development, as Robert Young bears witness of. The playfulness of hackers proves to be more productive than the estranged wage relation that programmers are caught up in, as is suggested by Linus Torvalds. And the possibility to involve users as co-developers in free software development projects, a factor stressed by Eric Raymond, is obstructed by the commodity form which separates consumers from producers as decisively as buyers are separated from sellers. In conclusion, the achievements of hackers cannot be told as the history of any single event—an ingenious form of organising people, the utilisation of a novel technology, or a bunch of larger-than-life individuals. Neither is it sufficient to combine these factors into an explanation. This phenomenon must be analysed in relation to the totality of capitalist relations. The FOSS movement is unique only because, in exploiting the failures of the capitalist system, it has demonstrated a prototype for struggle that is generic. In the following chapters, a closer engagement with Marxist theory will be made to substantiate this claim. It will be argued that self-organised labour can outrun firms in all sectors were the concentration of fixed capital (i.e. large-scale machinery) and the division of labour (specialised knowledge) is not an insurmountable threshold.

POWER RELATIONS INSIDE AND OUTSIDE THE HACKER MOVEMENT

The image of FOSS development presented so far in the argument, as a single, monolithic model for writing software code, needs to be modified. Each project differs from the next in the way that decisions are made, work is delegated, and credits are given. Neither can FOSS coding be clearly separated from the corporate sector. All of the major projects are hybrids that muddle along as half enterprises, half community efforts. A survey discovered that 41% of all FOSS projects were initiated and managed by corporations. A majority of the projects turned out to be driven by individuals, and only 6% were organised in the loose collaborate networks of the kind usually associated with FOSS development.[35] The numbers do not necessarily tell the whole story about where most hackers are engaged and to what level of involvement. Projects initiated by firms often aim at customising code made available by the FOSS community. The most well-known and influential FOSS projects, GNU/Linux, Apache etc., are organised in open, collaborative networks.

It bears to be stressed, though, that network organisation does not imply an absence of power relations. Hierarchies are based on reputation, charisma, contacts, shrewdness, and demonstrated technical skill. These values are embedded in a shared norm system that, on the one hand, holds the community together, and, on the other hand, stratifies internal relations and raises barriers to outsiders. All sizeable development projects depend on a core group of chieftains and/or a charismatic leader for taking final decisions. The top 10% of the most productive developers of FOSS projects contributes 72% of the code, with further lopsidedness in the top tier.[36] Arguably, what matters is not that there are no asymmetries in power relations and performances. Demanding such purity would paralyse any effort to organise in this messy world. What matters is that power in these communities is not fixed in economic, legal, or architectural dependencies. Common to all FOSS licenses is that they guarantee everyone the option to fork a project. Inertia against forking rests on the commitment and size of the user base. It is the number of devotees which determines the relevance and the future prospects of a fork. The ease by which people can walk away from a project is therefore a significant constraint on how power can be exercised. If a leader is perceived as abusing his position, his basis of power can vaporise very quickly. It is on basis of how the subculture is internally organised in respect to power, rather than a freedom from power *per se*, that the egalitarian claim can be made.

Similarly, qualifications must be made in respect to how the hacker movement relates to the surrounding world. The self-image of hackers markedly differs from their track record. In *A Hacker's Manifesto*, a pamphlet that circulated on bulletin boards in 1980s and that has become something of a founding charter of the computer underground, it was declared that hackers: 'Exist without skin colour, without nationality, without religious bias'[37] A quick glance is all it takes to confirm that the social base of the hacker movement is heavily skewed towards middle-class males living in the West. The demography has its roots in those days when only a privileged few could access computers during their college years. The monetary restrains have since been considerably eased. Prices of computer equipment are no longer a barrier to entry since five year old computers with zero market value work perfectly fine for the purpose of writing free code. The main cost is the leisure time and the peace of mind which it takes to engage in frivolous computing. Spare time is, however, one of the few resources which the unemployed among the western working class have in abundance. Geopolitically speaking, the dominance of USA and Europe will be history once China, South America, and India commit to free software.

But the monetary aspect is not a catch-all explanation, as is shown by the extreme gender imbalance of the hacker movement. According to one policy document, only 1.5% of FOSS community members are female.[38] The statistic is puzzling not the least since there are no economic incentives for male hackers to keep women out as there would be in the labour market. Indeed, another survey found that 66% of the men agreed to that the FOSS community as a whole would benefit from more female participants. In spite of this, a majority was of the opinion that it was up to the women to make the effort.[39] The voluntaristic and meritocratic ethos in the subculture makes male hackers, and indeed, some female hackers too, impervious to structural explanations to the gender bias. Admittedly, those structures go far beyond the scope of the FOSS community. Because of the division of domestic labour, women on average have less time to devote to improving their computer skills. The gendering of technology as masculine keeps girls from ever getting in contact with free software, or, they do so much later in their lives than the boys, again resulting in less training.[40] These are major drawbacks in a community where demonstration of technical skill is deemed to be of paramount importance. Even with the same level of knowledge, female hackers attest to that they have a harder time to gain recognition from their male peers. Often they end up doing tasks with lower status, such as documentation and writing manuals, while men drift towards more prestigious and technologically more challenging assignments. It is not surprising then that out of the small number of female recruits; many quickly drop out because of a general lack of encouragement.[41] The absence of public institutions within the community means that these structures cannot easily be counterbalanced with positive discrimination and targets for equal opportunities. Lots of hackers prefer to keep it that way as a matter of self-determination of the community vis-à-vis the outside. Government initiatives of the sort, which can be expected to follow with a more official role for FOSS applications, will not be welcomed by everyone.

Though the union between hacker priorities and feminist politics is far from harmonious, the two groups have things in common. The portrayal of the early feminists and the media image of the hacker are unnervingly alike. Scaremongering against hackers as criminals is only outdone by the stereotype of the male, geek misfit in popular culture. The representation of the geek is similar to the stigmatisation of educated women in the nineteenth century, who were then described as ugly, un-feminine, and unfit for marriage. Now as then, people are discouraged from seeking knowledge that would have increased their autonomy. In order for women to defend their positions in a computerised society, skills in programming are essential. It is with awareness of this fact that a number of women's groups, such as Haeksen, LinuxChix, and Debian-Women, have started. They support each other and female newbies that are about to join the hacker movement. Additionally, they try to change the attitudes among male hackers. In theory, at least, the graphic interface could be a leveller in respect to gender, race, and appearance, something hinted at in *the Hacker Manifesto*. Similar thoughts are echoed in cyber-feminism. This brand of feminism expects that everyone will end up as cyborgs in a society that relies increasingly on technology. When the human-machine distinction breaks down they hope that essentialist separations between man/woman will crumble too.[42]

The inclusion of women in the hacker community is not an act of charity by male hackers but is a fateful question. The emancipatory potential of hacking exists precisely in that it crosses the line of who can access technology. While legal obstacles to entry have been reduced thanks to free and open licenses, know-how required of FOSS users continues to be a barrier. The difficulty to engage ordinary computer users in free software are hotly debated and its grave importance is recognised within the hacker community. In addition to legal, technological and monetary constraints, however, community norms are another barrier that prevents diversification and growth of the base of users and developers. If the goal of making non-proprietary software a standard on desktop computers is ever to be realised, the other half of the population must be let onboard. Techies within the hacker movement have to come to terms with that the implications of FOSS development run deeper than narrowly defined cyber-politics. Hacking affects labour relations, the standing of developing countries, and gender issues. These realities of the mundane will weight heavier upon the hacker community the more integrated FOSS development gets in the global economy and the world of business.

BUSINESS MODELS BASED ON FREE SOFTWARE

From a liberal perspective, FOSS development is understood as simply another business model that better approximates the free market. The economist Joseph Schumpeter's idea about 'creative destruction' is often invoked at this point. According to him, the creative destruction of capitalism continuously leads to old monopolies being undercut by better technology and smarter entrepreneurs. The appeal of this narrative is twofold. Firstly, legislators, judges and the general public are more receptive to the arguments of FOSS advocates if the challenge to intellectual property rights is framed within a liberal discourse. Secondly, there is a reassurance to hackers in the belief that information technology and free market forces inevitably will defeat the Enemy, artificial monopolies and intellectual property. The liberal interpretation of how free software development and free markets relate to each other needs to be complemented with critical theory.

Corporate involvement in FOSS development is *not* a final disclaimer of the proposition that hacking is subversive and possibly anti-capitalist. Readers familiar with Marxism know that individual capitalists sometimes respond to contradictions in the capitalist system, in such a manner that the economic system is pushed further into deepened contradictions and decline. Putting it even more poignantly, communism is plausible when the choices which are rational to an individual capitalist, simultaneously, on an aggregated level, are disastrous to capital as a collective class. Corporate backing of the FOSS movement might be such a case. That is the belief of Darl McBride, executive officer of the software company SCO. In the computer underground, SCO is infamous for litigating distributors of GNU/Linux. The company claims that vendors of GNU/Linux have appropriated software code owned by SCO. In a letter to the U.S congress Darl McBride outlined the dire consequences if the government sided with FOSS developers, and the fallacy of other executives in doing so: "Despite this, we are determined to see these legal cases through to the end because we are firm in our belief that the unchecked spread of Open Source software, under the GPL, is a much more serious threat to our capitalist system than U.S. corporations realize."[43] Of course, Darl McBride is keen to portray the special interest of SCO as the common interest of all capitalists. Many hackers would protest that the FOSS model threatens monopolies (especially Microsoft's) but not markets. The corporate backing of FOSS seems to confirm their argument. They are probably correct, at least for as long as the issue is narrowed down to the provision of software services. From this horizon, the collective capitalist class can do without Darl McBride and a few more unfortunate individual capitalists. Reformist critics of copyright are eager to point out that capitalism can benefit from a commons in software, since it frees up circulation of capital in other sectors. Toll-free roads is a standard example of a public good that does not threaten private property, but quite to the contrary, facilitates the automobile- and petroleum-industry. The comparison might not be entirely justified in this case. Much more is at stake than the sale of software services. In the second chapter it will be argued that the commodification of information is at the heart of the so-called information age. Key to the privatisation of information is capital's control over code architecture and over electronic, global communications. If the constituent power to write software remains out in the wild, capital faces an uphill battle when enclosing information commons. The sharing of music and films on peer-to-peer networks is only the beginning.

To discern the complex symbiosis between capital and community, a closer look at the motivations and the business models are required. We must not get stuck in a black-and-white dramaturgy of profiteering villains exploiting unaware idealists. The hacker subculture has a pragmatic attitude in this regard. Even the leftwing camp endorse business models as long as these are based upon free licenses. Commercialisation is only possible because it is carried by a strong current within the hacker movement. Most hackers believe that if corporations get a vested interest in FOSS development, corporations will help to diffuse FOSS to the public. Without doubt, corporations played a significant role in elevating GNU/Linux from the shadows of a student project to the echelons of a competing industrial standard. More questionable is the underlying assumption, however, that Open Source is emancipating no matter how (and for whom) it is put to use. Coupled with the agenda of the pro-business camp are individual hopes to make a living out of hacking, ultimately in order to escape other kinds of dull employment. It is not the decisions by a few corporate managers that are the motor behind commercialisation. Instead, commercialisation is driven by individual ambitions among hackers. Many strive to professionalise the hobby so that they can work full-time on writing free code. But focusing on the ambitions of individual hackers is yet again to lose sight of the bigger picture. Their hopes are rational within the irrational world in which they are forced to make a living. The hacker movement is commercialised not primarily by pull from individual capitalists but by push from generalised conditions of plight in a market economy. Capitalist relations are the 'culprit' in this drama, if we are to designate one, not any individual capitalist or a band of 'disloyal' hackers.

Free software, Richard Stallman never tires of pointing out, means free liberties as in 'free speech'. It does not mean free prices as in 'free beer'. Against this viewpoint it can be objected that the distinction between a public/political and a private/economic sphere is not as clear-cut in postmodern capitalism as Stallman makes it out to be. In any case, the GPL permits commerce in so forth that copies of a GNU program can be sold, even if this opportunity is limited by the fact that GPL also allows sold copies to be copied and given away for free. The great surprise is that in this impossible space, where the same object is simultaneously available for free and for a price, some people volunteer to pay. Richard Stallman supported himself initially by selling tapes with copies of GNU Emacs. This niche has been populated by a small but prospering flora of firms committed to the ideals of FOSS development. The first company to base its operation on GPL was Cygnus, founded in 1989. A slogan by the company sums up the contradictory logic behind their business model: "We make free software affordable". Cygnus expanded steadily for many years without making much fuss. It employed more than a hundred software engineers when it merged with another company based on free software, Red Hat, in 1999. Red Hat is the major symbol of the union between the FOSS movement and commercialism. Changes in policy by Red Hat, and by other commercial distributors of GNU/Linux, have cast doubt on their commitment to 'the Cause'. Concentration of capital (the merger with Cygnus—euphorically hailed as the establishment of a 'free software powerhouse') has been followed up with a narrowing of the service to high-paying, commercial customers.[44] It is tempting to brush over the past years of experimentation with free software business models. We could call it a rudimental phase in waiting to be decomposed into a mature form more consistent with capitalist relations (and, as it happens, Marxist doctrine). That would be a bit too convenient of us. It is undeniable that both Cygnus and Red Hat were raised in the free software community and have been loyal to the ideals of free software for many years, while at the same time being highly profitable. For the fiscal year of 2007, Red Hat reports total revenue of $400,6 millions.[45] And many small garage firms survive on this peculiar business model. Taken together, it is enough of an anomaly to call for a closer investigation and possibly a revision of Marxist theory. Red Hat earns revenue from selling its own branded packages of GNU/Linux bundled with customer support. Even though variants of GNU/Linux are easy to access for free on the Internet, and even getting a Red Hat version for free is quite possible and entirely eligible, the company manages to charge a price for its product. The chairman of Red Hat, Robert Young, explains this phenomenon with branding. Additionally, it might be cheaper for a company to pay Red Hat for technical support than hiring a programmer of their own. Though Red Hat and a few other 'bumblebees' do fly, it is a mistake to jump from these marginal cases to the conclusion; that they embody the business model of the future. This irrational but non-coercive source of income, Young ads in a critical comment, generates only a fraction of the profit compared to proprietary software. Corporations established in a proprietary software model would never volunteer to decommission copyright protection.[46]

Robert Young's last comment hints at Red Hat's role as a niche provider. To identify how 'free software'-based companies earn their profit, it is therefore not sufficient to focus on the operations of the individual firm. The hidden riddle is in the conditions surrounding free software firms. To carry the analysis any further, we need to plunge into a theoretical discussion a little pre-emptively. According to Marxist theory, labour is the source of 'surplus value' (in short, profits). The amount of surplus value that can be accumulated depends on the number of labourers which are set in motion by capital. It is possible, however, for the individual capitalist to acquire more surplus value than he employs labourers. Sometimes the capitalist manages to position his venture so favourably that the surplus value of labourers hired by competitors flow to his pockets instead. The schoolbook scenario is when a capitalist invents a superior way of producing goods. The expense for producing an item then falls below the social average, i.e. that average cost which competitors pay when they produce the item. The units are produced at different cost levels but since they are identical, all items sell in the same market for the same price. Hence, the most cost efficient capitalist (producing the unit at the lowest cost) earns his efficiency gain as a bonus from the other capitalists. This boon is known as 'surplus profit'. The advantage is only temporal since other capitalists will try to catch up with the inventor.

When the majority have adopted the superior way of doing things, the average production cost will even out at the new equilibrium. The surplus profit vanishes for the individual capitalist. It is not efficiency gains in 'absolute terms' that provide the sought-for benchmark. It is efficiency gains vis-à-vis other comparable producers. Point is, surplus profits exist per definition as a deviation from the norm.

The existence of the FOSS business model can be understood as a variation on this theme. Companies like Red Hat and Cygnus hire labourers, to customise software code, to provide supportive services, and to brand their products. These activities generate a modest amount of surplus value. The input of waged labour is marginal in comparison to the vast amount of volunteer labour that has been involved in writing the software application.[47] Gratis labour is not, though, automatically voided of value. It has value if it duplicates waged labour performed somewhere else in the economy. In other words, the worth of non-waged labour of FOSS developers stands in relation to the waged labour of in-housed programmers. Both are working towards equivalent code solutions. For as long as the social average cost of solving a computer problem is determined by waged labour and intellectual property relations, volunteer labour (hackers) and copyleft licenses cut costs below this social average. Surplus profits do not derive from the reduction of staff by means of technological innovation. It is created when work is emigrated from paid labourers to un-paid users thanks to organisational innovations. It is an open question whether the copyright-dependent fraction of the capitalist class (Microsoft, Hollywood, record studios) can follow suit and close the gap in production costs, without disbanding themselves in the process. Microsoft's 'shared source' policy, where selected customers are given restricted access to Microsoft's source code, could be seen as an attempt to close in on the distance between proprietary software and FOSS. However, the priority to stay in control will probably spoil their efforts. Quite possibly, these companies are unable to appropriate the FOSS model and still sustain high profitability.

If that statement is correct, Red Hat's surplus profit business model will prosper for a long time in the margins of society, leeching off the differential level in the cost of production. Taken to its logical end-point, this reasoning leads to the conclusion that shareholders of GPL-based firms like Red Hat are not freeriding on development communities. Through the so-called 'equalisation of social surplus value', as it is known by Marxists, Red Hat's shareholders are exploiting the programmers employed by Microsoft. The second conclusion, more pressing to our inquiry, is that FOSS enterprises will never supersede and replace proprietary business model. The belief is commonly held by libertarian hackers who imagine that as long as entrepreneurs are left to work their deeds, intellectual property monopolies will eventually crumble under the superior rationality of the free market. They fail to see that Red Hat can only be profitable in relation to the inflated social average production cost set by Microsoft. Subsequently, even those firms dedicated to GPL can't afford to do away with the intellectual property regime altogether. Individual capitalists might have different opinions on how to optimally configure the intellectual property regime. But the demand for an absolute abolishment of intellectual property rights is incompatible with capitalism. As we have now demonstrated, that statement is not falsified by the existence of non-proprietary software business models.

Speaking from the standpoint of Marxist theory, all firms, irrespectively of their policy on free versus proprietary licenses, are based on the exploitation of living labour. Saying that does not mean that executives cannot act with the best of intentions and even do some good from time to time. It is by no means automatic that entrepreneurs within the movement will push for commercialisation at every given opportunity. The involvement of competitors can even create checks in defence of the information commons. This paradox attests to the resilience of the GPL. The race for a graphic interface for GNU/Linux proves the point. Having an object-oriented desktop interface for GNU/Linux, i.e. using a mouse instead of typing in the commands on the keyboard, was a crucial step for the free operating system to become competitive. One attempt to create such an interface was an application called KDE. Though the code was licensed under the General Public License, it depended on a proprietary graphical library named Qt. Without the library to draw from the program becomes rather pointless. Qt was owned by Troll Tech, a Norwegian company, and in most circumstances they charged a developer's license fee. Consequently, KDE did not meet the conditions of a free license. Though one branch of GNU/Linux users decided to overlook the impurities and move on, others were alarmed by the danger of leaving one company with legal claims over critical parts of the free operating system. A team of developers launched a project called GNOME that would compete with KDE while using a completely free graphical library. Another group of developers chose a second path to circumvent Troll Tech's property claim. They sat down to create a Qt clone under the project name 'Harmony'. The technological inferiority of GNOME at the outset did not prove an infeasible hindrance to the success of the non-proprietary fork. Strong community norms abiding to the ideals of free software proved sufficient to compensate for Troll Tech's first-mover advantage. Eventually, as GNOME and Harmony gathered steam, Troll Tech was forced to renounce its hold over Qt. As will be argued extensively in later chapters, this suggests a high threshold within labouring communities against the crystallisation of private property relations. The second important observation to make is the strategic decision by Red Hat. At an early stage the company decided to throw its weight behind the GNOME-project and stand up for an information commons. The firm took some financial risks by not shipping their Red Hat version of GNU/Linux with the most advanced Troll Tech features. It made more sense for Red Hat to stick to a free license where they could race on a levelled field with other firms, rather than giving up some legal rights to a competitor. (*Moody*, 252).

To denounce all involvement by firms as a matter of principle can therefore be misleading. Activists must not forget that the pragmatic attitude of hackers towards commercial involvement partly explains their stunning successes. Garage firms are initiated and run by people in the subculture. They share the same values and depend on the support of the community, to the point where the two are at times indistinguishable. Undeniably, software start-ups have helped extending the political influence of the hacker movement, especially when campaigning against copyright legislations and software patents. And then again, a bridge runs in two directions. In the end, the most prominent role of garage firms will probably have been as bridgeheads for major corporations to enter the movement.

THE OPEN SOURCE INITIATIVE

The invitation to the movers-and-shakers was sent in 1998 with the staging of the Open Source Initiative. If any single company could be said to have been responsible for setting off the avalanche, it has to be Netscape Communications. It is telling that the company began as a direct assault on a public-funded project to create a common standard in web browsers. In the early days the most widely used browser for navigating on the World Wide Web was Mosaic. It had been developed by the University of Illinois. A veteran within the software industry, Jim Clark, watched the browser grow in popularity and realised its commercial potential. Clark recruited a handful programmers from the team who had been working with Mosaic at the university, most noteworthy among them Mark Andreessen. They created an improved clone of the original browser and released it for free under the same name. Their infringement on the intellectual property rights of the university was never resolved. The only demand eventually imposed on Clark and Andreessen was that they must not call themselves 'Mosaic' any more. Instead they took the name Netscape.[48] Ironically, many hackers would later hail Netscape as one of the good guys in the fight against proprietary software. In 1995, Microsoft recognised the importance of the Internet and began to push its own web browser, Internet Explorer.[49] A year later, Netscape was in difficulties. Its share of the browser market was declining fast and a drastic change in policies was called for. The company decided to publish the source code of its browser. In January 1998, Netscape made its announcement to a baffled team of journalists and an exited audience of programmers. Netscape had consulted many 'superstar hackers' when drawing up an appropriate license. The General Public License was out of the question since it treats all users equally in terms of legal rights. Netscape had to balance the need for control with the urge to involve as many participants as possible in their development project. Their solution was to split the software code and the license in two projects running in parallel. The two licenses were Netscape Public License (NPL) and Mozilla Public

License (MPL). While NPL kept some privileges for Netscape and third parties, MPL was fashioned for community development. Mozilla[50] was run as a parallel development project backed by the company. The intention was that innovations made in Mozilla's code would be fed back into Netscape. The company hoped to gain an edge over Internet Explorer by riding on the free labour of the computer underground. Despite the hype, Mozilla failed to attract a critical mass of free developers outside Netscape's own corporate team. Commercial and communal coding does not mix well. In his seminal study of the Free and Open Source Software movement, Glyn Moody attests: "Netscape's rise and ultimate fall is, in part, a monument to the failure of the commercial coding model—and a pointer to fundamental weaknesses in other companies that employ it." (*Moody*, 203). Mozilla couldn't save Netscape in the browser war. In the aftermath of the company's decline, Mozilla developers have staged a comeback with the Firefox browser. Maybe the challenge to Microsoft's Internet Explorer will be of a more noxious breed this time.

Despite its eventual downfall, Netscape had staked out the path when it published the source code of its key brand product. The road taken by Netscape's initiative caused a split in the computer underground. In April 1998, all the chieftains of the hacker subculture minus the politically most outspoken of them, Richard Stallman, met up at the Freeware Summit at Palo Alto, to discuss the future direction of the movement. They wished to encourage big businesses to get involved in the computer underground. A crucial element in this strategy was to choose a label that sounded less threatening to *status quo* than the term 'free software'. Free software, as the Free Software Foundation never fails to point out, concerns first and foremost the question of freedom. Freeing up technology is a means to deepen democracy. Such notions are just not helpful when corporations are to be courted. The preferred label decided upon at the meeting was Open Source. The focus of Open Source 'revolutionaries' is technological superiority while social concerns are tactfully left to the side.[51] The term Free and Open Source Software used here is a compromise worked out after much debate within the community. In addition to launching a new brand name for the movement, Open Source differed in a crucial aspect from the GPL license. Like GPL, Open Source requires licensed software to be distributed freely; it guarantees that the source code is kept transparent, and it ensures the user the right to create modified versions of the original software without first notifying the author. All of these clauses are necessary to unlock the creative potential of volunteer labour collectives. Open Source does not, however, demand that the open license is attached to derivatives of the original code. By removing the 'viral' feature of GPL, Open Source provides firms with a back-door for appropriating code. Software licensed under Open Source can be 'ripped, mixed, and burned' and released under copyright. That is how Mozilla Public License was intended to work for Netscape. This is what repeatedly happens with software licensed under the terms of the Berkeley

Software Distribution (BSD) license. In Marxist terms, Open Source licenses can be described as an organisational principle for systematising 'primitive accumulation', by which is meant theft, of the social labour taking place in developing communities and in the commons.

The opportunity was amazingly quickly recognised in corporate board-rooms. In the weeks following the launch of the Open Source initiative, IBM announced that they would switch to Apache. Their rationale for hitching onto the Apache project merits a closer look. It testifies to that the size of the user base can bear more clout as a strategic asset than concentration of capital and the expertise of the personnel. In 1998 the software market for web servers was jointly held by Microsoft, Netscape, and Apache. IBM had tried to enter the market but came to realise the strong tide of network externalities working against newcomers. It made sense for IBM to drop their in-house project and jump straight on to the very large user base held by Apache. The fact that IBM abandoned its own undertaking in favour of a non-proprietary project had a strong psychological impact on the business community. IBM has since made considerable investments in GNU/Linux and paraded its high-profile commitment to the FOSS movement. Other multinational corporations jumped on the bandwagon following the Free-ware Summit. Oracle and Informix, two giants providing software for busi-ness applications and databases, declared that they would release products that supported GNU/Linux. And hardware vendors, most notably Compaq, Dell, and Hewlett Packard, followed suit. Another important backer for the FOSS movement is Intel. In addition to porting commercial products to GNU/Linux and offering the free operating system to their customers, many companies are paying employees to write free and open source code. Sun Microsystems, for instance, bought a word processor from a German com-pany and released it to the FOSS community. OpenOffice, the name of the program, is challenging Microsoft's Word.

The willingness of hardware manufacturers, vendors and software inde-pendents to line up behind FOSS developers must be understood against the backdrop of Microsoft's grip over the market. Because corporations have little to gain or lose in face of Microsoft's *de facto* monopoly, they can free-ride on non-commercial projects and hope to enlarge secondary profits, by cutting costs for software development, or by distributing software to pro-mote sales of hardware, or to sell support services, or through advertising. But since these profits tend to be inferior to Microsoft's, this is a peripheral strategy. The preferred option for a firm is monopoly profits. We can there-fore stipulate that corporate engagement in FOSS prerequisites an existing monopoly. Though the backing of FOSS developers is the second best option to a corporation, there are some solid economic reasons for bypassing the proprietary software development model. Microsoft's restricted capacity to upgrade its software imposes time-lags on downstream businesses. Because of the long process that is required in proprietary development models for debugging and releasing software, Intel's shipments of new processors have repeatedly been stalled.[52] To reap the full benefit from advances in semiconductors, hence to persuade consumers to buy the latest technology, software applications need to be optimised for the hardware. The gravity of this concern might be better appreciated when we consider the speed by which fixed capital is devalued. Martin Kenney reports how stations for assembling computer chips, previously outsourced to sweatshops in Asia, are moving back closer to the consumer market in United States. In the two-three weeks it takes to ship a central processing unit (CPU) across the ocean, the product loses 5–10 percent of its value.[53] Open source is attractive to fractions of the capitalist class because it solves expensive and dangerous time-lags in development cycles. Based on a public standard such as GNU/Linux, Intel is free to optimise the software for its hardware sales without having to wait for Microsoft's 'cathedral builders'. The restrictions imposed by intellectual property are impeding the circulation of capital and, consequently, limited commons in information looks increasingly attractive to companies in order to boost market sales.

Our understanding of the issue is clouded by the crisp line between FOSS and propietary licenses routinely drawn in the intellectual property debate. When critics make 'open' versus 'closed' into the central cleavage, mirrored in the moral distinction between good, innovative firms and bad, protectionist companies, more important divisions go unnoticed. In particular, we fail to see the extent to which both violations of and alternatives to intellectual property law has always already been overappropriated by the intellectual property regime. Intellectual property does not work by being simply 'closed'. A fisherman catches no fish if his fishing net stays closed all the time. From this perspective, corporate experimentation with free and open licenses makes perfect sense as a complementary to copyright. Corporations are not unfamiliar with supporting public goods provided that they have control over the situation. A direct parallel to computer giants backing the Open Source Initiative is the sudden change of heart among biotech corporations towards private ownership of genetic discoveries. Pfizer, Merck & Co and other pharmaceutical and chemical industries were the chief architects behind extending patentability to life-forms in the US. Later they were alarmed when small start-ups and universities rushed to file patents on genetic information and act as patent trolls against the corporations. In 1992, the *Pharmaceutical Manufacturers Association* advised against government ownership of gene sequences, and the *Industrial Biotechnology Association* insisted that the U.S. government put gene sequences in the public domain.[54] When the Human Genome project was launched it came up against an offshoot of rampant greed. A rivalling project was run by venture capitalists and two researchers, Craig Venter and William Haseltine. They applied a method allowing them to rapidly generate sequences of human genes. The drawback with their method was that the data they collected was too fragmented and random to be of much scientific use. Instead, their research was aimed at hijacking the legal and financial control over the Genome database.

The peril from such an outcome was so terrifying that Merck & Co invested substantially in public research to race Craig Venter and William Haseltine and to ensure that the data would stay in the public domain.[55] The costs for Merck & Co were relatively small. In fact, it was cheaper for the company to initiate a public research project and create a free-for-all database, than it would be either to set up their own private database, or to pay for access to another company's private database. Merck & Co gambled that it had the market position to make a net profit even from discoveries made available to its competitors.[56] Major computer firms count in the same way that they can get the better out of information commons due to their sheer size. Their rallying around an industrial standard open for competition is not dissimilar to the American 'open door' policy in the colonial annexation of China by Western powers. FOSS licenses establish a standard to work from which maximises the pool of consumers, skilled workers, and business partners. This advantage will gain in weight the further capital gets in restructuring its operations into a network of subcontractors and freelancers, and the more global this network grows.

The ultimate prize for companies involved in the hacker movement is to engage a pool of gratis labour in one end of the balance sheet and to sell the output in the other end with no discount. It's a 'have-your-cake-and-eat-it' business model. If a company sets out to make money in this way it can't advertise its intent since most developers refuse to contribute to projects under such terms. Often it is pulled off as a one-off violation against the terms of a free license. Despite occasional baddies, most companies have come to the conclusion that they have more to gain in the long run by playing by the book. While this fact is a sigh of relief to FOSS project leaders, the same remark looks entirely different from a Marxist vantage point. To a Marxist it suggests that a more systematic way of exploiting labour has been found. Our critique must therefore not stop at the companies that violate the free licenses, or else we will fail to detect subtler forms of exploitation that sidesteps the direct point of sale. For example, if the FOSS community is being engaged to reduce the administrative and overhead costs of a firm while the firm maintains a constant level of earnings from its proprietary services and hardware sales (income in part deriving from purchases by hackers), then it could be argued that exploitation has been intensified. Not only do corporations thereby cut labour costs in individual programming projects. They also impose an overall downward pressure on the wages and working conditions of in-house computer programmers. Cutting to the chase, this is the main reason for corporate enthusiasm for the Open Source Initiative. The labour process of programmers is being outsourced and opensourced. The threat will eventually be felt by people in the computer underground too, since many of them rely on the privileged status and high salary of programmers to fund their passion for hacking. Hackers usually respond to this objection by saying that free software code does not compete with proprietary code since they occupy different market niches. That might be the case for now, however, if companies have it their way, they certainly will try to steer volunteers in such a direction. The outcome depends on if FOSS development communities can fight off attempts at channelling their labour power into avenues that undermines the position of in-housed programmers. Only then will hackers be more of a threat to capital than to organised labour.

To fully appreciate the significance of the open source initiative it must be set in context with other user-centred business models. Once we start looking, it becomes evident that quite many corporations base their strategies on putting users to work. For instance, search engines and databases are constructed so that users automatically add information to the database as an unavoidable side-effect from visiting the site. Though the input from each user is insignificant, the number adds up and, as is shown by Google and Yahoo, the financial worth can be gigantic. To gather more intricate electronic texts requires a greater degree of participation from visitors. This creates a trade-off between the numbers of users and the efforts asked of them. A possible solution is to bundle a service or, in the best case scenario, a community, to the gathering of information. Gracenote is a good example of how volunteer labour can be utilised in this way. The company owns the database CDDB which provides information on music titles. The database was built up by encouraging ordinary users to type in details of one or two of their own favourite albums. In this fashion, Gracenote eventually ended up with the world's largest database on music. Paying a staff for doing the same job might have been quicker and better coordinated, but also prohibitively costly.[57] By allowing the service to stay free for end-users, the company is ensured of a continuous upkeep of the latest information on music. The continuity of volunteer labour is crucial in a rapidly changing landscape of music fads. Revenue comes from charging commercial uses. The business model of Gracenote demonstrates how the pooling of volunteer labour can be combined with a partial closure by discriminating against different uses of a service. The version of the Creative Commons license were the artist preserves rights over commercial uses of her creation works in exactly the same way. Ironically, the open-ended invitation to a pool of unpaid contributors pared with a fee for commercial uses are often wrapped up in an ideological 'let the business pay, it serves them right' mentality. The foresightedness of the General Public License is underlined by that it does not permit discrimination of any kind of uses, not even commercial uses. It radically annuls exclusion as a concept and becomes all the more threatening to the world of commerce by not excluding it. The FOSS development model is a two-edged sword, even for hardware manufacturers and software vendors. Proprietary software applications such as Windows continuously demand more computing power. Thus the customers keep upgrading both software and hardware devices on a regular basis. Free software slashes this need in half and makes ten year old computers viable again. In the long run, hardware manufacturers and software vendors risk shrinking the size of their own market, unless they can inflate it by other means, by fashion and prestige of having the latest upgrade, for instance. Secondly, Microsoft cooperates closely with 'content providers', i.e. the Record Industry Association of America (RIAA) and Motion Picture Association of America (MPAA), to design software in support of Digital Restrictions Management (DRM) technology.[58] It will be hard for content providers to enforce intellectual property rights on the Internet if a free computer architecture becomes the standard.

FIRMS CONFRONT FOSS DEVELOPMENT

Hardware manufacturers are striking alliances with consumer pressure groups in a bid to outdo the influence of content providers. There is an obvious risk that the movement for alternative licenses, if activists sail too close to one branch of the industry, is reduced to a pawn in the game between warring fractions of capital. Campaigners for 'information com-mons' should keep in mind that the whole of the collective capitalist class depends on the intellectual property regime. The clash between Japanese hardware manufacturers, Sony and Matsushita, and American record stu-dios over the introduction of digital audio tapes (DAT) in the late 1980s, is instructive. The record studios were unhappy about the lack of restrictions to private copying of digital audio tapes. They demanded technological fixes that would restrict duplication of tapes. Their demand was backed up with the threat not to give Sony and Matsushita access to their music catalogues. Faced with the prospect of shipping a technology with no content running on it, the manufacturers were forced to back down. As a direct consequence of the conflict, Sony acquired CBS records in 1988 and Matsushita pur-chased MCA with a record division in 1991, bringing content suppliers in to their corporate portfolios.[59] The lesson is that both intra-industry pressure and acquisitions to stay independent of such pressure amounts to the same thing: a convergence of interest towards the protection of intellectual prop-erty. In fact, manufacturers of hardware are just as dependent on intellectual property law for their high profitability as software producers and content providers. The inflated price of high-tech consumer goods is upheld by pat-ents, trademark law, *sui generis* directives on circuit boards, and protection of trade secrets. Essentially the rift within the capitalist class centres on the distribution of profit and rent between different sectors and industries. From a Marxist outlook it is obvious that the exploitation of labour can never be abolished in these rows, since exploitation is the source of profits over which capitalists are haggling.

Likewise, the interaction between capital and the capitalist state in relation to FOSS developers is a complex web of rivalries and mutual dependencies. Conflicts of interest arise between authorities at national and local level as well as between states in different regions of the world. For example, strong intellectual property protection works favourable to the US foreign trade balance. The US administration is therefore very receptive to the demands of movie- and record-studios.[60] The same fact, however, is the primary obstacle when American businesses confront governments abroad. Initiatives in Third World countries and by local municipals in Europe to mandate the use of free software in public administration and schools, in part to save public money previously spent on proprietary licenses; have alarmed Microsoft and U.S. authorities. Sometimes their heavy-handed approach backfires. In India, Venezuela and Brazil, among other places, the governments have publicly endorsed the use of free software. But not even the different arms of the U.S. state have a unified front against the FOSS movement. A report prepared for the U.S. Department of Defence ended up advocating extended use of Open Source since it was considered to improve national security.[61] From a quick glance at court orders and announcements by government officials, the capitalist state might appear to be more supportive of GNU/Linux than of Windows. However, if it comes to a stand-off between the two, hackers donate no campaign money, they have no influence over employment figures, and they do not steer global capital flows. While different branches of the state advance contradicting policies, the fundamental bias is in the existence of the State as such. It is true that Microsoft has been hassled by anti-trust investigations for over a decade, first in America and then in the European Union.[62] However, the monopoly which the governments are prosecuting against is also upheld by the same state powers enforcing the patents and the licenses claimed by Microsoft. At the same time as the company was fined by the European Union for unfair competition, the EU commission pushed hard, in part on Microsoft's behalf, for the introduction of software patents in Europe. Software patents can only strengthen Microsoft's stranglehold over the market. In this light, the fine which Microsoft was asked to pay looks more like a bribe to pass favourable legislation.

The weakest link of the FOSS movement is its relationship with commercial, educational and institutional allies. By questioning the legality of FOSS licenses its adversaries hope to scare away supporters of free software. The SCO/Caldera's lawsuit against IBM, Red Hat, and other businesses investing in FOSS utilities, is a case in point.[63] Through a succession of acquisitions over the years, some property rights over UNIX have ended up with SCO/Caldera. The company has claimed that parts of the UNIX source code is incorporated in GNU/Linux and has been distributed by IBM and others. After several years of suits and countersuits the U.S. court system has come down against most of SCO's claims. However, the litigations were as much about public relations as about law enforcement. The worst case scenario is that small businesses and municipals are discouraged from investing in FOSS because of the perceived legal and technical uncertainties of such applications. To counter these fears, the Open Source Development Labs quickly established a legal fund to shield GNU/Linux users from litigation risks. Intel and IBM contributed to the fund while Novell and Hewlett-Packard offered its GNU/Linux customers indemnification from the SCO/

Caldera lawsuits.[64] One outcome of the SCO/Caldera debacle is irrespective of the fortunes in the court. FOSS developers end up seeking protection under the wings of their corporate allies. Litigations further an interest that both the plaintiff and the defendants have in common, namely: Capital stays relevant to FOSS development. The greatest danger to the community comes from within. IBM, while fighting the lawsuit of SCO/Caldera and parading its support for Apache and GNU/Linux, has also lobbied aggressively in favour of the introduction of software patents in Europe. The company holds one of the world's largest patent portfolios in the world. IBM has even been awarded an information process patent on an Open Source-like model for developing software.[65] In other words, IBM is the owner of the concept of this mode of development. It is a small comfort that IBM has pledged not to go after FOSS developers with its patents. By creating a legal power and withholding it, IBM ensures that it stays a partner worthwhile talking to.

HACKING AND CLASS STRUGGLE

The skirmishes between the hacker movement and corporations and governments have deeper roots than is shown by the confrontations over treacherous code, hostile legislations, and public smear campaigns. More fundamental is that the norms and aspirations motivating people to be hackers are at odds with at least some aspects of capitalism. The central claim of this book is that the hacker movement is part of a much broader undercurrent revolting against the boredom of commodified labour and needs satisfaction. These sentiments, however, can be made to cut in two ways. In business literature, managers are often advised to encourage a 'hacker spirit' among their employees.[66] Dennis Hayes gives a good account of how such a hacker spirit among engineers in Silicon Valley educes them to work harder without asking for anything in return. While he acknowledges the autonomy that software engineers enjoy, he doubts that any serious political agenda can arise from it. "Capital and modern technology apparently have seduced the computer builder with rare privilege: a genuine excitement that transcends the divide between work and leisure that has ruptured most industrialized civilizations. [. . .] When computer-building becomes an essential creative and emotional outlet, any politics larger than those governing access to work and tools seem distant concerns"[67] Dennis Hayes' doubts are very justified, though his observations are limited to in-house programmers. The demand for 'access to tools' becomes political dynamite once it is articulated outside the wage relation, i.e. by people who are denied access to the tools. When the 'hacker spirit' sticks among workers with no foothold in the creative business, the spirit warps into a 'refusal of work'. The ranks of these people by far outnumber those of the professionals in the media and information sector. And even among the lucky few who enjoy stimulating jobs, many of them will in due time find themselves deprived of their privileges. Programmers are being thrown into the lower tier of the labour market since the computer industry is maturing. Occupations that recently were felt as gratifying, such as writing software code, are becoming as routinised as any other field of activity that has fallen under the spell of exchange value. The shift of control over coding practices from programmers to managers is a major topic in the computer industry. This debate is also reflected in the hacker community in its concern about superficial knowledge in programming languages among volunteer contributors.[68]

Ironically, the deployment of computer technology has been decisive in degrading work elsewhere in the economy. Its impact on work was highlighted by the sociologist Richard Sennett when he examined the changes that have taken place in a bakery in New York over a period of twenty-five years.[69] In the 1970s, baking was an endeavour coupled with physical effort and toil in a hot and sometimes hazardous milieu. On the upside, baking required artisanship and rewarded the baker with some satisfaction. In the modern work environment, computerised ovens oversee the process of baking. It is clean, user-friendly, comfortably tempered, and, by any objective measurement, more 'civilised'. But the employees are left with no clue about how to bake bread. They only know how to push a few buttons and to call a technician when the bakery machinery breaks down. In the bakery, the source code is the dough, the spices, and the baking recipe, skills which the old bakers had mastered and exalted their peers in. In modern, computerised baking, the source code has been hidden away from the bakers. The growth of the software sector, which is providing exciting new jobs for computer programmers, rests in no small part on the usefulness of software as a means for deskilling the workforce in other sectors. This connection is laid bare when we consider the role of the first computer engineers employed by the industry. These programmers worked in the same company and side-by-side with the blue-collar workers who were subjected to computerisation. David Noble has documented how the embryo of computer software: templates, hole cards, recordable tapes, and numerical control (N/C), was deployed in heavy industry exactly for the purpose of intensifying the techniques of Taylorism. "By making possible the separation of conception from execution, of programming from machine operation, N/C appeared to allow for the complete removal of decision-making and judgement from the shop floor. Such 'mental' parts of the production process could now be monopolized by managers, engineers, and programmers, and concentrated in the office".[70] Crucial to this strategy was to keep the workers 'in the dark' about the source code. In the same breath as N/C technology was designed to lock workers out, workers were held in contempt for being too simple-minded for programming tasks. Nonetheless, supervisors attested that workers learned on their own to read the program language backwards. It was useful for them to know the program in order to anticipate the next move by the machine, and to foretell malfunctions and possible accidents. Workers were not meant to have this knowledge though. The routine was that upon discovering a bug, the worker had to report it to an engineer. It was a cumbersome and frustrating procedure to both the worker and the programmer.[71] Instead of following the correct procedures, workers often showed ingenuity in fixing bugs by themselves. Such initiatives by workers were beneficial to the bottomline of the firm. In order to take full advantage of the N/C technology it had to be opened up to allow feedback loops from the workers back into the work process. But managers had embraced the technology for exactly the opposite purpose. The machinery had been devised to regulate the performance of workers and to force a higher work pace upon them. With insight into how the machinery and the software functioned, workers also knew how to use the technology to their own advantage. They could now alter the instructions of the machinery and reduce its speed. This practice spread spontaneously yet rapidly in factory districts and was occasionally discovered and documented by supervisors. Managers fought back by trying to make the clockwork of the machinery impregnable and incomprehensible. Antagonism between capital and labour was contested on code level and 'access to tools' was the name of the game.

The dream of managers to build away workers' discontent through black-box technologies has continuously been frustrated by hacking. Computerisation has not eradicated workers' resistance but displaced it, from the execution stage to the conception stage. When more and more people are assigned to conceptualise rather than execute work processes, capital must economise this labour force too. The same tight regime is imposed on engineers and programmers as has previously been, with their help, forced upon blue-collar workers.[72] At this point, however, Taylorism runs into its own limits. There is no easy way to deprive 'knowledge workers' of knowledge and still have them working. One unexpected outcome from the mechanisation of the office is that the opportunities for hacking and sabotage abounds. A high-profile case of employee hacking occurred in 1996 when Timothy Lloyed discovered that he was going to be fired from Omega Engineering. He wrote six lines of code that erased the design and production programs of the company and allegedly resulted in $12 million dollars in damage. According to a survey in 1998 conducted jointly by Computer Security Initiative and the FBI, the average cost of successful computer attacks by outsider hackers was $56,000 while the average cost of malicious acts by insiders was $2,7 million.[73] A culture of spontaneous sabotage among employees contributes for most of the computer downtime in offices. The fact that these attacks are charged with labour discontent almost always goes unreported. Managers are anxious not to inspire other employees to work the same deed. With these reflections in the back of the mind, Andrew Ross insists that the perspective on hacking must be broadened. The media image of hackers as apolitical, juvenile pranksters belittles the issues at stake: "While only a small number of computer users would categorize themselves as 'hackers,' there are defensible reasons for extending the restricted definition of *hacking* down and across the case hierarchy of systems analysts, designers, programmers, and operators to include all high-tech workers—no matter how inexpert—who can interrupt, upset, and redirect the smooth flow of structured communications that dictates their position in the social networks of exchange and determines the pace of their work schedules."[74] Employees crashing the computer systems of their employers gives a clear indication of that hacking can be an act of labour resistance. How does this observation reflect upon hacking done by students, unemployed, and spare-timers, in other words, hacking unrelated to the workplace? After all, both the self-image and the stereotype of the hacker portray someone positioned outside and against the profession.

First it must be acknowledged that the site of production is fuzzy in net-worked capitalism. The production process has gradually shifted from the factory and office to work-at-home schemes and commissioned freelanc-ers.[75] Computerisation is closely related to this larger picture of a restruc-tured labour market. The availability of personal computers, mobile phones, and Internet connections has been pivotal for making telecommuting and work-at-home-schemes practical. Furthermore, to the arsenal of freelancers, leased workforces, and subcontractors, firms can now add FOSS developers. As Red Hat's and IBM's engagement in GNU/Linux demonstrates, commu-nities have become important sources of surplus value for capital. Hence, development communities confront capital just as waged labourers do. In order not to foreclose the many places where capital extracts surplus value and were there are a potential for labour conflicts, we need to take into account a much broader terrain than the direct workplace. The factory has spawned outwards to the whole of society. The concept of the 'social fac-tory' was first suggested by Mario Tronti in *La fabbrica e la società* back in 1962: "At the highest level of capitalist development social relations become moments of the relations of production, and the whole society becomes an articulation of production. In short, all of society lives as a function of the factory and the factory extends its exclusive domination over all of society."[76] The concept of the 'social factory' offers a promising avenue for analysing contemporary capitalism. The whole of society has been subjected to capitalist discipline and capitalist relations of production. For instance, everyday leisure activities like watching television or using a search engine on the Internet is turned into advertising revenue. Antonio Negri and Michael Hardt draw some far-reaching conclusions from this fact. The proletariat, who are defined as those being within capital and sustaining capital, are present everywhere. Not only wage labourers, but equally so home wives, unemployed, and students, are qualifying to belong to the proletariat.[77] This all-inclusive categorisation calls for a different description of how and why the working class opposes capital. Traditionally, Marxist theory has pinned down the workers' struggle to a contest over surplus labour. By surplus labour is meant the amount of working hours that people are forced to toil in excess of what they require for their own subsistence. Surplus labour is accumulated and becomes capital. Class struggle can thus be anchored directly in key concepts in Karl Marx's political economic critique. The collision between capital and labour is hell-bent since the employers desire longer and more intense working hours while employees want the very opposite. The definition is very elegant, perhaps a bit too elegant for its own good. During the twentieth century, under the influence of trade unions, the tug-of-war over surplus labour led to a narrow focus on pay levels and working hours, at the expense of other aspects of the class struggle. In the social factory, were the workday extends beyond the direct employment situation and even leisure activities have been put to work, the struggle over surplus labour cannot be read out of the stroke of the office clock. Antonio Negri and Michael Hardt make another drastic suggestion at this point. With inspiration from Michel Foucault, they argue that life is being nurtured and administrated by capital as an intrinsic part of the value-adding process. The resistance of the proletariat is therefore a bio-political struggle, at once economical, political and cultural, and centred on conflicting forms of life. They conclude their reinterpretation by stating that one way for the proletariat to fight back is to invent new public spaces and communities incompatible with the value form. (*Empire* 56)

These remarks assist us in our attempt at understanding the hacker movement in terms of labour struggle. The conflict over surplus labour that characterises the antagonism between labour and capital at the workplace has little explanatory power in the computer underground. Hackers volunteer to write software applications. They are more likely to be happy about spending an extra hour in front of the computer than trying to sneak a shortcut. As far as money is concerned, many hackers couldn't care less if a corporation profits from a project that they have contributed to. From the perspective of a trade unionist, amateurs labouring for free are nothing short of alarming. The unsuspecting hacker is ripe for exploitation, and what's more, while working away he is weakening the bargain position of employed programmers too. What hackers do care about, mainly free access to information, seems peripheral in comparison to social, labour, and environmental concerns. The glaring ignorance towards labour issues in the hacker movement has convinced Alan Liu to write off cyber-politics as subcultural 'bad attitude'. He charges that the demands for free information are individualistic, consumerist and entrepreneurial.[78] Alan Liu is mistaken because he portrays information in the same way as 'content providers' do, as merely a consumer product. From this perspective, the hacker's wish to have information for free appears like just another angry customer demanding more value for his money.

If we acknowledge that information also is a means of production, it becomes clear that the demand for free information is the same thing as 'access to tools'. With free licenses the tools to write software code are made accessible to everyone, thus they are free as in free from knowledge monopolies, white-collar professionals, and corporate hierarchies. Hacking undermines the technical division of labour that is pivotal to Taylorism.

Furthermore, the failure of hackers to mention labour issues is consistent with the fact that their politics is the politics of 'zero work'. At first it might sound odd, but the statement above is consistent with the extreme motivation and discipline of many hackers when they develop software code. The radicalism of the FOSS development model springs exactly from the distance it places between 'doing' and the wage relation. Hackers are contributing to radical social change because they prevent the labour market from being the sole determinant over the allocation of programming recourses in society. As a consequence, the economic rationality and instrumentality of technological development can not be taken for granted anymore, at least not in the computer sector. The model for developing technology invented by hackers is guided by the most non-instrumental of human activities: the play-drive.[79] Software code is not the end-purpose of hacking but rather an excess flowing from the playful form of life that hackers are choosing for themselves. Hackers may or may not be conscious about and motivated by the wider political implications from promoting access to computer tools. Linus Torvalds, for instance, has repeatedly proven his political innocence in rows with the Free Software Foundation. Nonetheless, he made the key decision to license the Linux kernel under a free license. The demand for free information is not grounded in ideological convictions as much as in the fact that the public space that hackers draw from can be sustained only if software technology stays open and accessible. It is the form of life of hackers that command resistance. Their commitment to sustaining the FOSS community is in conflict with at least some priorities of capital, though, admittedly, it also plays into the hands of capital in other respects. Would it not be fair to object that with corporations making millions of dollars out of FOSS applications, the liberating potential of hacking has been lost? In that case we must also say that the struggle of waged employees is non-existent since corporations make millions of dollars out of them. The fact that the hacker movement has partially been recuperated by capital does not falsify hacking as a radical praxis, unless we badly want to think so. The hacker movement is in continuation with more than two hundred years of labour struggle.

2 FOSS Development in a Post-Fordist Perspective

INFORMATION AGE LORE AND MARXISM

The politics of the hacker movement is anchored in a loosely defined conception of the world. The key to this narrative is the notion that we live in an information society, that information resources are different from tangible resources since information can be endlessly duplicated, and a strong bent for explaining historical change with technology. These beliefs are prevalent both in the libertarian and the anarchist camps of the computer underground.

In this chapter the world-view of hackers is contrasted with Marxist theory. It is argued that Free and Open Source Software (FOSS) development would be better set in the context of a restructured post-Fordist labour market. By taking labour as our point of departure, information appears no longer as a finished end product but as a continuous labour process. The demarcation line between information resources and intellectual property, on one side, and tangible resources and private property, on the other side, looks less absolute from this horizon. Permeating our discussion is the question about the causes of historical change, whether it can be attributed to technology or social conflicts. Not only are 'information age'-futurists separated from Marxists on this question, the divide cuts right through the Marxist tradition as well. The practice of hacking gives some clues about how human agency relates to technology. Furthermore, the FOSS movement provides a vantage point for updating Marxist theories on labour and value. The employment of user communities by companies is part of a more general trend where audiences and consumers become sources of surplus value for capital. In short, the hacker movement and Marxist theory can enrich each other, though at first sight they seem to stand very far apart.

Their differences start already with the notion of the information society. That idea underpins most Internet-related literature and it is the departing point for self-reflection within the computer underground. The genesis of the information society concept comes from writers in the 1950s announcing an end to class conflicts. The sharp end of their argumentation was pointed against Marx's prediction that capitalism headed towards a polarisation of two antagonistic classes, capitalists and proletarians, which would make a final showdown inevitable. These writers objected that the modern industrial society with its welfare provisions was moving towards diminishing social conflicts.[1] In the following decade, the claims about an end to ideology were coupled with the idea of a post-industrial society. The social causes for conflicts in capitalism would give way together with the manufacturing industry. One of the earliest and most scholarly inclined among post-industrial thinkers is Daniel Bell.[2] Writing in the 1960s and 1970s, Daniel Bell paved the way for more popularised works by futurists like Alvin Toffler, Peter Drucker and Robert Reich, just to mention the most influential names. With the advent of the Internet in the 1990s, similar thoughts surfaced yet again taking a slightly different shape, this time emphasising networks and information. A milestone is the three-volume study of the so called 'network society' by the sociologist Manuel Castells. While adopting the standard themes of the genre, Castells grounds his argument on a great amount of empirical data and treats his subject more critically than his peers. He acknowledges the continued existence of social conflicts in the network society but disputes the relevance of class-based struggle.[3] The latest, though hardly the last, outgrowth of this tradition is Richard Florida's announcement of the rise of the creative class. He proposes that monotonous work assignments are about to be replaced with stimulating jobs, not because of workers' resistance, but since creativity is more profitable to capital.[4] A common trait of this literature is the assurance that the downsides of old capitalism will be solved by a more advanced capitalism.

Though this loose family of ideas set out to attack Marxism, it was often conceived by people that once were Marxists themselves. Thus, at least superficially, there are many overlapping features between the inexplicit assumptions of post-industrial thinking and historical materialism. In the futurist outlook, history is divided into three periods according to a few key technological breakthroughs: the agricultural age, the industrial age and the informational age. Classical Marxism identifies epochs in history too but on very different criteria. Presented as a straightforward and somewhat simplified schema, these stages count to primitive communism, slavery, feudalism, capitalism, and eventually, communism. The categorisation is here based on how labour is organised in class relations. The Marxist writer Nick-Dyer Witheford pins down the key difference that separates Marxism from its post-industrial look-alikes: "That rewriting retains the notion of historical progress towards a classless society but reinscribes technological advance rather than class conflict as the driving force in this transformation".[5] The information-age literature is more plagued with technological determinism than any version of historical materialism ever was.[6] Despite that these shortcomings of the historical materialist theory have been severely criticised by opponents of Marxism, as well as by many self-critical Marxists, postulations about the information age often go unquestioned, except by Marxists. Being somewhat rhetorical, one could say that bourgeois thinkers enrolled historical materialism, and radicals dropped it, at the time when liberal market economy instead of communism seemed to be the fixed endpoint of history. Throughout the 1980s and 1990s, Marxists have responded by exposing the vulgarities and the ideological agenda behind post-industrial fancies.[7] The main objections are as follows. Writers abiding to the information-age concept fail to take account of power relationships in their new society. They forget that information is not a given end product but the result of human labour. They ignore that a staff of what Robert Reich calls symbol-analysts require a manual labour force that satisfies the material needs of those professionals. Finally, they downplay the continuity of capitalism and industrialism in the new era of information and services.

Though these objections are valid, the criticism is counter-productive if it goes too far and denies the importance of information altogether. If information is not given its due credit the implications from it cannot be drawn, but are left to apologetics to interpret for their own ends.[8] The insight of Roland Barthes on how mythology works can be of assistance here. He says that a myth, to be plausible, always contains a core of truth. The lie just casts the significance of the facts in a different light. When futurists jump on the Information-age bandwagon they set out to glorify digital capitalism. Thus they dig out all those potentialities in capitalism that are humane, in other words, that are the contradictory tendencies pointing away from capitalism, towards communism. The irony comes full circle when progressive scholars, anxious to reveal the ideological smokescreen of the apologists, respond by fiercely denouncing the same potentialities. We should therefore be cautious not to dismiss the futurists in a *tout court* fashion.

The recycling of topics from post-industrial literature is most forthcoming in the work of some autonomous Marxist writers.[9] Post-modern capitalism is here framed in discussions about networks, immaterial labour and communication, which surely has contributed to the popularity of the work of Antonio Negri's and Michael Hardt. A speculation on offer is that their readiness to borrow concepts first claimed by post-industrial ideology owes to them having distanced themselves from historical materialism to begin with. They trace their philosophical roots to other sources of influence. In the place of Hegel stand Niccolo Machiavelli, Benedict de Spinoza, and Friedrich Nietzsche. Maybe this has allowed them to jump straight at a post-modern, linguistic-centred reading of Marx. The ambition here is, however, to work towards roughly the same conclusions but from within a more classical Marxist terminology. This take on the subject matter is needed to anchor the post-modern, cyber-Marx in a longer tradition of Marxism. If the old school of labour theory is simply abandoned for something else, we will lose the many insights into labour struggle collected in this extensive body of study. In line with the mission statement above, the argumentation will be traced through a disparate collection of classic Marxist sources as they happen to run in parallel with the ideas presented more coherently by some autonomous Marxist authors.

HISTORICAL MATERIALISM AND LANGUAGE

The dynamics of history conceptualised in Marxism is heavily indebted to Hegel's philosophy. Hegel departed from his contemporaries in recognising that society was not a given static but was at every moment in the process of evolving into something else. The process of change consisted of a dialectical movement between opposites unfolding into a higher unity. Hegel's idea is best captured in the well-known dictum: 'thesis-antithesis-synthesis'. In the context of Marxism, capitalism (thesis) has created its adversary, the industrial proletariat (anti-thesis); which will bring about communism (synthesis). In Hegel as in Marx, the movement towards synthesis correlates to the idea of totality. By totality is meant that the parts are related to the whole in a meaningful way and that individual observations can only be explained with some knowledge about the systematic level.[10] While retaining the dialectic model of thinking, Marx replaced Hegel's idealism with materialism and famously declared that he had 'turned Hegel on his feet'. In opposition to idealism, the materialist world-view laid down that human consciousness is conditioned by its material existence and social relations. The materialist conception of history underlies Karl Marx's philosophy but it was Friedrich Engels that systemised the theory and gave it the name 'historical materialism'. The next generation of Marxists, most notably Karl Kautsky, inherited the historical materialist terminology and gave it a more rigid and simplistic articulation. In its popularised version the theory claimed that it could prove the scientific necessity of history moving dialectically towards communism. It had a big influence on the early labour movement and as a mobilising tool, if not as an intellectual tool, it might have been of some use. It is this strawman that is attacked when adversaries set out to dismiss Marxism in general. A brief summary of the propositions in historical materialist theory is required in order to criticise it and relate it to notions about the Internet and the information age.

Historical materialism deduces changes in society back to its material *base*. One part of the base is made up of the *forces of production*. Forces of production include the technical instruments of labour (machinery, tools) and the skills of the labourers. The second half of the material base is the operation and control over the forces of production. This is known as the *relations of production*. The class presiding over the relations of production is the ruling class of that period. In a capitalist society, relations of production are orchestrated through private property, and property is concentrated in the hands of the capitalist class. The ruling class favours a particular legal, political, and ideological setup of society, the so-called *superstructure*. Norms that acknowledge private property and sanction contractual agreements, and laws that punish violations of property and the breaking of contracts, for instance, are favoured by the ruling class since it supports capitalist relations of production. Having laid bare the hidden clockwork of society, the theory then gives some projections about how this mechanism operates over time. In the strict, orthodox version of the theory advocated by Gerald Cohen, the epic looks like this: forces of production develop continuously, as labour methods and tools are improved incrementally. The relations of production, on the other hand, are conserved by the ruling class, since they have a stake in preserving *status quo*. A growing mismatch between forces and relations of production fuels a revolutionary upheaval and ensures the victory of the suppressed class.[11]

The narrative of orthodox historical materialism corresponds with some very popular ideas in the computer underground. It is widely held that the infinite reproducibility of information made possible by computers (forces of production) has rendered intellectual property (relations of production, superstructure) obsolete. The storyline of post-industrial ideology is endorsed but with a different ending. Rather than culminating in global markets, technocracy and liberalism, as Daniel Bell and the futurists would have it; hackers are looking forward to a digital gift economy and high-tech anarchism. In a second turn of events, hackers have jumped on the distorted remains of Marxism presented in information-age literature, and, while missing out on the vocabulary, ended up promoting an upgraded Karl Kautsky-version of historical materialism. Among contemporary Marxists, conversely, the simplistic scheme of orthodox historical materialism has been discredited. Before we incorporate the lessons from the Internet and hacking into theory, we had better consult the latest developments in Marxist philosophy. For instance, as will be discussed towards the end of the chapter, the exceptionalism ascribed to information that underpins the claim about a digital gift economy and information commons, does not hold water when examined closer. It is crucial to problematise these concepts or else we might be tricked into singing in a different tune the official hymn of digital capitalism in a different tune.

The key controversy in the debate over historical materialism is to what extent technological development modifies class relations as opposed to the impact of class struggle in shaping technology. It is a question that cuts right through the Marxist tradition and is also present in Karl Marx's authorship.[12] A conceptual weakness with the first approach, the *technicist* line of reasoning, is that technology is here understood as a self-explanatory, coherent and delimited category. But tools only become useful in a certain environment that supports their utilization. This ambiguity was formulated by Wiebe Bijker, a student of technology, by saying that technologies are subject to *interpretative flexibility*. An out-dated technology cannot be assessed without knowing both the historical context and the semiotics of which it was a part. Bijker illustrates his claim by pointing at the passing from high-wheeled bicycles to safety bicycles. The temptation to dismiss, in hindsight, the high-wheeled bicycle as an inferior and unsafe prototype on the path to evolutionary perfection (the safety bicycle) must be resisted. High-wheeled bicycles were used by upper-class youths, not primarily for transportation but to show off their nerves and skills. The very qualities that made these vehicles unsafe from one perspective made them attractive from the view-point of its chief propagators. To be seated high above the heads of ordinary pedestrians was certainly part of the fun. Furthermore, some long-forgotten conditions of the time, such as muddy and bumpy roads, could even make it sort of practical. Bijker therefore rules out the common notion that the high-wheeled bicycle was a brief deviation from an otherwise linear path towards ever greater functionality.[13]

It is only in hindsight that a technology seems to advance along a fixed benchmark. The point of direction marked out in orthodox historical mate-rialism is therefore, at the very least, seriously confused. An innovation will never take hold unless it is in the interest of a class fraction to actively prepare the ground for it. The classical example hereof is Imperial China. Already back in the fifteenth century the material and intellectual resources seem to have converged for an industrial take-off. Instead of industrialising, the Ming dynasty was marked by stagnation, at least in terms of innovation, though the economy boomed and the population grew steadily. Industri-alisation came three hundred years later and on the western fringe of the Euro-Asian continent. The reason for this can be ascribed to the organisa-tion of the Chinese empire as opposed to the organisation of nation states in Europe. Class rule in China was intimately tied up with state bureaucracy. Often the imperial administration chose to impede inventions because cohe-sion and stability was its top priority. While making this argument, the his-torian of economics Joel Mokyr stresses the monolithic political culture of the Chinese empire at the time when technological stagnation took hold. In earlier and technologically more dynamic dynasties, politics had also been more pluralistic. On the European continent, in contrast, sovereignty was divided between several, rivalling nation states. If one monarch blocked an expedition or invention within his jurisdiction, the explorer or inventor could turn to the sovereign in a neighbouring state.[14]

Maybe this explains how the European ruling class came to ally itself so closely with disruption and change. Arguably, the longevity of capitalism owes precisely to its elasticity in capturing the innovations of the subju-gated class. The hacktivist group Electrohippies puts it well: "All resistance is fertile". Their motto could sum up the rewriting of the history of tech-nology by autonomous Marxists. Here the thrust of technological devel-opment is attributed to capital's responses to working class resistance.[15] A well-documented fact supporting such a reading is that machinery is often introduced after major labour conflicts. The sudden urge among managers to lay off obstinate workers and weaken unions overcomes the costs also associated with new technology. This observation, familiar to labour theory, is expanded by autonomists so that the changes we are living through at the moment, networks, computerisation etc., are attributed to the great social upheaval of 1968 which launched capital into a process of crisis and restruc-turing. The perspective is appealing since it challenges the common image of capital as active and labour as reactive or passive. It reverses the causality drawn up between technological and economical structures on one hand and class struggle on the other. And if the ontological claims are narrowed down to the context of computer technology, it does a fairly good job at describing the relation between the hacker movement and software development. But, at least as far as Antonio Negri is concerned, the effort to break away from set patterns within the Marxist discipline comes at a high price. He dismisses the dialectics inherited from Hegel and declares that the law of value has ceased to function. As we will return to later on, the law of value stipulates that the exchange value of goods is correlated to the amount of labour-time it takes to produce the goods. According to Negri, the productivity of social and scientific labour disqualifies this correlation and makes labour immeasurable.[16] Without the law of value, however, much of Karl Marx's political-economical critique is left hanging in the air.

The law of value is not only consistent with capitalism after 1968, but the hypothesis is rather helpful when investigating the high-tech, information-rich computer sector. In this task, lead will be taken from the Belgian Trotskyite Ernest Mandel. Mandel covered roughly the same terrain as Antonio Negri; studying the increased use of scientific labour in a period which he tentatively labelled 'late capitalism'. Later on, Fredric Jameson based his acclaimed study of post-modernity on Mandel's analysis, declaring post-modernism as "the cultural logic of late capitalism".[17] Jameson was attracted to the Marxist version of an epochal breach in capitalism because it provided him with a position from which the post-industrialist notions could be countered. This vantage point was succinctly phrased by Ernest Mandel in the saying that the superstructure has been mechanised.[18] By that he meant that the economic instrumentality previously perfected in the factory had now embarked upon culture, law, politics, and society at large. Where post-industrialists claimed that political economy has dissolved into a cloud of culture and meaning, Mandel retorted that the economy has become near omnipresent.[19] Antonio Negri attests to the same phenomenon, though speaking from a very different tradition within Marxism, when he announces that society has been subjected to *real subsumption*. The terminology is borrowed from Karl Marx. In a draft for the first volume of *Capital*, Marx compared *formal subsumption* to real subsumption. Formal subsumption describes how the early capitalists hired craftsmen to produce goods for a market but without reforming their working methods. Real subsumption arose as the workers became more dependent upon the capitalist and the whole enterprise was restructured according to capital's needs. The craft methods were broken down into the organisation of the factory. Negri says that the same thing is now happening to human relations, to language, and to life, a development culminating in the social factory.

The mechanisation of the superstructure, or, if preferred, the real subsumption of society, provides a framework for analysing the heightened relevance of communication in the economy today. Part of the reason why classical Marxism looks outdated is because of its one-sided focus on manual labour and the production of tangible goods. Language was of little concern at the time when Karl Marx wrote. When the Frankfurt School begun scrutinising the culture industry in the 1930s and 1940s they departed from traditional Marxist themes.[20] But they too saw communication primarily as a question of propaganda and ideology. For a long time, mass media was a political rather than an economical problem. Today it is clear that language is a key element of production. Indeed, the Italian Marxist Paolo Virno assigns communication industries a heightened order within the echelons of production. In the twentieth century, this privileged position was held by heavy industries that made machinery tools. Since machinery tools had an impact on downstream production, Marxist doctrine considered it to be of particular importance. Nowadays the skills and the motivation of the staff are more important than tools and machinery. Accordingly, Virno argues, it is the communication industries that create the means of production most relevant to all the other industries.[21] It is through this prism that the surge of post-structuralist theory and the pivotal role given to language by thinkers such as Michel Foucault and Jacques Derrida can be seen, though they would have objected to being framed in such a context.

An emphasis on language does not mean that the materialist conception of history is abandoned for a turn back to idealism. Quite the opposite, the materialist outlook is reaffirmed by recognising that communication has been mechanised.[22] Nothing illustrates this point better than computer algorithms. In source code, signs have become mechanics in their own right. Software shifts between being a consumer product, a process technology, an infrastructure, an instrument of regulation, a subculture, and a language. This provides a concrete example of Negri's claim that the forces of production and the relations of production have blurred into an indistinguishable one. What happens in one area, a changed self-image in the computer underground, for example, directly translates into the other area, the advance of a different technology.

The struggle for free source code is an excellent point of reference when we contemplate over the determination of structures versus the agency of humans, the Gordian knot of Marxist philosophy. The strong inclination towards technological determinism in the computer underground is a contradictory mixture of thought and praxis. Just as with their endorsement of information-age literature, everything is not what first meets the eye. For hackers, in contrast to almost everyone else, technology increases their collective strength. Technophilia reassures hackers of their eventual victory just as dialectical historical materialism did to revolutionaries in those days when communism was thought of as the fixed endpoint of history. In most other cases, references to the inevitability of technological progress are meant to discourage people from taking action. Decisions over technological development are firmly located in the hands of a profession, and, by extension, investors. Often it is hard to discern a field of technology as under dispute at all. It is near-total defeat, not the absence of antagonism, which has rendered technological development to appear as a neutral, self-directed process, floating freely outside the universe of political choices. Radical scholars, anxious to reveal the political stakes behind technology and the possibility of intervention into these flows, spare no energy in attacking deterministic viewpoints. Raymond Williams, a stern critic of technological determinism, lays down that: "The moment of any new technology is a moment of choice."[23] Conversely, however, for a choice to be of any meaning, it must delimit in some way the choices available after it has been made.[24]

The fascination in the computer underground for Marshall McLuhan's contemplations (declared by *Wired Magazine* as their protective saint and Raymond Williams' favoured target when attacking technological determinism) should be seen in this light. The influence of McLuhan among hackers must somehow be consistent with their grasping of technology as a politically contested field. This insight is inseparable from the praxis of hacking because capital has lost its monopoly over software development. Hence, the recognition that code design is underpinned by political choices is immediately transparent in hacking. While ascribing to the convictions which Raymond Williams criticises, the hacker subculture epitomise the very opposite of his worst-case scenario where people are pacified because of the overbearing force of technology. If hackers do not ponder over the hidden agendas that shape technology and restrict their life and freedoms, it is because they are in the position of setting such agendas themselves. Their attention is instead on how their choices in code design confine the possible options thereafter, for them and for less skilled computer users. Questions first brought up by progressive architects on how the cityscape affects the conduct of its inhabitants are rebounding in the computer underground. The issue at stake is best captured in the slogan of the cofounder of the *Electronic Frontier Foundation*, Mitch Kapor: '*Architecture is Politics*'.[25] It could be objected that ordinary users are prey to the design choices of hackers as much as to those of companies. Indeed, part of the attraction with being a hacker is to perceive oneself as an elite vis-à-vis 'newbies', 'scriptkiddies' and 'lamers', some of the many names given to less experienced users. But with the mainstreaming of the Internet, a countervailing awareness is growing on the people in the computer underground. Since the least skilled users also are by far the most numerous, it is their decisions that add up to setting the standard of computers. And in communication networks, standards are everything. Free software can not be written exclusively "by engineers, for engineers" since hackers too will be hurt if the majority of users side with proprietary technology enclosed behind electronic locks. The goal of making free software accessible to ordinary computer users has grown into a real concern among FOSS developers. In conclusion, the decision over what the next generation of computer technology will be like is spread out to every computer user.

INFORMATED AND AUTOMATED PRODUCTION
IN POST-FORDIST CAPITALISM

Marxists tend to use Fordism and post-Fordism to categorise the historical transformation that elsewhere is talked about as the industrial and informational society. The categorisation of Fordism/post-Fordism centres on differences in the labour process, out of which technology is one component.[26] Liberal commentators understand Fordism as a period when productivity in society was rapidly increased but with some unfortunate consequences for workers. Those downsides have now been resolved, the same writers believe, thanks to the passing of Fordism. Labour theoreticians, on the other hand, insist that Fordism from the beginning was a strategy to control and deskill workers and make them expendable. They argue that it was not the advancement of science and technology, but the resistance of workers, that spelled the end to Fordism. When workers organised against the old factory regime, Fordism became increasingly costly to keep up. Post-Fordism is a renewed attack on the positions of workers and, in this regard, it is in complete continuance with Fordism.

The passing from Fordism to post-Fordism was first noted in the 1970s by a group of Marxist scholars known as the French Regulation School. One of the leading names of the school, Michel Aglietta, characterised the labour process of Fordism as semi-automatic assembly-line production.[27] At the time he wrote, managers had come to the conclusion that the strategy of Fordism was failing. It could not fulfil their dreams of a factory run entirely without skilled workers. Knowledgeable employees were still called for to bridge the gaps in the semi-automated production line. Furthermore, Fordism created new vulnerabilities to capital's valorisation process. An interruption at one point on the conveyer belt resulted in a standstill of the whole chain. The monotonousness of the tasks provoked spontaneous absenteeism with devastating consequences for profitability. Another drawback was that large investments in machinery locked production into long production runs. Mass production of single products made the point of sale of the goods all the more risky. The rigidities of Fordism provided a foothold for workers' resistance. Bogged down by labour conflicts, capital opted for a more flexible *accumulation regime*, what Michel Aglietta tentatively called neo-Fordism. The labour process was made flexible by shortening the feed-back loops between the worker and the work done. Michel Aglietta observed that this strategy required that the production line was both *informated* as well as *automated*. The seminal economic importance of software can be attributed to its usefulness in this regard. Separate stages of semi-automation are integrated in fully automated production flows thanks to the implementation of algorithms. Arguably, the informated and automated factory is a step closer to the qualitative turning point envisioned by Ernest Mandel: "*The automatic production of automatic machines would hence be a new qualitative turning point*, equal in significance to the appearance of the machine-production of machines in the mid-19th century" (*Mandel*, 206–207, *italics in original*). Claims that capitalism is heading in this direction can find support in a few sentences by Karl Marx. In the celebrated paragraph *Fragment of Machinery*, he sketched out the trajectory of big industry. The future predicted by Karl Marx is a close call to the world we live in today: "But to the degree that large industry develops, the creation of real wealth comes to depend less on labour time and on the amount of labour employed than on the power of the agencies set in motion during labour time, whose powerful effectiveness is itself in turn out of all proportion to the direct labour time spent on their production, but depends rather on the general state of science and on the progress of technology, or the application of this science to production." (*Grundrisse*, 704–705). Karl Marx proposed that at this stage a 'general intellect' would emerge as a productive force in its own right. The brief remarks in the *Fragment of Machinery* strengthens the statement, common in post-industrial literature, that the informational sector is transforming the industry in the same way as industrialisation transformed agriculture. According to this view, information and networks are rendered important because of their productiveness. Sceptically inclined Marxists explain the rapid growth of the tertiary sector in the very opposite way. Instead of attributing it to the productivity of information, the service industry is looked upon as a 'surplus dump' that resolves the vast overproduction in monopoly capitalism. If that assessment was correct, however, the information age would be over with the first downturn in the economy and the following destruction of surplus capacity. The sustained and growing importance of information to the industry calls for a closer engagement.

A number of radical scholars, most notably Antonio Negri, Michael Hardt and related thinkers, have married the concepts of a general intellect with post-Fordist restructuring. This fusion of ideas underpins their claim about a novel class composition, variably named cyborgs, immaterial labour, the social worker, or the multitude. The communicative, affective and scientific processes engaged in by these people constitute the general intellect. In announcing the rise of a different class, Negri, Hardt, and others, are contributing to a two-hundred-year-old tradition with roots both in the liberal and the socialist camps. Liberals have invariably heralded the new social stratum as the bearer of an end to class conflicts, while radicals of course have made the very opposite judgement.[28] Revolutionary hopes were attached to the high-tech worker already in the 1960s when Serge Mallet wrote about the New Working Class. The subjectivity of the young workers in the automated factory, Mallet attested, was particularly disposed to seeing through the contradictions of the capitalist system.[29] Thirty years down the road, Maurizio Lazzarato makes a similar argument about workers in the cutting-edge sector of our day. Immaterial labour, as he calls it, is a hegemonic form of labour in post-Fordist capitalism. He defines immaterial labour as the labour that produces the informational and cultural content of the commodity. Firstly, it refers to the changes taking place in the labour process in the industrial and tertiary sectors. The change consists in that the subjectivity of the labourer has become as important to productivity as the trade skills he is in possession of. Secondly, immaterial labour includes activities that cross the boundary between work and leisure, such as setting aesthetic standards, developing tastes, creating consumer norms, and shaping public opinion. Admittedly, the number of immaterial labourers in the world is very small. Lazzarato justifies his interest in them, in affinity with the devotion that Karl Marx showed for the marginal group of factory workers, by projecting that immaterial labour indicates the future direction of capitalism.[30]

Even so, the idea of a new class of immaterial labourers has been criticised on the grounds that the vast majority of the world's population live under very different conditions compared to professionals in the media and computer industry. Undue focus on privileged workers in the West mirrors post-industrial ideology where everyone is said soon to become a member of the creative class.[31] It should be evident that a plurality of labour relations coexists in the global economy. Far from decomposing old forms of making and living, post-modern capitalism feeds on inequalities and differences between regions. It draws together feudal and patriarchal structures in some provinces with 'Fordist' wage labour and 'post-Fordist' networks of freelancers and petty commodity traders in other places. Indeed, George Caffentzis has argued convincingly that the more technologically advanced the industrialised countries become, the worse the exploitation of labour gets in the remaining parts of the world. In an article in the *Midnight Notes Collective*, Caffentzis based his case on a vision of the computer scientist John von Neumann about a self-replicating, automatised factory. In this hypothetical scenario, where the production process involves no living labour whatsoever, there will be no value generated for the capitalist to exploit. The law of value postulates that only human labour can add value to a product. Human labour is unique in that it enlarges the value of a product above the sum of its own inputs. In this narrow, economistic sense, the value of the human input equals the amount of food, clothing, education, and recreation that is necessary for the worker to reproduce her labour power at a given moment.[32] The extra value which human labour adds to a product, above this input of 'necessary labour', amounts to surplus labour/ surplus value. That is to say, labour time which the worker is not compensated for. Accumulation of capital is precisely the build-up of surplus value. The more human labour an individual capitalist can set in motion, the more surplus value he derives from the enterprise. On the other hand, adding more inputs of dead labour, by which is meant tools and raw materials, will not add any more value to the end product above the value of the inputs themselves. Dead labour in production is dead weight. Hence, Neuman's self-replicating automatic factory would never add any value to the goods it produced above the value of the factory itself. Whatever surplus value gained from running this factory would have to derive from a transfer of wealth from more backward sectors in the economy. Caffentzis concludes that the exploitation of African peasants and workers in South-American maquiladora factories has to be intensified in order to compensate for the automation and absence of living labour in high-tech, Western industries. It is these people that the capitalist world system really depends on, rather than the symbol-analysts in the tertiary sector.[33]

Caffentzis has relentlessly criticised Lazzarato, Negri, and likeminded scholars on this ground, advising them to expand their geographical horizon. At stake is the question where to best strike against the capitalist system. In affinity with Maoist strategic thinking, Caffentzis takes the desperation of the most wretched people as a stepping stone for revolutionary action. The opposite point of view contends that capitalism is closest to being superseded where it is most developed. It is the second tradition of thought that this book ascribes to. Nevertheless, George Caffentzis' insistence on the importance of the proletariat in the Third World to the existence of cutting-edge, digital capitalism provides a healthy reality check. His reasoning is theoretically sound, though it does not provide an exhaustive explanation. As will be argued at length, capital has more options for sustaining profitability than increasing the rate of exploitation of workers in the periphery. Shifting production from waged employees to unpaid users is another possibility, a trend that is persistent in the industrialised economies. A scholarly preoccupation with these changes in the labour process is not a manifestation of Eurocentrism, since it has global ramifications. Governments in developing countries have come to embrace Free and Open Source Software (FOSS) as part of national strategies to increase technological and economical independence vis-à-vis Western powers. When municipalities and schools in the South are spared the expense of buying software licenses from multinational corporations, the flow of revenue from the periphery to the centre, that were to compensate for automation in the West, is somewhat reduced. The concrete gains of FOSS development to Third World populations is not invalidated by the fact that the software code has mainly been written by a marginal group of middle class males living comfortably in the rich countries.

SOFTWARE ALGORITHMS AND SURPLUS VALUE

The what-if scenario of total automation, which George Caffentzi elaborates with, also puzzled the mind of Ernest Mandel. He wrote that the extensive enrolment of science in production delivers capitalism close to the point where the: "[. . .] *mass of surplus-value itself necessary diminishes as a result of the elimination of living labour from the production process in the course of the final stage of mechanization-automation.*" (*Mandel*, 207, italics in original) Ernest Mandel builds on the Marxist theory of the 'falling rate of profit'. The tendency towards a falling rate of profit owes to the decimation of human labour in production. Capital seeks to replace living labour with machinery—dead labour—to increase productivity, stay competitive and combat labour militancy. However, as we saw before, dead labour does not add any extra value. The overall output from production rises with more and better machinery. But the amount of living labour in relation to dead labour falls. It follows that a smaller quantity of surplus value is divided up on the larger amount of goods produced. Profit falls in relation to the amount of capital invested in the undertaking. This is the law of the 'falling rate of profit'.

The expectations of early Marxists, that capitalism would spiral downwards into aggravated crises and eventually self-destruct because of falling profitability, has by now been thoroughly discredited. Nevertheless, the law of the falling rate of profit does portray a gradual movement towards a logical endpoint, suggested by Ernest Mandel—total automation, which simultaneously is inconceivable with capitalism. A state of total automation, as it was envisioned already by John von Neumann, would be reached when machinery, without any injection of living labour, spits out an infinite volume of goods at instant speed. It is hard to imagine a machine with such dimensions, less than visualising science fiction gadgets or, just slightly more down-to-earth, nanotechnologic fantasies. Or alternatively: software algorithms. That is what is meant by saying that information can be copied infinitely without injecting additional labour. Digitalisation has leapfrogged capitalism to the endpoint of total automation. The extreme situation is, of course, confined to the software industry and related branches. However, if we subscribe to the concept of the general intellect, it follows that informational production stands to become hegemonic in the economy.

Readers are justified in objecting that individual capitalists are doing very well in the software business. How does the statement above square with Microsoft being one of the most profitable companies in the world? Capitalism is not coming to an end because of a future state of total automation. On the contrary, the economic system is currently busy at adapting to the challenge and is doing very well at it. George Caffentzis points to one solution, namely increasing the rate of exploitation in labour-intensive sectors, primarily in underdeveloped, low-tech economies. The surplus value extracted in these countries is then channelled to capital in the high-tech sector. The pattern of growing mechanisation on one side, and growing poverty of labour on the other, is business-as-usual in the market economy, extending a logic that was familiar already to Karl Marx. But the option to intensify exploitation of the Third World proletariat is not endless. Limits are set by the unionisation of workers, growing militancy among the population, and the prospect that western-oriented, neoliberal governments will be toppled, either by nationalist reformers or religious fundamentalists. To the extent that capital is restrained from taking this route, it has to find other ways to solve the problem of automation. A possible route has been uncovered by Tessa Morris-Suzuki. She has elaborated on Mandel's work to answer how capitalism can sustain the exploitation of surplus value together with a partial, asymmetrical state of automation, but with a twist: "This fission of labor inherent in the nature of robots, in other words, creates a situation where it is only in the design of new productive information and the initial bringing together of information and machinery that surplus value can be extracted. Unless this process is continually repeated, surplus value cannot be continuously created, and the total mass of profit must ultimately fall."[34] She calls this state of affair the *perpetual innovation economy*. Tessa Morris-Suzuki's reasoning provides a theoretical backbone for understanding the heightened relevance of innovation and collective learning processes in late capitalism. Valorisation of capital is concentrated to the starting-up of a production line, rather than the running of the production line. Capitalism has always sought to increase profitability by accelerating product cycles. When this logic turns on the innovation process itself, creative destruction enters 'warp speed'. The odd situation is particular forthcoming in the computer sector. Since the manufacturing process here consists of little more than "copy-and-paste", efforts are placed in the invention of new software algorithms. Software code is developed and made obsolete at such speeds that the product form of computer applications, i.e. boxes wrapped up and marketed in yearly releases, is dissolving into a continuous process where the application is upgraded every two weeks. Point-of-sale is replaced with subscription services as the favoured business model. The experimentation with novel ways of doing business in the computer sector shows that the reasoning of Tessa Morris-Suzuki, that surplus value is exploited in the stage of innovation instead of manufacturing, has profound consequences for Marxist theory. Her thought can be stretched yet a bit further. Most innovations in post-modern capitalism are what Fredric Jameson has called 'aesthetic innovation'. It is primarily the invention of style and meaning. Only a tiny portion of society's aesthetic innovation takes place in science laboratories and advertising agencies. In other words: within the wage relation. The overwhelming majority of aesthetic innovations are made in the street, in communities, in language, by users. It is thus we can start to outline the dimensions of the social factory.

AUDIENCES AND USERS AS SOURCES OF SURPLUS VALUE

In order to include users and audiences in the production process we need to re-examine the commonsense categorisation of production and consumption. Starting with Jean Baudrillard, post-modernists have relentlessly charged that Marxism is outdated because it fails to give due consideration to consumption as well as production. While post-modernists and mainstream economists recently became aware of the overlapping between the consumer and the producer role in the cultural economy, Karl Marx had a more complex picture to start with. In *Grundrisse* he wrote:

Consumption produces production in a double way, (1) because a product becomes a real product only by being consumed. For example, a garment becomes a real garment only in the act of being worn; a house where no one lives is in fact not a real house; thus the product, unlike a mere natural object, proves itself to be, *becomes,* a product only through consumption. Only by decomposing the product does consumption give the product the finishing touch; for the product is production not as objectified activity, but rather only as object for the active subject; (2) because consumption creates the need for *new* production, that is it creates the ideal, internally impelling cause for production, which is its presupposition. (*Grundrisse,* 91, *italics in original*)

The key point is that a product becomes a full product only when it is consumed. In other words, the user plays a part in producing the product. This was the case long before post-modernists, management gurus and, more recently, critics of the intellectual property regime, made the discovery. The fact that it has caught their attention at this late hour is, nonetheless, an indication of the heightened importance of the user in the cultural economy. Culture is nothing if not communication and communication is a continuously ongoing process between the 'producer' and the user. This aspect is plainly obvious in collective and oral forms of culture where the exchange between audience and performer is immediate. With the advent of mechanical reproduction of the art work, the performance of a work of art and the site of the performance were separated. Divorced from its context, art could be moved, owned, scaled, and sold. It is thus we have come to think of cultural content as one-directional information and not as communication running in both directions. But something is inevitably lost when art is mass produced. Walter Benjamin's seminal article on how the artwork fares in the age of mechanical reproduction offers some guidance: "Even the most perfect reproduction of a work of art is lacking in one element: its presence in time and space, its unique existence at the place where it happens to be."[35] Far from grieving the loss of authenticity, Benjamin anticipated the involvement and appropriation of the film medium by the audience. A void was left to be occupied by the audience, opening up exactly in the limitations of mass-communication. It remains for the film audience to close the cognitive loop and 'take the position of the camera', as Benjamin put it. Even something as passive as watching a film requires a learning process from the viewer. The viewer must place the message in a narrative for the signals to be of any meaning to her. Hence, the dialogue is not so much stifled as postponed and obscured by the commodity form of culture. This is essentially the rediscovery made by the British Cultural Studies. In the 1980s they began to focus on the decoding process of audiences instead of the encoding process by the broadcasters.[36] Their research developed in opposition to the tradition inherited from Max Horkheimer and Theodor Adorno, where television audiences tended to be seen as duped and pacified by the culture industry. The reassessment within British Culture Studies was part of a more general trend at the time. Acts of defiance were searched for within popular culture and the perception of active producers and passive consumers was questioned. A centrepiece within this literature from the 1980s is Michel de Certeau's study of everyday resistance in consumer society.[37] He objected to the popular notion that the only resistance worth counting is observable acts of self-conscious and articulated protests. Pointing at how colonised people subvert the religious beliefs which are forced upon them by their conquerors, Certeau argued that similar tactics were used by consumers. The ambition to find new grounds for struggle is commendable. Conversely, the pitfalls of this approach are illustrated by those media scholars who came to describe the zapping between tv-channels as an act of resistance.[38] It is unsurprising that these thoughts branched off into the liberal notion of changing the world through consumer choice and, among post-modern leftists, an unwarranted gravity ascribed to the criticism of representations. Opponents of British Cultural Studies have rightly protested that the decoding process by audiences is blown out of proportion, that broadcasters hold infinitely more power over the message, and that the political economy of communication still matters the most.[39] The decoding process by audiences does not offer much ground for resistance. As a cognitive and emotional investment and a source of surplus value for capital, on the other hand, the decoding process is a sizeable factor. Thus, the hardliners of political economy are mistaken too when they respond to the adepts of cultural studies by downplaying the importance of audiences.

Dallas Smythe has made an important contribution by applying the Marxist law of value to television audiences. He started with a maxim known since the advent of radio, 'the Sarnoff Law', which states that the wealth of a broadcasting network stands in proportion to its number of non-paying listeners. Smythe deduced that the commodity sold by media networks is the attention of audiences. The consumer buying into this product is the advertiser. It follows that the audience has the role of the producer, together with, to a lesser extent, the paid actors making the tv-shows. Mirroring the Marxist term labour power, Dallas Smythe introduces the word *audience power* to describe the work performed by audiences.[40] He runs into some difficulties when explaining why people volunteer to watch television and listen to commercial radio if it is a kind of unpaid, unsolicited work. Smythe starts with a fact familiar to working class women: Work does not end with the labourer leaving the factory gate. In their spare time, workers must prepare themselves for the next day in the factory; by cooking, cleaning, and sleeping; and preparing the next generation of workers, by sexual intercourse and childrearing. Prior to the advance of monopoly capitalism, reproduction of labour power was sorted out inside the household. Bread was baked, clothes sewn, tools tinkered with, and mating of adolescents seen to, inside the family or the extended family. Today the purchase of consumer goods fills the same purpose of facilitating the reproduction of labour power. It is therefore, according to Dallas Smythe, that audiences have to sacrifice their spare time in order to stay informed about available goods.[41]

Smythe did not expand on the similarity between the reproductive labour of audiences and that of women. Still, the experience of women demonstrates that capitalist exploitation of unwaged, reproductive labour is neither a marginal nor a novel phenomenon. In the 1970s feminist Marxists brought attention to the fact that housewives and children link up to capitalist circulation. Women devote necessary labour and surplus labour time to cleaning, cooking, caring, childrearing etc., out of which the surplus labour is appropriated by the husband. The relationship between the members of the family is feudal while the household relates to capital through the man's employment. The exploitation of the woman's reproductive labour affects the ratio between necessary labour and surplus labour at the workplace. Hence, the man is basically relaying surplus value from his wife to his employer.[42] With women entering the labour market *en masse* since the 1970s, coupled with expanded commodification of the household, some of that reproductive, un-waged labour is now carried out by audiences.

It might still be objected that it does not take the average six hours a day of televised indulgence to learn about life-supporting consumer goods on offer in the local corner shop. But if Smythe's thought about the need to reproduce labour power is given one more twist, his idea gets really interesting. Our concern is not with the needs of the individual to reproduce her labour power, but the need of the system for the individual to do so (which, one way or the other, is often experienced by the individual as the same thing). Reproduction of labour power goes beyond the satisfaction of anthropological needs (eating, sleeping) required for bare, human survival. It also includes the education of the worker with the skills she requires to be employable. What it means to be employable, however, changes with the mode of production. Fordism, for example, took advantage of a higher standard of public education that had previously been forced upon capital in working class struggle. Large-scale industry could now build on, and soon demand, a workforce with basic training in writing, reading and counting. In the same way, the post-Fordist economy calls for certain skills from consumers and audiences. Speaking the language of brands and navigating in the graphical interface of a computer are productive, overhead costs of a cognitive, semiotic-based and post-Fordist accumulation regime. Though it all began with workers defecting from drudgery in the Fordist factory, the pursuit of subcultural identities and leisure activities have grown into an educational requirement of the system to operate smoothly.

Television audiences are not the best example for making this case since their efforts are very minor and it is open to dispute if they can be said to do anything at all. It is easier to think of computer audiences. A remark by Martin Kenney, writing on the economy of the high-tech sector, is enlightening: "But the software requires its users to learn how to use it. This means that the ability of software companies to capture value is related to our willingness to learn how to use their programs. [. . .] From this perspective, in the aggregate the users have invested far more time in learning how to use a software program than did the developers."[43] The key strategic asset of computer firms is not their fixed capital, not their employees, but their user base. Know-how of a product among a large audience creates a high switching-cost in the market. Even if an individual customer wants to switch to a competitor, he is often held back by the inertia of the mass of users with whom he needs to stay in contact with. Hence, the user base is the chief source of stability for a firm in a highly volatile market. The step is a short one from a computer user who learns how to navigate in a graphical interface and a user-developer who improves on the application. It now becomes clear that the engagement of FOSS development communities by capital is not an isolated event. The software industry has merely refined something much more generic. The concept of audience power provides a backdrop against which the toil of users in the social factory can rightly be assessed.

Many other businesses are following suit in more actively taking advantage of user communities. The music industry has a long history of outsourcing the development of music fads to youth subcultures. But user-centred development models are going beyond mere aesthetic innovation. It can be found in everything from surfing boards to advanced medical equipment.[44] According to Tiziana Terranova, free labour is structural to the cultural economy. She objects to the leftist romantic notion of authentic subcultures and countercultures that are besieged by commercialism. 'Independent' cultural production takes place within a broader capitalist restructuring which has always-already anticipated and shaped the 'active consumer'.[45] The involvement of users and audiences in the production process answers the question how capitalism can sustain profits despite approaching a state of near total automation. Extensive use of machinery has not abolished the law of value but it certainly has changed the terms of its operations. Living labour has been expulsed from inside the production process and the jurisdiction of trade unions. But labour returns from the ashes with a vengeance. The investment of living labour must be made perpetually in order to create the setting in which decontextualised, mass-reproduced, digital use values are to be consumed. The making of the product by employees and the use of the product by users are intertwined into a continuous labour process. The importance of emotional and educational investments made by user communities and audiences is reinforced in proportion to digitalisation and the corresponding downsizing of in-housed workers. In some parts of the economy, especially in the cultural and informational sector, user communities can be assumed to be the main source of surplus value for capital. The surplus profit model of Red Hat, examined in the first chapter, is but one example of how capital manages to sustain profits in this circumstantial way.

The exploitation of the surplus value of audiences is not an exhaustive answer to the question why and how FOSS development communities are engaged by capital. Other aspects to be considered are capital's wish to externalise labour costs, to circumvent organised labour, and the incapability of capital to organise the labour process and get creative results. On the flip side of the coin is the defection by working class youth from monotonous jobs and monotonous mass consumption in favour of playful and communicative doing. The thought model is useful though to give a frame of reference from within Marxist theory. It provides an antidote to the much unwarranted optimism about digital media empowering consumers from the passivity of old media. Furthermore, it encourages us to look for new kinds of labour conflicts arising out of the enrollment of volunteer developers, such as black-hat hacking, cracking and pirate sharing.[46] From this vantage point we can proceed to look at the themes debated in the computer underground with more of a critical distance.

INFORMATION EXCEPTIONALISM

'Information wants to be free' has long been the rallying cry of hackers, crackers and file sharers. The words were first coined at a hacker conference in 1984 by Stewart Brand, a senior figure in the American counter-culture movement. The saying has since come to live a life of its own among devotees. Likewise, sceptics have commonly dismissed cyber-politics by replying that 'information doesn't want anything'. Looking closer at what Stewart Brand actually said makes it clear that his thought was a bit more sophisticated than is given away by the catch phrase: "Information wants to be free. Information also wants to be expensive. Information wants to be free because it has become so cheap to distribute, copy, and recombine—too cheap to meter. It wants to be expensive because it can be immeasurably valuable to the recipient."[47] As is shown by the full quote, Brand counterposed two warring forces and situated them in the political economy of information. The intentionality ascribed to information was strictly metaphorical. Still, the question remains if the contradiction pointed out by Stewart Brand is unique to the political economy of information? That seems to be the conclusion of mainstream economic theory. The economist Fritz Malchup commented in the 1960s on the unusual properties of information: "If a public or social good is defined as one that can be used by additional persons without causing any additional cost, then knowledge is such a good of the purest type."[48] Public good has played a minor role in liberal economic theory. The concept was briefly touched upon by John Stuart Mill and he exemplified with lighthouses.[49] He advocated that the service provided by lighthouses should be administrated collectively as a public good. Mill's remarks on lighthouses correspond with Thomas Jefferson's often quoted comparison between light and ideas, where Jefferson acknowledged that just like light, ideas can be freely shared.[50] Thomas Jefferson, head of the US patent commission, concluded that inventions cannot, by their very nature, be subject to exclusive private ownership. Some Marxists, especially those researching the cultural economy, have noticed the peculiarity of information. The two pioneer critics of the culture industry, Max Horkheimer and Theodor Adorno, made some suggestive remarks: "Culture is a paradoxical commodity. So completely is it subject to the law of exchange that it is no longer exchanged; it is so blindly consumed in use that it can no longer be used"[51]

Summing up, there are plenty of observations supporting the idea that the political economy of information is queer in some way. Campaigners for information commons are eager to stress this discrepancy between endless digital resources and limited tangible resources. The non-existent marginal cost of reproducing knowledge is in conflict with its treatment as a scarce property. Though this statement is undeniably true, there is something fishy about making the uniqueness of information the cornerstone of an analysis. A few quotes from Stanford law professor Lawrence Lessig's *The Future of Ideas*, help to demonstrate the shortcomings of this thinking. It should be said, however, that the erroneous assumptions are shared by almost everyone who campaigns in favour of information commons. Lessig is a good example since he is widely read and he sums up the matter in a few succinct words. In the book he strongly advocates that information and culture should be distributed in a commons. He then immediately reassures the reader that markets and commons can coexist peacefully: "Not all resources can or should be organized in a commons", and: "While some resources must be controlled, others can be provided much more freely. The difference is in the nature of the resource, and therefore in the nature of how the resource is supplied"[52] It is in the nature of informational, non-rival resources to be organised in a commons. In the same vein, rivalrous, tangible resources are thought of as optimised for markets. Since it is the nature of the resource which determines if a product is rivalrous or non-rivalrous, the proportion between the two categories is assumed to be constant over time. Hence, policy makers face a straightforward, technocratic task of deciding between commons or market for each resource.

We can now see what is wrong with the 'information exceptionalism' narrative.[53] It serves to brush over any destabilising implications to *status quo* from information commons. In an effort to unwind policy makers and the business community, some people even campaign against the word 'intellectual property' in favour of 'intellectual monopolies'. The message is clear: The challenge to intellectual property is not a threat to private property. While intellectual property is seen as creating artificial scarcity, traditional property is assumed to be grounded in objectively existing limitations. Ownership of tangible, rival goods is therefore taken as 'operational', or even 'optimal'. In the Marxist discipline, on the other hand, scarcity is always a social institution. It is part and parcel of the property relation. In his study of archaic societies, Marshall Sahlins makes a comment on the modern society that is instructive: "The market-industrial system institutes scarcity, in a manner completely unparalleled and to a degree nowhere else approximated. Where production and distribution are arranged through the behaviour of prices, and all livelihoods depend on getting and spending, insufficiency of material means becomes the explicit, calculable starting point of all economic activity."[54] The historical roots of scarcity date back to the enclosure movement in fifteenth and sixteenth century England. Land that previously had been held in common by villagers was parcelled and fenced in.[55] Law transformed these turfs into private property assignable to individual rights holders. Accordingly, Marxists prefer to look upon intellectual property as an extension of traditional property, and highlight the continuity rather than a discontinuity between the two. This is evident from a sentence by Dan Schiller, a long-time sceptic towards the enthusiastic claims about information systems: "As against the postindustrialists' assertion that the value of information derives from its inherent attributes as a resource, we counter that its value stems uniquely from its transformation into a commodity—a resource socially revalued and refined through progressive historical application of wage labor and the market to its production and exchange."[56] Additionally, Marxists would question the analytical procedure of taking the informational use value and its inherent characteristics as the referential point for an analysis. The product is, after all, not an entity in its own right, but a stage in the metamorphosis of the labour process. If there is a discontinuity, which is probably the case, it should not be sought in a discrepancy between non-rival goods and tangible, rival goods. It should be located in a rupture in the labour process. As we saw previously in the chapter, the hunch that work has changed in a qualitative way has caught the imagination of numerous scholars. They have tried to name this rupture by inventing new names for labour, i.e. immaterial labour, social labour, scientific labour, etc. With such a line of attack, it follows that the contradictions arising from the political economy of information ought not to be phrased as 'infinite reproducible information treated as a scarce resource'. It is more appropriate to think of it as private property being straightjacketted onto a socialised labour process that only exists in communication. Such a description allows for a more dynamic analysis of information systems. It now becomes evident that commodification is underway long before copyright and patent law move in to privatise knowledge.

As Katherine Hayles has vividly shown, the term 'information' is itself part of the problem. The notion that it is possible to abstract information patterns from the material body was a cultural invention made in the natural sciences in the 1940s and 1950s. It met the needs of an ascending techno-scientific industry. The industry wanted a definition that allowed reliable quantifications and Claude Shannon's theory of information satisfied the requirement. He specified information as a signal that is indifferent to the meaning that it conveys to the receiver. Competing definitions, where information and the message it conveys were treated as inseparable, also surfaced at the time. To assess 'information as meaning', however, would necessitate a measuring of the changes taking place in the mind of the receiver. It was such practical considerations, Hayles laid down, which persuaded the scientific community to side with a narrow, mathematical, and de-contextualised definition of information.[57] Information defined in this way is a substance that can be divorced from the labour process and owned as private property. It can be equipped with an individual author. Intellectual property is merely a logical consequence of such a mindset.

We need a language that makes visible to us that so-called information goods are continuously co-produced at multiple points of creation and reception. Information is, in other words, embedded in a perpetual labour process that we know better as communication. With this perspective, focus is placed on the labourers producing information and therefore the antagonistic relation is brought to the fore in our discussion. The systematic enrolment of data in the economy has affected all kinds of work assignments. It is surely ludicrous to propose that labour has been replaced by information, since information itself is a product of labour. However, informated and automated production does not just decimate the quantity of labourers employed by industry. It diminishes labour in a qualitative sense too. Since objectified labour can be stored infinitely in binaries, the need for reproducing the same labour twice is effectively erased.[58] A quick glance at the precarious situation for freelancing workers in the information sector uncovers the economic interests in force. Contracted workers can be compelled into creating information products that outlast their contracts and make them at least partly redundant on the labour market. Hence, the queerness of information has not emerged out of sheer randomness, as many believe. Digitalisation is consistent with capital's quest to disband workers and uproot the remaining strongholds of organised labour. Some fields of work can more easily be attacked than others. 'Symbol-analytical' labour is particularly vulnerable since its output is pure information. In the case of the manipulation of affects, if that implies person-to-person services, a difficulty arises in divorcing the labour performed from the context of the performance. The respite in these sectors will be a short one though. In higher education, for example, multimedia and recording technologies are pushed in order to replace teachers with interactive instruction manuals.[59]

It is therefore plausible that more and more fields of the economy will be made subject to digitalisation. Competition and class struggle are animating the labour process and races it along this vector. Though the challenge to organised labour is daunting, digitalisation cuts in both ways. The call to arms by filesharers, hackers, and progressive lawyers, rallying against the current intellectual property regime under the banner of 'information exceptionalism', is a case in point. Their moderate vision of information freely provided in a commons and, side by side, property markets in rival, tangible goods, is more subversive than they would like to think. Ever more of the market society is falling pray to the logic of infinite reproducibility. Though limited commons in information is compatible or even beneficiary to capitalism today, that might not be the case with capitalism of tomorrow. This point can be clarified by elaborating on a famous catchphrase by Richard Stallman, the founder of the Free Software Foundation. In agreement with the 'information exceptionalism' hypothesis, he insists that free software is free as in free speech, not free as in free beer. In other words, commons in information is about civil liberty and not about price. However, as Paolo Virno has shown, the boundary between the public and the private sphere is not absolute in post-modern capitalism. Free beer is indistinguishable from free speech, in: "[. . .] *the era in which language itself has been put to work, in which language itself has become wage labour* (so much so that 'freedom of speech' nowadays means no more and no less than the 'abolition of wage labor')"[60] If we save free speech, we have won free beer.[61] Such a scenario is not likely to come true in the near future. Even so, this potentiality is that dark, unseen force which bends the arc of all those events that we can see. Abolition of wage labour is the void in the rhetoric of moderate critics of the intellectual property regime; it is at the heart of the contradicting policies of IBM towards free software development; and it explains the paradox that the culture industry simultaneously profits from filesharing networks and litigates against individual filesharers. In conclusion, if information commons prove resilient to commodification, it is not because 'information wants to be free', but because the labourers producing information want to be free.

3 Commodification of Information

FIVE SCHOOLS ON INTELLECTUAL PROPERTY RIGHTS

The politics of the hacker movement is influenced by their opposition to intellectual property. A critique of the intellectual property regime from the horizon of FOSS development highlights that intellectual property is not primarily about generating revenue for content providers. On a more fundamental level, patents and licenses are about fixating a certain subjectivity of individual authorship. The licenses advocated by hackers answer instead to an ambiguous and multifaceted form of authorship. At stake is not just free access to information, but, more importantly, the subjectivity of the labourers that are producing information. When the constitutive power of labour is seized upon by an ambulant and anonymous mob of developers, the loss of control can be witnessed in paper-tiger statutes, the mass picking of electronic locks, and defiant norms among broad sections of the population towards intellectual property law. The commodity form of information is simultaneously contested on the legal, technological, and cultural arena. Resistance against commodification is the prism through which the intellectual property regime ought to be seen. Such an approach is at variance with the way that intellectual property is usually understood, both by its supporters and most of its critics.

The justification for intellectual property within mainstream academia comes in four shades of grey. The utilitarian camp postulates that intellectual property is beneficial to everyone's social welfare. Economic incentives are said to increase the production of culture and information in society. Another tradition borrows from John Locke's classic defence of private property. It is a moral argument stating that the individual is entitled to an ownership right over the product of his labour. A similar approach draws loosely from the thinking of Hegel and Kant and argues that private property rights are instrumental to ensure the integrity of an author. Only with such a right is he able to prevent unwanted appropriations and distortions of his artistic work. After listing these three schools on intellectual property, William Fisher introduces a fourth stance which he calls 'social planning theory'. This tradition puts emphasis on third parties affected by intellectual property rights such as consumers and citizens. William Fisher sympathizes with the fourth school which approves of shorter terms of copyright protection, expanded fair right use, and wider use of compulsory licenses.[1]

Proponents of the social planning theory are critical of the present intellectual property regime. In their objections they appeal to US constitutional rights, a truly free market, the economic benefits from increased circulation of information, or concerns about consumer and citizen interests. But William Fisher and his colleagues fail to see the property relation as a power relation, thus they stop short of questioning the legitimacy of intellectual property as such. When power and exploitation have tactfully been removed from their narrative, the intellectual property regime looks perplexingly counter-productive and dysfunctional. The liberal critic is at pains to explain the growth of intellectual property laws. Some blame badly informed decision-makers in Washington/Brussels that need to be provided with the right information. A few trace it all back to a historical misnomer, the transformation of 'copy' into 'copyright' in 1709 *Statute of Anne*. Many suspect a conspiracy of self-prudent lawyers. Others point at the oligarchs in the media industry who, nonetheless, are said to be entrenched, obsolete, and eventually doomed. All these explanations carry some weight. Ultimately, however, they are insufficient in themselves to explain the forces set in motion. Not even the culture industry on its own has the power to advance a global intellectual property regime and corresponding punitive measures, often at the expense of other fractions of the capitalist class. The stakes are much higher than the well-being of a guild of selfish lawyers or a few outdated media oligarchs. The collective capitalist class considers intellectual property as so vital that it is willing even to sacrifice some revenue to the image rentiers in the media business. This is the mighty force against which the champions of the information commons are up against, and hence, their arguments—no matter how well articulated and informed and circumscribed for tactical reasons—will always come up short in Washington/Brussels. William Fisher's four schools need to be complemented with a fifth, critical standpoint.

MARXIST PERSPECTIVES ON LAW AND THE OUTLAW

The intellectual property debate looks entirely different from the perspective of Marxist theory on the law and the outlaw. Marxists have interpreted bourgeois law in one of two ways. Either it has been perceived as an index of deeper currents within the relations of production, or focus has been on the use of law by the ruling class to stamp down on working class resistance. The classic Marxist study of bourgeois legal rights was presented by the Soviet jurist Evgeny Pashukanis in the 1920s. His ideas are known as the 'commodity exchange theory'. It states that the rights given in a market society are essentially the right of the individual to hold private property and the right of contractual agreements. For commodity exchange to proceed smoothly it is crucial that every agent on the market is assured that property and contracts will be respected by everyone else. The prism of capitalist relations makes humans see themselves as monads relating to other monads through exchanges of legal rights and responsibilities. According to Pashukanis, this sentiment is reflected in all other aspects of the law in bourgeois society. When the commodity exchange theory is stretched to include cases very remote from property law, such as violent assault, it comes close to reducing all aspects of life to mechanic, economic laws. Despite his blemishes, for which Pashukanis was criticised already by his contemporaries, the commodity exchange theory has a lot to contribute to an understanding of how law assists the creation of bourgeois, legal subjects.[2]

The other tradition within Marxism, the "class instrumentalist" approach, stresses law enforcement as a method of class dominance. From this outlook, the State apparatus employs law as one weapon among many in its arsenal against the working class. Police, militia, prisons, and other insignia of law enforcement, play a central role to curb and deter insurrections and petty transgressions against the *status quo*. At the turn of the last century, state violence against workers was commonplace and brutal. However, as Hugh Collins points out in his survey of Marxist interpretations of bourgeois law, this approach has difficulties in explaining those instances when workers and fractions of the capitalist class jointly advance progressive legislations. Such counter-examples go as far back as the *Factory Act* of 1802 that gave workers some minimal protection, and it culminates in the social-democratic welfare state. According to the class instrumentalist theory, the ruling class enrols law to subjugate the working class. And though their ability to do so is always contested and constrained by class struggle, the ruling class will on average win more terrain than they lose. If this assumption is valid, Collins asks rhetorically, how it is that there is a relatively strong approval for law authorities among the working class?[3]

The idea of the criminal as a public enemy has surely contributed to the broad support for law-and-order. The case can be made, however, that the consent of the law-abiding majority is a historical exception. The historian Eric Hobsbawm sketched out a very different outlaw of past centuries that he called the 'social bandit'. Hobsbawm's bandit was set apart from the villagers by his military training, his mobility, and his daredevil attitude. On the other hand, he came from the village and he depended on the goodwill of the villagers to survive. In medieval Europe, outlaws were often poachers and run-away serfs, while law authorities were symbols of the feudal rule sweeping down against all poor with equal vengeance. The myth of the outlaw as a folk hero flourished in most parts of the world up until the establishment of strong, central governments.[4] Michel Foucault argued that the reformation of the penalty system of the *ancien régime* repositioned the outlaw within a new discourse of criminality. Law authorities from now on posed themselves as protectors of poor people against other poor people. In the ideal scenario, law even staged itself as a guarantor of the rights of the weak against more powerful interests in society. Indeed, this is the ideal of 'equality before the Law'. It suggests that legislation is neutral towards those over whom it rules. Of course, when law enforces equal treatment over two unequally strong parts, as in a dispute over an employment contract between a manager and a worker, neutral law enforcement sides with the stronger part. But it would be a mistake to dismiss the Rule of Law too quickly, especially in a time when it no longer can be taken for granted. Franz Neuman and Otto Kirchheimer made important contributions to Marxist theory on law. They wrote in the period leading up to Nazi Germany, and while they clearly saw the hypocrisy of the liberal juridical system, they still thought it was worth defending. For instance, Franz Neuman asserted that the limited, formal and negative generality of law in liberal market societies not only makes possible capitalist calculability, but that it also ensures a minimum of liberty.[5] The ideological side of law that makes it such a powerful ally of the *status quo* is also the factor that contributes to the, limited but real, progressive aspect of law. Jane Gaines sums up the doubleness of law in a sentence: "[Law] cannot rule without seeming to be fair, and without seeming to be fair it cannot secure the consent of those whom it governs".[6] According to Hugh Collins, it is this ideological grip of the Rule of Law that is the secret of its hegemonic force. Law is conjured by the common sense, convictions, and ideology held by legislators and judges, which in turn is a result of their daily practices. It is in this circumstantial way that one class tends to win out over the other in verdicts and legislation. Thus, Collins argues, the relations of production do make an imprint in the law book. It is an outgrowth of the beliefs and allegiances that follow with a particular class position in the social division of labour.

This claim is too weak to satisfy us in our search for a Marxist explanation to the rapid expansion of intellectual property law. The key to the puzzle has been provided by Bernard Edelman. In his study of the invention of ownership over the photographic image, Bernard Edelman borrows from Pashukanis' work on how bourgeois law sanctions commodity exchange and private property. In Pashukanis' view, the overriding priority of law is to stabilise the commodity form. Edelman stretches this point a bit further. The chief commodity in capitalism is the human being, or, to be more precise, her labour power. As a legal subject, the human being takes the general form of a commodity.[7] In emphasising law's role in shaping subjectivity, Edelman draws from a second source of influence, Louis Althusser's famous essay about ideology and the State.[8] Louis Althusser differentiated between two arms of the State Apparatus. First there is the repressive state apparatus, embodied in the Army and the Police. It is flanked by an ideological state apparatus. Althusser mentioned the Church, the Family, the Educational system, and the Legal system, though the Army and the Police also works in part through ideology. The Ideological State Apparatus affirms *status quo* by upholding the category of the subject. When the individual is hailed by a court order as a defendant (or, for that matter, a plaintiff, a witness, or even, an absentee) he responds in a certain way that confirms his status as a subject of the law. In the final instance, this operation is geared towards the reproduction of the relations of production. Bernard Edelman extrapolates that the invention of intellectual property rights over photographic images is geared towards fixating the photographer as a labourer. Edelman's observation on intellectual property rights is no less applicable to alternative license regimes. In the computer underground, FOSS licenses are the key issue which hacker politics gravitate towards. In organising the labour power of play movements, these licenses have the same central role as the employment contract has in organising waged labour. A license both dictates how developers relate to each other and to future and past developers, and it specifies the legal claims over the output. FOSS licenses seek to break away from individual authorship but do so while negotiating a new compromise on the Author. From the very beginning a process of reterritorialisation is underway in the movement. This is overt in the forking by the open source initiative and in the creative commons project, but can equally apply to free licenses depending on the circumstances under which they are used. For instance, by mandating that the name of the original programmer must be included with modified copies of free software, free licenses allow for a new point of closure based on brand recognition. Of course, this is not to say that the collective authors of FOSS and CC licences are essentially the same as the individual author of traditional intellectual property law.

A historic parallel can be made with the abolition of slavery. When slaves won their freedom from their masters the freedom was quickly countered with the imposition of wage labour. The transition was in no small part a change in subjectivity. A human must initially be free, if he is to be able to sell his work as a commodity. That was the well-known insight of John Locke when he stipulated the foundations of property. In his view, property is a premise for freedom, beginning with the ownership of oneself and one's own labour. The toil which a free man exerts is returned to him as his rightful property. With this mythical foundation, based on the absolute individual, law must refer all creations/infringements back to a single source of stimuli, an author (whether it is an author of a book or of a crime). The case of intellectual property rights demonstrates how law modifies and creates literature and culture, together with the concept of originality, by authorising some models of creativity whilst pathologising other models. Law sanctions the individualised author-creator as the norm. Concurrently, law tends to criminalise amphibious, collective and anonymous forms of creativity.[9] It must now be clear that intellectual property law is only partially about generating revenue by controlling public access to information. On a more fundamental level, patents and copyright law shape subjectivity and prescribe a way of organising labour relations. Ultimately, we face the question of who is privileged to be the author our reality.

THE AUTHOR AND THE
COMMODIFICATION OF THE SELF

Intellectual property rights in a non-trivial sense are only purposeful within the context of an advanced market economy. Still, a glance at the prehistory of intellectual property can be instructive. The bourgeoisie inherited copyright from the censorship powers of the absolute monarchy. Control over the written word became an urgent concern for the English authorities, the country generally credited with the first modern copyright law, after the printing press had been introduced to the islands by William Caxton in 1476. In the following century, English politics were tormented by the royal defection from the Catholic Church. Writings of heresy and treachery flourished and were combated with censorship decrees. This was the historical cradle for the early formative years of copyright. For example, the custom of giving credit to the author and the publisher by including their names in the book—now a right fought for by culture workers—was then a practice originally forced upon authors by royal decree. Listing their names became an efficient method for the sovereign to keep track of disobedient writers and publishers.[10] In France too the author's privilege was a product of the absolute monarchy. Subsequently, those decrees were abolished in the French revolution. After the revolutionary leaders had consolidated their power, however, they substituted the author's privilege with a weak property right. The reform was justified by the need to create accountability and to prevent the spread of libellous and seditious pamphlets that circulated after the collapse of royal censorship.[11]

The transition from censorship rule to property right came gradually in England. In the sixteenth century the emergence of a commercial book market, responding to an ascending bourgeois class with an appetite for casual reading, made it difficult for royal appointees to keep apace with the flow of new books. As a response to the surge of printing, the Worshipful Company of Stationers London was created in 1557 as the sole body with permission to publish books. A symbiosis was found between the autocrat's need for political control, and the economic interests of private actors.[12] Three centuries later the publishers anticipated an end to censorship acts and feared for their prosperous trade. Consequently, they lobbied the English parliament for new forms of protection. By then the Stationers' Company was thoroughly unpopular and they could not expect any sympathy from the legislators. Instead, publishers highlighted the legitimate, moral claims of authors. The members of the Stationers Company knew that rights assigned to authors would eventually end up with them. The result was the *Statute of Anne* of 1709. It was primarily a trade-legislative act and not a copyright act. Its thrust was directed against the old monopoly, and yet, the statute played right into the hands of the publishers. In the disguise of an author's right, legislative protection became much stronger than it had been as a publisher's right. The *Statute of Anne* established a full-fledged private property right, involving not just the right to copy a work but also rights to change the work, to exclude others from the use of it, and the option to transfer the rights over it.[13] Copyright's heritage in censorship and autocratic rule must not be forgotten in the current discussion on intellectual property. It is against this background that we can appreciate Michel Foucault's denouncement of the author as a point of control. In his essay "What is an Author", Foucault writes: "[. . .] The author is not an indefinite source of significations which fill a work; the author does not precede the works; he is a certain functional principle by which, in our culture, one limits, excludes, and chooses; in short, by which one impedes the free circulation, the free manipulation, the free composition, decomposition, and recomposition of fiction."[14] If we broaden our definition of authorship, from the writing of fiction to the writing of source code, a new horizon opens up to our investigation. Foucault's words lend weight to the claim that the mass defiance of intellectual property law on the Internet is of a deeper, political significance. Once the straightjacket of the bourgeois author-programmer has been blown apart by the peer-to-peer model of near-anonymous programming, the flow of free software code becomes cancerous and subversive. The hacker movement is turning out file-sharing applications like Freenet for routing around censorship, encryption programs like Pretty Good Privacy that prevents governments from eaves-dropping on citizens, spy programs like Back Orifice that distributes the powers previously held by system administrators and employers and used to spy on their employees, and so on. Crucially, Foucault's reminder helps us to recognise the significance of the intellectual property regime beyond generating revenue to owners.[15] While liberal critics are happy to call for the downsizing or even abolition of the intellectual property regime, they regularly express their concern for preserving individual authorship, without ever recognising that these two claims are in conflict. They fail to see that the construction of authorship is an integral part of the labour market and property relations. And property relations, intellectual property being no exception, are at its heart a relationship of power and domination.

Authorship, together with capitalist relations, is reproduced each time new media technology is introduced in society. By looking at the early development of photography and the ownership over the photographic image, Bernard Edelman captured these dynamics in the making. The invention of the 'photographer' is preserved like a fossil in French juridical history. When the first cameras were being experimented with, courts refused to recognise any authorship belonging to the man handling the apparatus, i.e. the photographer.[16]. Photographs, judges decreed in the 1840s, are merely copies of reality, stealing from streets and landscapes that which belongs to the public or is the private property of someone else than the photographer. In short, taking photos is plagiarising nature by optical means. The photographer-as-a-technician had no particular rights over the output from the gadget which he handled. His claims were not treated differently from the labourer's claim over the output from the machine in the factory. Bernard Edelman shows how the attitude gradually changed as a market developed in photography, resulting in foreign exports of photographic imagery and the embryo of a cinematic industry with clout to lobby for state protection. Courts begun to express their sincere appreciation for the work of art of filmmakers and photographers. Bit by bit, the photographer-as-a-technician was turned into the photographer-as-an-artist. The image was provided with an author that held property rights over the image. And once rights had been installed over the image-object, those rights were transferable. Thus, the photographic image entered into commodity circulation.

The example above shows how the recognition of authorship is tied up with the organisation of the labour process. It is individual authorship that makes the photographer into a 'petty commodity trader'. The petty commodity trader is defined by that he, as opposed to the wage labourer, owns his own means of production and produces commodities for simple exchange. In contrast, the wage labourer does not own the means of production and he has no artistic claim over his output. The wage labourer sells his time to work rather than the products of his work. Karl Marx expected that capitalism would shovel out self-employed traders and replace them with wage labourers. As can be seen in the software sector today, however, capital is organising more of its operations around freelance workers instead of in-house employees. The 'discovery' of authorship in new walks of life, computer programming being one example among many, is directly related to these changes taking place in the labour process and the expansion of market relations. Authorship, first worked out in the publishing industry, has become a widespread model in the post-Fordist economy as a whole.

Celia Lury gives a good account of why individual authorship became an organising principle in the cultural sector to start with.[17] In the eighteenth and nineteenth century, publishing houses reached out to consolidate their grip over the production of literature in response to a prospering book market. They then confronted the same question now posed by all self-respecting management consultants: how to spur the authors to creativity while at the same time ensuring that the firm reaps the lion part? The problem was solved by dividing literature production into two tiers. Low literature was produced according to a standardised formula. Conditions for writers resembled those of workers in the Fordist factory. In this tier, the name of the author and his creative rights were aggressively subsumed under the company name. Carl Barks working anonymously for Walt Disney springs to mind. In the tier of high literature, on the other hand, where the quality of the text was paramount, writers had to be given optimal working conditions. Direct commodification of the writing process had to be avoided. Instead, the author's persona, her subjectivity, was commodified.[18] The ideals of romanticism played its part as an ideological supporter for this constellation of the author-publisher relationship. Romanticism veiled the crass market forces working behind the scenery and whose disclosure would rip apart the authenticity of the product. The image of the author-genius sealed the commodity form of the text and raised a barrier towards the readers.

Conversely, romanticism was the best bargain chip of authors and artists when they negotiated terms with publishers and staved off the dreaded situation in the lower tier of literature production. Hence, authorship was constituted with strong support from established culture workers as well as publishers. When European copyright law was codified in the Berne convention towards the end of the nineteenth century authors such as Victor Hugo played a key part.[19] The custom of identifying a strong intellectual property regime with labour issues is continued by contemporary cultural workers. They reckon, and not without some justice, that they will be worse affected than the media companies if copyright law is undermined. Consequently, the cultural workers often end up as an angry vanguard of the expansion of market forces into previously unexploited cultural expressions.

Not only writers and film actors but equally so waitresses, stewards, receptionist, all occupations involving some element of affective labour, are experiencing that their very subjectivity is put to work. Because subjectivity is productively engaged in many different fields of the economy, the author stands out as a favoured model for organising this kind of labour power. Ownership rights are projected onto the image of the individual just as property rights over the photographic image have over-appropriated other kinds of sceneries (landscape, cityscapes) before. In the U.S., though still not in Europe, the 'right of publicity' doctrine has developed into a full-blown property right. It protects the name and appearance of an individual from unwanted appropriation, as well as her nickname, signature, physical pose, characterizations, vocal characteristics, frequently used phrases, style, and gestures. Everything that is distinctive and recognised by a wider public is subject to the doctrine of publicity. Just as with the French courts in mid-nineteenth century, American judges in the 1920s and 1930s turned down the first complaints about unwanted and uncompensated exposure. But with growing economic stakes in celebrity the juridical system gave in to the demands of the Hollywood industry.[20] Authorship, the instrument of sixteenth century autocratic rule, has been internalised and is carried on in the very subjectivity of the worker. When censorship was imposed on the writer by royal decree he had a fair chance to dodge it by distributing his pamphlets anonymously. Today it is in the self-interest of the worker to keep tabs on himself. In order to make a living he must cultivate his image and strive to be named, in other words: willingly take the form of a commodity. The extent to which commodification has permeated society and human relations is indicated by the fact that the arc of a nose or a peculiar accent is recognised by law as a property right.

THE INTELLECTUAL PROPERTY REGIME TODAY

It is an unfeasible task to detail the changes taking place in international intellectual property law. Furthermore, such a list would quickly become obsolete. The tendency is, however, easy enough to spell out and is likely to remain in force for some time. The intellectual property regime is growing in strength on all fronts. This growth is shown in an expanded scope of patents, a lengthening of the duration of copyright protection, the invention of new forms of intellectual property, co-ordination of law on the international level, as well as new legal powers to monitor and enforce violations of intellectual property and a heightened willingness among courts to rule in favour of rights holders. A few highlights will be given for the sake of orientation.

Many changes in copyright law run back to the *WIPO Copyright Treaty* (WCT) of 1996. In the United States the commitments made in the WCT were endorsed 1998 in the *Digital Millennium Copyright Act* (DMCA). The key note in the DMCA is that it prohibits the circumvention of digital locks. Also prohibited is manufacturing and distributing technology which is principally designed or used to circumvent digital locks. Even the dissemination of knowledge which could be used for circumvention is in a legal greyzone under the DMCA. Hackers and civil liberty campaigners protested that free speech would be stifled by the law, and they have largely been proven right.[21] Europeans are subject to similar laws after the passing of the *EU Copyright Directive* in 2001 and the *EU Directive on the Enforcement of Intellectual Property Rights* in 2004. Copyright protection has successively been extended both in US and in EU. The American congress passed the *Sonny Bono Copyright Term Extension Act* in 1998. Copyright protection was prolonged with 20 years *after* the death of the author, from 50 years to 70 years. The longer period of protection had then already been introduced in EU in the *Directive on Harmonising the Term of Copyright Protection* of 1993. It is hard to believe in the justification given, that an extension of post-mortem protection of creative works would spur authors to industriousness. Rather, among other things, the extension of copyright protection saved Walt Disney from losing its exclusive rights over Mickey Mouse and other classic Disney characters, that otherwise would have entered the public domain in 2003 and 2004. Subsequently, the extension was mocked on the Internet as the 'Mickey Mouse Act'.

In addition to extending the length and scope of copyright protection, the patent law has grown to eclipse areas that recently were covered by copyright or not conceived as a form of property at all. The major difference between copyright and patents is that patents protect the idea behind a work while copyright only protects the expression. So, for instance, while Disney's copyright over Mickey Mouse prevents others from drawing that particular character, everyone is free to use the idea of a cartoon mouse. In the same vein, if a unique line of software code is written to solve the same problem as a competing program, it is not a violation against copyright laws. Software patents, in contrast, ensure that all different ways to tackle a problem, and there are always several in computer programming, can be claimed by the owner of the patent. It is very difficult to work around a solution patented by a competitor. Such powers are of major advantage to big companies with large patent portfolios and the clout to cross-license with other major players. Software patents are particularly damaging to Free and Open Source Software (FOSS) developers who lack a war chest to fight lawsuits and a patent portfolio of their own to bargain with. In the US, software patenting goes back to the *Diamond vs. Dierh* case in 1981. The patent claim concerned a computer program that aided the process of making rubber. The Supreme Court ordered the US Patent and Trademark Office to grant the patent claim since the computer process was part of an industrial process. In Europe, the extension of the patent system to software applications is championed by the European Patent Office. The organisation has registered more than 30.000 software patents in defiance of its own instructions and the fact that software is not recognised as patentable by European treaties and national laws among most E.U. members.[22] An alliance of small and midsize computer businesses and hacktivists has, at the time of writing, stalled the introduction of software patents in Europe. Their case has been strengthened by the many failures of the US patent system. The extension of patentability in the US to cover information processes has turned out to be a slippery-slope. In 1998, a circuit court of appeals upheld a patent of a method to pool financial assets into a single portfolio fund held by multiple investors. The court decision was a landmark in enabling business methods to be patented. Even sport styles are now subject to patent disputes. Sport is big business and business needs protection.[23] Of graver concern is the trend towards patenting life-forms and genetic information.[24]

The expansion of established forms of intellectual property is coupled with the invention of entirely new categories of ownership. One case that was mentioned previously is the right of publicity doctrine in the US. The right of publicity doctrine originated as a protection clause against unwanted coverage in the media. Over the years, celebrities and the film industry have wrestled case law into a fully fledged private property right. Through a series of court rulings, the right of publicity doctrine has gone from a law protecting privacy to an ownership right over peoples' appearance. The difference is that as a private property, the right to display a celebrity can be signed away to a third party and be enforced in court against non-paying infringers. Another up-and-coming invention is the *Broadcasting Treaty* currently under discussion in the World Intellectual Property Organisation. If the treaty is passed, a new right will be constructed that gives cable networks, broadcasters, and, possibly, Internet portals, a fifty year monopoly over the material which they are transmitting. The right would exist on top of copyright legislation. Material not claimed by copyright or licensed under alternative schemes would still be subject to the broadcasting right.

The account given above is by no means exhaustive, but it gives the reader a sense of the direction we are heading in. There are, as is usually the case, countervailing forces too. The many inefficiencies of the intellectual property regime have encouraged some business leaders to look for a fix among the alternative licensing schemes invented by hackers and activists. A pointer is the grassroots campaign for flat rate taxes on Internet access. The initiative originated with left-of-the-centre activists that hoped that filesharing would be permitted if the culture industry was compensated for their alleged losses. It is quite likely that a settlement on flat rate taxes between reformist critics, the state, and media companies will be found at some stage. Such a compromise can only be a 'combined and uneven' dismantling of intellectual property. People will be granted the right to share information within a gated common. Surveillance and law enforcement will still be needed however to police the gates. As the flat rate tax initiative amply illustrates, the void left after the market will immediately be filled with an administrating, monitoring, capitalist state. The collective capitalist class will never bargain away the cash nexus. For as long as there is a point of closure somewhere in the system, a looser intellectual property regime will count for little more than faster circulation of capital and intensified exploitation of users and audiences.

INTELLECTUAL PROPERTY IN THE WORLD-SYSTEM

One difficulty for the protection of intellectual property rights is that information flows easily across national borders. Though the fluidity of information has been accentuated by the Internet, legislators and rights holders had already been familiar with the problem for a long time. The world's first international copyright treaty, the *Berne Convention for the Protection of Literary and Artistic Works*, signed in 1886, answered to an emerging global audience and an equally global market in books. Back then it was United States who objected to the enforcement of copyright law. English publishers tried to persuade the American congress for the better half of the nineteenth century to ban unauthorised printing of English books. Charles Dickens sailed over the Atlantic in 1842 to educate the readers in America about paying royalties. But the English claim for compensation was repeatedly refuted by the US congress. The congress argued against abiding to English copyright law since national resources would then be transferred to foreign monopolies. A second concern of the congressmen was that the diffusion of reading and literacy would be slowed down if books were made unnecessarily expensive. Not until 1989 did US sign the Berne Convention. The major reason for United State's resistance to the Berne convention was that for most of the century US was a net copyright importer, while Europe was a net copyright exporter.[25] Over the years the tide of export revenues has turned, and so has American policy on intellectual property. The bulging market value of information is coupled with the need to protect this economic interest in the global marketplace, as is neatly summed up in a book with the title 'Cross-Border Enforcement of Patent Rights': "Companies that invest large amounts of money in commercializing new products and processes must operate in as many countries as possible to recoup these high costs.

Besides easily obtaining patents in a number of countries, these companies expect to be able to enforce their patents without excessive bother and cost against third parties."[26] Extending law across national borders is however controversial. The new requirements of global capital are in conflict with the historical alliance between national law, national capitalists, and the nation state. Monopoly rights over trade, such as patents, have traditionally been a power exercised by the sovereign over his territory and his citizens and only extended to subjugated colonies and colonised people. The concept of law itself is intimately connected with territoriality. The linkage between jurisdiction and place was largely adhered to by nation states up until the First World War. Then legislators began to pass national laws that could be extraterritorially applicable if some prescribed conduct had a harmful impact within the territory of the state in question. Legal theory continued to pledge the territorial connection even when the law was enforced across national borders. Only recently have hearts among legal theorists warmed to the principle of a truly universal jurisdiction in international criminal law.[27] The soft power legitimising this sea change in attitudes is the idea of a human rights code that is valid irrespectively of national borders. The moral case for universal human rights is hardwired in global financial markets, cross-border regulations, and mutual economic interdependency.[28]

A global body with considerable powers to monitor and enforce intellectual property rights in membership states was established with the signing of the Trade-Related aspects of Intellectual Property rights (TRIPS) agreement in 1995. The treaty specifies minimum requirements for the protection of copyright, trademark, industrial designs, and patents. TRIPS came as part of the World Trade Organisation (WTO). The settlement procedure established in WTO gives a plaintiff the power to impose trade sanctions against nations that fail to comply with the TRIPS agreement. TRIPS is the most ambitious effort as of yet to write a global constitution on intellectual property law, though it adds to a rich flora of bilateral, regional and multilateral agreements. As was feared by critics from the start, WTO and TRIPS have predominantly led to a reinforcement of global asymmetries. The consequences have been unfavourable to developing economies, resulting in an annual net transfer of billions of dollars to industrialised nations, with the United States as the main beneficiary.[29] Writing in *Monthly Review*, Michael Perelman compares intellectual property to oil in its strategic importance for the Western economy: "Intellectual property rights have become the financial counterweight to deindustrialization, because the revenues that they generate help to balance the massive imports of material goods."[30] Perelman's observation is in accordance with an estimate made by Marcelo D'Elia Branco, coordinator of Brazil's Free Software Project. For every license paid for Word plus Windows, the country must export 60 bags of soybeans.[31] It appears as if the transfer of wealth from periphery to centre will increasingly be paid as royalties instead of as interest payment on foreign debt and direct investment. Occasionally, this outcome of intellectual property is acknowledged, or even appealed to, by the advocates of property licenses. Executive officer of SCO, Darl McBride, fears that the US economy is jeopardised if FOSS spreads in developing countries. In a letter to the US congress, he states: "For more than 20 years, software has been one of the leading examples of innovation and value-creation in our economy. When software becomes a commodity with nearly zero economic value, how will our economy make up for this loss?", and: "Instead of UNIX from any number of US companies or Windows from Microsoft, governments throughout Europe and Asia are using Linux, often downloaded for free from the Internet."[32] The surge of international treaties on intellectual property cannot, however, be understood solely as a redistributive measure at the world system level. Otherwise it would be hard to explain why corporations in America and the European Union lobby for stricter legislation in their home regions than is exported to countries in the South. The globalisation of intellectual property law begins in the general conflict level between capital and labour. Let us make a few stipulations on this. Global communication networks have enabled living labour to coordinate its operations over a smooth space spanning the whole earth.[33] The mobility of labour inverses the stabilising force of geographical segmentations, in particular nation borders. National jurisdiction has become a rigidity in the constituted power of the state and law.

A good illustration hereof was the prosecution against Jon Johansen in 2002. He was a Norwegian teenager singled out by law enforcement agencies for distributing a program known as DeCSS.[34] The program decrypts a DVD disc that has previously been encrypted with the Content Scrambling System (CSS). One motive for hackers to remove CSS was to be able to run DVD discs on GNU/Linux machines, though the added benefit of enabling unauthorised copying of DVDs surely contributed to the popularity of DeCSS. Jon Johansen, however, had bought his DVDs and he did not distribute illegal copies. In short, he had not violated the Norwegian copyright law. Still, the joint complaint by DVD Copy Control Association and the Motion Picture Association of America was acted on by Norwegian prosecuters. Both the district court and the appeal court freed Jon Johansen from all charges. The case ended when the Norweigian Supreme Court dismissed a final appeal by the prosecution. Though Jon Johansen eventually was freed of charges, it is quite remarkable that he could be prosecuted in the first place for a practice that had recently been criminalised in the US in the DMCA. His error consisted in trafficking in software that facilitates illicit copying, rather than having committed the act of illicit copying *per se*, which was the only offence acknowledged in Norweigian copyright law at the time. The Norweigian exception was a short-lived one since the country is a signatory of the WCT, which calls for national parliaments to ban circumvention technologies. National laws on intellectual property are integrated into a jurisdiction that is becoming global. The US connection is shown by the fact that the legal action against Jon Johansen had repercussions on American soil as well. Eric Corely, alias Emmanuel Goldstein, is a publisher of the legendary hacker magazine *2600: The Hacker Quarterly*. The magazine had posted the source code of the DeCSS utility. Eight motion picture studios filed suit against him under the anti-circumvention provision in the DMCA. Both a district court and an appeal court barred the *2600: The Hacker Quarterly* from publishing the DeCSS code and from linking to websites with the source code.[35] But the controversy provoked a mass posting of the DeCSS code on the Internet and it was even printed on t-shirts and chanted in songs.[36] The court system had no means to prevent the code from being spread about. The DVD-Jon debacle is a showcase of the consequences when information can be accessed from any point in a network spanning the whole globe. The commodity form of information is threatened by pirate sharing from every place irrespectively of the distance in real space. Subsequently, law enforcement needs to be equally spread out. Omnipresence of markets is typically taken as a proof of the triumph of liberal capitalism and the 'end of history'. Alternatively, it can be argued that the necessity of markets to be omnipresent is what constitutes the vulnerability of market economy at this point in time. The presence of a single void in the global fabric of law enforcement is sufficient to cause destabilisation to the intellectual property regime everywhere. Markets in information must be upheld globally if they are to exist at all.

TECHNOLOGICAL DESIGN AS A LAW ENFORCER

The story about DVD-Jon also points us to how technology is designed to regulate the behaviour of consumers and citizens. One advantage derived from having consumer technology policing its user is that the inertia of national jurisdictions can be circumvented. Technological design as law enforcement by other means is a recurring theme in Lawrence Lessig's extensive writings. His dictum is known to all students of this topic: "Code can, and will, displace law as the primary defence of intellectual property in cyberspace"[37] Lessig warns his readers that when architecture substitutes for law, society is tumbling into a 'privatisation of the law'.[38] In addition to strengthening the protection against illicit copying, the manufacturers can now build away consumer rights which the law otherwise would have forced them to honour. Reformist critics of intellectual property have come out in defence of consumer choice and fair competition. They are mistaken, however, in thinking that the current situation is particularly novel or alarming. In *Capital* volume I, writing on the deployment of machinery in large industry, Karl Marx made the following note: "In the factory code, the capitalist formulates power over his workers like a private legislator, and purely as an emanation of his own will, unaccompanied by either that division of responsibility otherwise so much approved of by the bourgeoisie, or the still more approved representative system."[39] History is full of examples of how 'factory code' is arranged to govern the behaviour of workers. The parade example is the speed of the conveyor belt. It forces upon the labourer an activity and a work pace which he has no influence over. Not only does the conveyor belt enforce industriousness; it has advantages in domesticating the workforce as well. By scattering the workers throughout the factory and fixing them at points along the machine, workers are prevented from communicating with each other. This is but one example of what Richard Edwards called 'technological control'. He argued that machinery is designed with three purposes in mind: to direct work tasks, to evaluate the performance of workers, and to reward and discipline them. In short, technological control is implemented to check any suspected leakage between labour power and paid labour time.[40]

Richard Edwards contributed to a current within labour theory in the 1970s and 1980s that investigated how technology aids the agenda of management. The aim of these writers was to prove wrong the popular notion that technology is a neutral force for the common good. Their investigations, and the controversies which they caused, influenced the young discipline of science and technology studies. Contemporary scholars in the field are objecting, however, that technology cannot be reduced to the wishes of powerful elites. They stress the unpredictability of innovation and the flux of the motives of social actors.[41] These qualifications are valid but must in turn be qualified. The fact that a technology rarely fulfils the expectations of its inventors does not rule out the existence of an agenda behind designing the technology in a particular way. The reason that a design falls short of regulating the behaviour of users is because the users are opposing the agenda. Workers and users intervene in the process of (prod-)using the technology. Indeed, this is exactly what hacking is about, taking the system at hand and bending it to serve a different purpose. It is justified to reproach the old school of labour theoreticians to the extent that they analysed machinery as a top-down affair and failed to emphasise how living labour subverts technology, or even creates a technology of their own. Given this provision, however, their case studies of the struggle over factory code between managers and workers are instructive in our present inquiry into the struggle over software code in the social factory.

The infrastructure of the Internet is currently being rebuilt to respond better to the needs of law authorities. The computer network has the same strategic importance as the central squares on the chessboard. All activities have to pass through them. The Internet is believed to become the major production centre and distribution channel of goods and money in the near future. Dan Shiller, highly sceptical of the emancipating claims commonly made about the Internet, identifies it as the central command structure in a global market economy. He points at the long series of corporate take-overs and mergers, Time Warner and America On-line to mention the biggest one, which have decorated the grab for power over the Internet.[42] However, since companies can only buy and sell what they control, financial acquisitions provide no straightforward indication of the consolidation of corporate influence over the Internet. The infrastructure of the Internet must be laid down so that order replaces anarchy and surveillance cancels out anonymity. According to one business consultant, five requirements must be met to build the architecture of an ethereal, global market place: "(1) Authenticitation (assurance of identity); (2) Authorization (that the party is sanctioned for a particular function); (3) Privacy or confidentiality; (4) Data integrity (proof that the object has not been altered); (5) Nonrepudiation (protection against someone denying they originated a communication or data."[43] These are conditions that commodity exchange theory tells us are necessary for the operation of a market economy. In most situations in real space, however, the criteria listed above are taken for granted. When we look at the virtual world it becomes obvious to us that these conditions are crafted. The architecture of the Internet is rebuilt with three main purposes in mind. To protect the commodity form (obstruct infinite reproducibility and identify violations), to speed up commodity circulation, and to prevent users from acquiring technical know-how. The last point is crucial since the security system will be disabled by users the moment they acquire the skills that give them control over the computer technology. In fact, fences against intruders are only the tip of the iceberg in protecting the intellectual property regime. Its real momentum lies in the strategy of social Taylorism.[44] In the same way as Taylorism aimed at curbing the skills of the factory worker, social Taylorism attempts to lessen the required skill level of the average user. The obvious method to do this is by hiding source code behind binaries and forbidding users from accessing the information. A more subtle method is to seduce the user through convenience, as is summed up in the treacherous word 'user-friendliness'. It is worth recalling that Frederick Taylor often stressed 'friendliness' when advising managers on how to treat workers to 'get the job done'.

There is no way to foretell to what extent capital will succeed in pushing this agenda. Faith in that the Internet is inherently anarchistic, a belief common to cyber-libertarians in the early 1990s, looks rather out-of-date today. Capital has successfully restructured other sectors over which it initially held no influence. The introduction of hybrid seeds in farming is a case in point.[45] The result of hybridisation is that the second and following yield from the same crop dramatically drops. Though it is possible, biologically speaking, to sow hybrid seeds a second time, it is economically suicidal to do so. Hybridisation is often perceived as a neutral improvement of agricultural methods for the greater social benefit of increasing yields. However, as Jack Kloppenburg has demonstrated, the increase in yields from these crops did not necessarily owe to hybridization. It was a predictable outcome of the vast amount of resources poured into research for improving this particular strain. Hybrids had to be made economically superior to traditional varieties. Otherwise, farmers would simply not have grown hybrids when it was so obviously to their disadvantage. Competition from farmers growing hybrids would do the trick. The point is that if the same amount of research had been invested in open-pollinated varieties capable of self-reproduction, then they might be just as productive as hybrids are today.[46]

The case with hybrid seeds goes to show the many options that capital has at its disposal to ram through a particular technology. The equivalent of hybridization on the Internet is of course Digital Rights Management (DRM) technology. Up until recently, DRM technology has relied on encryption. The drawback with this approach is that encryption has to let through legitimate consumers. The door is a weak point that hackers can exploit. The DVD-Jon incidence demonstrates how a group of dedicated youngsters equipped with ordinary consumer technology can defeat an industrial standard. The battleground is therefore shifting from software code to a contest over the hardware and the network. Stuart Biegel identifies a number of strategic points in the infrastructure of the Internet susceptible to centralisation.[47] One is the root servers that keep track of the location of all the addresses on the Internet. When clients access a website, they first call up a server 'closer to home', held by the Internet Service Provider. If the requested website is not available at the local server, then the Internet Service Provider forwards the call to one of the root servers. After many years of bitter fighting, control over the root servers was turned over to the Internet Corporation for Assigned Names and Numbers (ICANN). It was the product of a bargain between the major players, notably the U.S. government, E.U., and a few major e-commerce and telecommunication firms. WIPO and ICANN cooperate closely since both recognise that control over the root servers will play a key role in enforcing intellectual property on the Internet.[48]

Another easy target is the companies that connect clients/customers to the Internet. Trough Internet Service Providers the Internet traffic of their customers can be regulated. Sensitive material can be filtered, passwords can be imposed, and elaborate systems for identification of users can be set up. Distributing censorship and surveillance to Internet Service Providers has one drawback, from the perspective of regulators, in that counterfeiters can hire the services of another company, or set up their own shop. But the options are declining fast since ownership over the network infrastructure is concentrated into ever fewer hands. After a number of mergers, ownership over the cables is for all practical purposes divided up between AT&T and AOL Time Warner. These giants can easily strangle access to a large part of the network and pass decrees down to smaller Internet Service Providers. No less detrimental is their intent to turn the Internet into an interactive cable TV set.[49] The next generation of wires would realise this scenario by discriminating the traffic going upstream from the client (user) to the server, while giving priority to traffic going downstream (downloading of data) from server to client. Peer-to-peer transmissions, where traffic runs from client to client and where uploading is simultaneously downloading, would be hampered.

In addition to replacing the infrastructure of the network, there is the option of changing the network by replacing the consumer hardware that connects to the Internet. The first step in this direction was taken in 1999 when Intel hard-wired a unique serial number in its Pentium III processor. The serial number was meant to enable copyright holders to identify the computer of individual transgressors.[50] Public outcry forced the company to pull back. But a broader alliance between software and hardware firms, including Microsoft, Intel, IBM, HP, and AMD, has come together in the Trusted Computing Group. The industry needs to cancel out consumer choice if it is to market a product which adds features and increases costs while reducing the value to customers. The technology pushed by the industry is called Trusted Computing (TC) but hackers know it as Treacherous Computing. TC is a computer platform where software cannot be tampered with, and where the individual terminal is integrated in a centralised network. Applications running on TC computers are able to send information and take instructions from the network without allowing the user to interfere. The basic feature of these systems is identification. The computer of an individual user, the client, has to certify itself to other clients and servers, and, once identified, the computer will deny or permit the user access to the requested information. A drawback with the technology is that it only works in a closed loop with TC-compatible terminals. As soon as the TC-computer confronts clients outside the circuit, the integrity of the design is compromised. In other words, the entire network needs to be refurnished with TC computers. Mark Stefik, an advocate of this technology, acknowledges the difficulty in overcoming the cacophony of computers making up the 'network of networks', i.e. the Internet. It is a near infeasible task, he admits, especially since a limited introduction of certified terminals will leave a larger market outside than inside the closed TC loop. Thus the unprotected market share will have a stronger pull on content providers.[51] Throughout his writing, Stefik regrets that the Web was not drawn up in advance with a trusted system in the back of the mind of the architect.

Unfortunately for rights holders, identifying who's the owner of a computer does not resolve who is using the machine at a particular moment. The gap between body and machine causes a major uncertainty when cases are brought to court. It's no wonder then that much effort is put into expanding software-mediated schemes for identification outside the landlocked desktop computer. Following this development, the engagement of many hackers in the right to be anonymous on the Internet is growing into a concern for anonymity in the public space as well. Two technologies in particular have alarmed the hacker movement, Radio Frequency Identifiers (RFID) and biometrics. These technologies will enable the same degree of regulation and control in real life as is now possible inside the computer network. RFID are microchips, no bigger than a grain of sand, which scan for radio queries and transmit their unique identification number to the sender. The movement of the body in real space can thus be pinpointed in a virtual, Cartesian grid. RFID tags have been used for many years to track shipments and monitor inventories, and are expected to be used extensively on ordinary household products, branded cloths, and money. The other major concern is the advancement in biometrics. Researchers in biometrics claim that they can offer a near-hundred-percent reliable method for identification by locking it to the human genome. Up till now, most methods of identification have been hampered by frictions. Since the object of identification is something other than the object to be identified (the individual), the identification can be lost (a key), forged, or forgotten (passwords). Even if this is not the case, the mere possibility of an error will always give the benefit of doubt to the contester. Not so with biometrics. Research has got to the stage where most human features, DNA, voice, iris, fingerprints, heat patterns, odour, even gait, can be used to nail down a specified individual. In combination, these techniques create an extensive system for identification where a person can be scanned from a distance without even noticing it happening. Researchers in the field do not mumble about the purpose of their work: "The need to authenticate ourselves to machines is ever increasing in today's networked society and it is necessary to close the air gap between man and machine to secure our transactions and networks."[52] Software allows flexibility in design that approaches surgical precision. This technique of near absolute control is limited only by the 'air gap' left between the body and the virtual grid. But the rewards from regulating the behaviour of terrorists, criminals, counterfeiters, consumers, workers, citizens and immigrants are very compelling, and thus the motivation to close the air gap is equally so. A closed air gap would mean no escape from capital's transactions and capital's networks. Fear of such a scenario underpins the long-time scepticism towards information systems among many leftists. But those who dismiss the Internet with a reference to its origin in Pentagon's nuclear warfare strategies are mistaken. The spin-offs from a technology can be as enigmatic to its instigator as the backing of the Taliban movement in the 1980s was to the U.S. government.

RESISTANCE BY TECHNOLOGY

Previously in the chapter it was said that up until the breakthrough of capitalism, nation states, and a modern juridical system, commoners tended to identify themselves more with outlaws than with law authorities. Indeed, the social bandit as a champion of the little man is a recurrent theme in folk lore stretching from ancient China and feudal Europe to nineteenth century America. The argument put forward here is that the hacker movement might signal the return of the social bandit. The status of hackers as either social bandits or criminals depends on their relation towards the majority of ordinary computer users and citizens. Law, norm systems, and technology are intertwined in a struggle over fixating the public image of the hacker as either one or the other.

File-sharing networks provide a good example of how a particular architecture can strengthen the social aspects of lawbreaking. The open invitation to millions of regular computer users to share copyrighted files with each other has contributed to undermining the legitimacy of intellectual property. Efforts by law enforcers to isolate infringers and identify ringleaders are frustrated by the response of hackers to dislocate information flows, involve more people, and boost the heat losses of the juridical system. In the old days, a single pirate sold thousands of copies of a copyrighted work for profit, mirroring the position of the official vendor. In file-sharing networks, the position of the distributor has been replaced by thousands of individuals all acquiring a single copy from disparate sources. Since every petty violation of copyright is, in its aggregate, equally destabilising to the intellectual property regime as any other, the law has to track down every single perpetrator. Hence a growing number of ordinary computer users come to know the punitive side of law and order. Just as with a light bulb, the way to counter for heat losses in the juridical system is to scale up energy. In other words, the penalty for violating intellectual property must be set much higher than is called for by the nature of the crime in order to compensate for the small likelihood of getting caught. At the time of writing, copyright infringers are being fined and sued; however, judging by the current trends, they might soon find themselves behind bars. The distinction which courts traditionally have upheld between for-profit and non-profit motives, corresponding with the separation between civil and criminal offences, is being erased from both European and American copyright law. The reason is that if any safety vaults are left in the statute book, whereby some conditions must be met to merit a harsher sentence, hackers will quickly reorganise information flows beneath that minimum criteria. Likewise, the other hallmarks of the rule of law, predictability of outcomes and checks on law authorities, provide loopholes that can be exploited by hackers. Consequently, directives on intellectual property are made obsolete and have to be replaced at an accelerated pace. Ideally, in order to be effective, the police would need a penalty system that could be adjusted at the same speed as hackers write code. That would require an open-ended law, providing corporate lawyers with a *carte blanche* for making up enforcement policies as they go. It would require, in other words, a permanent state of exception. The reflections above suggest a similarity in strategies between hackers and the Baader-Meinhof league, though hackers are considerably more peaceful, playful and effective in their course of action. Namely, the idea that by provoking the democratic state into exaggerated and indiscriminate violence, the masses will be forced to choose sides. When legislators become increasingly out-of-step with public sentiments on intellectual property law, people tend to identify themselves with the cause of hackers. It is thus hackers can reclaim the status of social bandits.

These observations clarify the proposition made in the introduction of the book: Intellectual property law ought to be read out as a negative shape in the struggle of hackers. The inability of legislators to affect outcomes and enforce policies owes to capital having lost its monopoly over the means to dissolve and reorganise the virtual, networked space. This statement can be examined in more detail by borrowing from the anthropologist David Harvey. He says that the means of distributing space is continuously being revolutionised by capital in the same way as it revolutionises other means of production. In this drive, the incentive to reduce spatial barriers and to shorten circulation time are two guiding principles, in addition to the priority of removing strongholds of working class power. But to dissolve rigidities in one dimension necessarily implies the construction of a new rigid structure on top of which the previous terrain can be restructured. In Harvey's words: "In order to overcome spatial barriers and to 'annihilate space with time', spatial structures are created which themselves ultimately act as a barrier to further accumulation. These spatial structures are expressed, of course, in the fixed and immovable form of transport facilities, plant, and other means of production and consumption which cannot be moved without being destroyed."[53] The Internet is a showcase of how communications and logistics have been reorganised to undermine national borders, overturn traditions, redefine power relations, accelerate product-cycles, unlock financial flows, and expand global markets. Concurrently, however, the optical cables, the computer terminals, the Internet protocols, the widespread familiarity with a particular graphical interface, to mention just a few factors, cause a temporary fixation of the current setup of the Internet. Note to be taken, capital is not hindered from replacing the Internet because the structure is deeply entrenched. It is the other way around. The Internet is the most fluid form of structure allowing the widest scope of flexibility and perpetual restructuring within its set framework. The benefits are easy to spot. Nationally based working class organisations have been mortally wounded by the removal of frictions to capital, in part made possible by electronic networks. The advantage capital has won in this regard against organised labour is, however, offset by a new challenger. At least in some respects, capital and living labour meet on near equal terms in the computer network, since everyone is moving at the same (instant) speed. If capital finds a way to dissolve the current setup into an even more fluid form, it certainly will. But that would, (1) level the balance of power between living labour and capital/dead labour yet further, and, (2), this time around, it might be labour that dissolves and redefines the latest fixation of space.

The very flexibility and precision by which code can be tailored for technological control; the same ease allows many more to partake in the process of writing it. People are free to modify source code for their own ends, which on average will be in conflict with capital's intentions. The social division of labour will always leave the greater number of computer users outside capital's direct supervision, i.e. as not-employed, not-waged non-programmers. And since the number and the heterogeneity of the contributors are key factors in software development, capital will be at a disadvantage in setting software standards. Capital is therefore shifting the battle over free versus proprietary computer standards from software to hardware architecture.

Trusted computers prevent users from accessing the software layer by having instructions hard-wired into the machinery. In the long run, the hacker movement might have to craft their own machines in order to protect the gains made in the area of free software. Of course, free hardware projects are much harder to bootstrap than FOSS projects. Production costs, demands on logistics, and patent laws are major obstacles preventing a take-off of a free hardware movement. Despite the difficulties, some comfort can be taken in remembering that the personal computer was the invention of radio amateurs and hippies. And a few hardware projects are up and running at the time of writing. OpenCores is a portal gathering of about 2000 developers collaborating on free hardware devices. The seriousness of the undertaking is suggested by the fact that the industry keeps a close eye on OpenCores, to the point that companies have threatened the developers not to enter their business, while other companies have invested money in the project. Flextronics, a manufacturing-for-hire company that made the game console x-box for Microsoft, has engaged in discussions with the developers on the possibility of producing OpenCore designs. Even if the task of manufacturing the items was solved, however, difficulties would remain in marketing and shipping the goods. In the future, an alliance with developing countries is at least conceivable to overcome these difficulties.[54] Provided that the research has been made available free of charge under a GPL-like license, Third World countries have all the experience in the world to manufacture the devices. For the time being, however, governments in the South have not shown the same interest in free hardware as they have in adopting free software. What hardware hackers are waiting for is that the computer industry will commit itself to flexible hardware designs.[55] A prototype that has been under development for many years is printable circuits. These machines print electronic circuits just like ink is printed on paper. Another product in the pipeline is Field-Programmable Gate Arrays (FPGA). It makes the hardware reprogrammable as if it was a line of software code. It is plausible that hardware equipment will be developed along this trajectory for the same reason that capital has pushed for wide implementation of computer algorithms in society. Increasing the flexibility of hardware increases the flexibility of the labour market.[56] While, on the one hand, reprogrammable machinery risks to pull the rug from under organised labour, on the other hand, the ground is levelled for hackers to contest capital's monopoly over hardware design, just as they have in the field of software development before.

In addition to the struggle over software and hardware architecture, a third confrontation looms over the infrastructure of the network. Again, we can take consolation in the history of hacking. The Internet was predated by a grassroots network, the Bulletin Board System (BBS). The software and the hardware devices necessary to hike on to the telephone lines and to send electronic text and code through it, were largely developed by phone phreaks.[57] Though by now the BBS is eclipsed by the Internet and partly incorporated in it, the history of BBS demonstrates the possibility of side stepping an infrastructure overtaken by censorship and surveillance. The tradition of phone phreaks is continued by community activists experimenting with gratis, wireless access to the Internet. Wireless Internet access is carried in a narrow unlicensed patch of the spectrum that has been set aside from the regulated, commercial spectrum. The frequency is shared with such devices as garage door openers and heart monitors. Urban 'mesh networks' can operate in this tight space by utilising the spectrum in a novel way. Communication is relayed from sender to sender, instead of having to pass through a central transmitter. The capacity of the network is improved as the density of senders grows. A spirit of cooperation follows from the necessity to add together the transmission capacity of all the neighbours. Another consequence of open mesh networks is anonymity, or, at least, plausible deniability. Since anyone that happens to be in range of a sender can hike onto the network with her computer, it is impossible for law enforcers to pinpoint who has done what on the network. But the ramifications of mesh networks depend on the number of people and information it attracts. A serious drawback is therefore its short range, usually only covering a city block or at most a city. A historical difference that worked to the advantage of the Internet was that its backbone of globally-spanning cables and satellites was invested in by US government during the cold war.[58] To get worldwide coverage, mesh networks have to hook up to the Internet and that makes the points where the mesh network connects with the Internet a vulnerable spot for policing and control. Judging from recent experience, however, people will find the means to establish communication networks with each other independently of the state. By combining cheap, off-the-shelf equipment in a novel way, so-called darknets might be set up over the phone line, in the electricity grid, on the airwaves, through light signals, or by discovering another, today unforeseen, method. Binary data is similar to Morse code in its versatility. And Morse code, as we know, can be transmitted by an interstate telegraph line or by the wall separating two prison cells.

These examples highlight why a strategy of deskilling is essential to capital. But here capitalism encounters a difficulty of its own making. On the one hand, capital needs to suppress the skills of computer users in order to uphold the commodity form of information. On the other hand, it is beneficial to capital when technical skills are cheap and available, both to workers and customers. A large reservoir of qualified programmers keeps wages down; while a widespread understanding about how to use a technical system expands the consumer market of the product. Rather than dumbing down each and every computer user, social Taylorism is a strategy of 'combined and uneven' deskilling. Indeed, at a closer look, it is evident that Taylorism never was so much about removing skills as stratifying knowledge between different groups, separating white-collar workers from blue-collar workers, and professionals from laymen. Likewise, capital's restructuring of hardware and wires on the Internet does not aim at eradicating every single transgression. There will always be users that acquire advanced skills and employ that knowledge against the interests of capital. Design only has to raise the barriers of inconvenience high enough to separate the savviest users from the bulk of ordinary users. If the first group is marginalised, then their actions can be suppressed and branded as criminal. They will be no more of a headache than the more familiar transgressions against private property, shoplifting, theft, robbery, etc. When the outlaw is recast as a criminal, his actions is deflected by law upon ordinary citizens, who then come to embrace law enforcement as if it was one of their own. The social bandit is social only for as long as he in her transgression inspires everyone else to recognise law as class rule and to defy it.

That is to say that access to technology is not just contested on the level of design choices, i.e. free versus closed source code, but equally so on legal, educational, ideological and economic grounds. By inventing a free/open license, for instance, the legal barriers to entry raised by copyright law are minimised. Furthermore, the norm system within the computer under-ground, in particular a strong meritocracy rewarding the demonstration of technical skills, encourages individuals in the community to go beyond user-friendly interfaces. Know-how about information systems is thus spread outside the computer profession. Regrettably, the hacker identity inadver-tently creates new borders between insiders and outsiders, closing the door on women among others. Though it is an incomplete and conflictive pro-cess, the hacker movement contributes to a weakening of the stratifications created by social Taylorism. The authoring of technology is thereby opened up to an anonymous, ambulant crowd. As a consequence, the fixation of individual authorship, intellectual property rights, and market exchanges in information, are destabilised. The motive of hackers and crackers for doing this is not primarily, as is generally assumed, to access consumer goods free of charge. On the contrary, as will be argued in the next chapter, it is the lack of satisfaction from consuming pre-packaged information content, irre-spectively of price, which turns people to seek satisfaction in other activities, such as hacking.

4 Consumption and Needs of Information Goods

MASLOW AND THE AFFLUENT SOCIETY

In this chapter hacking is discussed from the angle of needs and consumption. The reader might ask what the relevance is of consumption and needs to a study of hackers. But production and consumption must not be treated as they appear at face value, as separate spheres of activities. They are two sides of the same commodity relation. To be sure, it is as crucial to understand the setting from which the hacker movement has emerged as it is to know about hacking as a practice. That setting is a semiotic-based, consumer-driven and post-modern accumulation regime. The leading question in the chapter is what kind of resistance is effective against this reformed, capitalist system. In the nineteenth and early twentieth century, socialists hoped that the advancement of the productive forces would eventually solve the problem of needs satisfaction without demanding sacrifices from the working class. That wishful thought has since been thoroughly falsified by the never-ending race for positional goods. It will here be suggested that hacking provides a different way of conceptualising scarcity, and, hence, a possibility of breaking out of the semiotic loop. In the computer underground, 'keeping up with the Jones' means writing the neatest software code or having access to a high-security server. In other words, distinction is not sought after primarily through conspicuous consumption but by demonstrating productive skills. The need to show distinction is thus satisfied at the very same time as the demand in society for software products is met. Since there are no trade-offs between fulfilling one's own needs and those of others, scarcity can be short-circuited by advancing a norm of 'convivial consumption'. The hacker movement will here be analysed as a producer of needs, to complement the established picture of the hacker movement as a producer of software code. The chapter argues that since those needs do not conform to the logic of scarcity, this aspect of the hacker movement contributes as much to their resistance against capitalist relations as the production of convivial tools, i.e. the making of free software.

It is noteworthy that the belief of early socialists, that humanity would be liberated from scarcity thanks to the development of the forces of production, is resurfacing in the technophilia of many hackers. When they reflect upon the ramifications of their hobby they tend to be heavily influenced by notions about the 'affluent society'.[1] The underlying assumption, explicitly argued in Pekka Himanen's *The Hacker Ethic*, is that the 'high-tech gift economy' on the Internet has emerged as a consequence of the abundant wealth in industrialised economies. Himanen is typical in referring to the psychologist Abraham Maslow's work on human motivation from the 1950s. According to Maslow, human needs can be arranged in a hierarchy where primacy is assigned to those needs that are most urgently requiring to satisfy for a human being when he lacks everything. When physiological needs are satisfied, such as food and water, attention is turned to safety needs. Among these are security, stability, freedom from fear, from anxiety and chaos, and the longing for structure. Once security is sorted, human yearning extends beyond the individual. Such needs are social in character, focusing on love and belonging. Self-respect, self-confidence and reputation among peers now capture the human imagination. Finally, if all needs are reasonably satisfied, the individual will be free to engage in self-actualisation.[2] The argument of Pekka Himanen, and many others, is that volunteer involvement in FOSS development projects can be explained by the extent to which primary needs have been satisfied in consumer society.

It is not alien to the Marxist tradition of thought that the quantity of social surplus, by which is meant excess productivity in society, modifies the conditions for struggle. Within Marxist scholarship it has been debated if the hunter-gather society could be said to have exemplified a form of 'primitive communism'. The lack of social surplus prevented a ruling class from forming in these societies. When productivity rose, usually assumed to have followed with the introduction of agriculture, enough social surplus was created to sustain a ruling class, together with ranks of people who worked with other things than providing for immediate subsistence, such as priests, scientists and philosophers. As was mentioned above, quite a few socialists have predicted that as productivity continues to swell, spurred on by the profit motive, the material conditions for transcending capitalism are being established. The same people tend to argue that the conquest of scarcity is a precondition for re-establishing communism proper. The conservative futurist Daniel Bell was so unsettled by this implication of his own writings that he felt compelled to denounce any likelihood of communism due to an end of scarcity in his post-industrial kingdom-come. In *Cultural Contradictions of Capitalism*, Bell charged that communism always was, always will be, unattainable. The reason is the human plight of eternal scarcity: "But what we have come to realize is that, the question of resources aside, we will never overcome scarcity. In the post-industrial society [. . .] there would be new scarcities which nineteenth-century utopians could never envision—scarcities of information, [. . .]."[3] Daniel Bell missed the point. Marxist theory is clear about scarcity is a social relation and that it cannot be done away with inside the confines of capitalism. In the case of intellectual property, it is obvious that scarcity is embedded in institutions and is deliberately enforced. But even where access to information is not restricted by legislation, scarcity crops up in new disguises in this society. A surplus of information leads to an insufficiency in the capacity of audiences to process the signals. Thus, some economists have begun to talk about an 'attention economy' on the Internet where the lack of attention is a source of new demand.[4] The market society is so tuned in to generating scarcity that abundance is coded as a 'scarcity of scarcity'. While Marxism holds that the conditions to overcome the market economy are developed inside the same society, these circumstances remain a potentiality until the capitalist relation has been overthrown.[5]

NEEDS IN CONSUMER-DRIVEN CAPITALISM

The popular adoption of Maslow in the computer underground, where needs are seen as ordered in a hierarchy and being quite constant to the human species, coupled with the belief that the hierarchy of needs is gradually being filled up like water poured into a vessel, is falling short on several accounts. Firstly, the impression that 'higher' needs among the population are set free in response to the peaceful and gradual build-up of affluence in western society, denies the antagonistic world in which wealth is created. Secondly, it fails to see the productive aspect of needs. Needs experienced by man as his own often correspond suspiciously well to the needs of the capitalist system. Thus, it is better not to think of needs as a consummative force liberated by the affluent society but instead as a productive force required by the operations of the economic system. Or, to put it differently, post-modern capitalism is as much about producing consumption as it is about producing consumer goods. This situation derives from the fact that circulating capital has surmounted productive capital and subsumed society under its own articulations. Leading on from Fordism, late capitalism requires a social norm of continuously high, working-class consumption matching the ever-larger output of mass-produced goods. Contrary to popular belief, the seeds of this mirror world that we now inhabit were noticed and commented upon by Karl Marx: "[. . .] Production of surplus value based on the increase and development of the productive forces, requires the production of new consumption; requires that the consuming circle within circulation expands as did the productive circle previously. Firstly, quantitative expansion of existing consumption; secondly: creation of new needs by propagating existing ones in a wide circle; *thirdly*: production of *new* needs and discovery and creation of new use values." (*Grundrisse*, 408, *italics in original*). At the beginning of the twentieth century, intellectuals of divergent allegiances foresaw a clash between an ever-expanding industry and the limits, then thought of as being quite constant, of consumers in absorbing the massive output. In his comprehensive study on the subject, *Time and Money—The Making of Consumer Culture*, Gary Cross tells how conservatives in those days feared a loss of economic incentives. They considered it to be a threat to the work ethic of the working class. Indeed, the same tunes are heard today from the ranks of the economic profession. Progressives, on the other hand, envisioned a utopian state of expanding 'democratic leisure'. It has since been proved, as much of a surprise to both sides, that private consumption can be expanded in much wider circles than was then imaginable. Gary Cross reminds his readers that the delight of consumption has consistently been downplayed by intellectuals and socialists. Part of the secret behind the longevity of consumption is, quite simply, that it is enjoyable. Despite the fact that consumption in Western societies has surpassed the reasonable many times over without losing any of its appeal, some absolute boundaries for use cannot be avoided quite irrespectively of our assumptions about the nature of human needs. For example, it is hard to overcome the length of the day in which a consumer can be an active, potential shopper. When mass production pushes even beyond these rock-bottom barriers, consumer habits must be rationalised, just as work was rationalised before. Nicholas Garnham describes how a racket of 'combined consumption' is devised for this purpose. One area ripe for combined consumption is driving. A sizeable portion of a consumer's day is spent in the car. The time when a driver cannot consume anything more than petrol represents a 'loss' to overall demand in society. According to Garnham, the invention of drive-in fast-food chains, motels and road-side cinemas are examples of how this bottleneck is solved through combined consumption.

Indeed, the sheer mass of individual consumption has itself become a boundary to consumer demand. The downward spiral of satisfaction from crowding was elaborated on by Fred Hirsch in *The Social Limits to Growth*. He calculated that the satisfaction that an individual consumer gets from a product derives less from her own individual choice and more from the consumption of others in her surrounding. The negative trade-off from crowding constitutes an 'economy of bad neighbours'. The parade example is the individual freedom that ownership of a car promises to a potential buyer. The appeal to freedom offered by the prospect of owning a car is compromised by the number of existing car owners. The dream of becoming a free, motorised ranger is bogged down in endless road congestions. Markets are inappropriate to satisfy such needs in an overcrowded environment. Fred Hirsch concludes that mass consumer goods must fail to satisfy the expectation of individual consumers.[6] We would, however, be erroneous to deduce from Hirsch's argument that the consumer market is running into a definitive obstacle because of this. On the contrary, a permanent erosion of the use value of individual consumer goods, paired with the delusion that buying more goods is a remedy to social ills, is instrumental in the workings of planned obsolescence. Consumption turns into an endless tail-chase to escape crowding. The market value of gated communities, remote beaches, and sport utility vehicles derives directly from the economy of crowding.

Crowding is one example of how specific, individual forms of need satisfaction are being saturated when consumption is pushed beyond the scope of use for the sake of exchange. The time it takes for consumers to digest mass-produced goods creates friction to the circulation of capital. Those frictions are better not thought of as rigid ceilings, against which infinite consumption eventually will collapse into (in a parallel version to Rosa Luxemburg's geographic boundaries to imperialism and world market expansion). Rather, they are thresholds that can be surpassed, as capitalism has proved many times over, but by which qualities in the conditions of exploitation and struggle are transformed as well. One such threshold is the passing from goods made for concrete uses towards positional goods where the primary use is to show distinction.[7]

THE BECOMING-IMAGE OF THE COMMODITY

The renowned thesis of Guy Debord, formulated at the verge of the 'mass-consumer society' in the 1960s, was that the image has become the highest form of the commodity. The image has given rise to an immense spectacle.[8] Though Guy Debord depicted the society of the spectacle as overwhelming, his writing and actions aspired to the disbandment of this state of things. When the French philosopher Jean Baudrillard picked up the same theme ten years later, his aim was to disprove the very notion of resistance. The principal target of Baudrillard was the Marxist distinction between use value and exchange value. He charged that use value is nothing but an alibi for exchange value and counterposed these two with the term 'sign value'. There is no escape from the endless semiotic game of sign values, Baudrillard exclaimed. From the 1990s and onwards, interest has surged in the so-called cultural turn or the aesthetisation of the economy. It is generally agreed that imagery has become a key factor in driving consumption and, thus, production. Academics researching the topic draw more from Jean Baudrillard than from Guy Debord. The concept of use value tends to be dismissed with a brief reference to Baudrillard's critique of Marxism.[9] This approach to the cultural economy is far from innocent. Class struggle is replaced with aesthetics, in parallel to post-industrialists who replace class struggle with technology. These writers have accurately described the changes in postmodern capitalism as it appears from the point of perspective of capital, but not as it comes across to the proletariat. It is thus they can declare that resistance against semiotic capitalism is futile, as Baudrillard did, or just take the futility of resistance for granted, as later-day theoreticians generally do. All they are saying, and they are correct in this, is that out-dated forms of struggle are out-dated when coming up against a reformed, semiotic capitalism. In the second half of the chapter, we will take the hacker movement as a springboard for theorising on what kinds of struggle that can be effective today. First we have to examine in more detail the claims about a cultural turn in the economy. In order to retain the centrality of class struggle, however, we will move in the opposite direction to those making the claim. We must deepen rather than abandon the discussion about use and exchange.

Wolfgang Haug did so already in the 1970s when he argued that the tendency towards image is latent in production for exchange. Karl Marx stressed that for a product to have an exchange value it must be of use to someone, i.e. it has to be a use value as well as an exchange value. Otherwise the item will not be purchased. Haug drew attention to the fact that at the point of sale, before the transaction has been carried out, use value does not exist but only the promise of use. It is the appearance of use, not actual use, which is decisive for the closure of a sale. Though this always was the case, in the period of early consumerism the look was taken for granted as identical with the object. When image becomes the highest form of the commodity, appearance of use is acknowledged as separate from use, and this recognition feeds back into the production process. The aesthetics of the commodity is now detached from the object and enters the calculation as an independent factor. Under the pressures of competition, Haug attested, it is ultimately necessary for capitalists to gain technological control over and start an independent production of this aesthetic process.[10] By shifting competition to the level of the aesthetic processes, where 'image fights image' as Haug puts it, corporations establish themselves as 'image monopolies'. The compression of time and space in post-modern, late capitalism is both catalyzed by and accentuates the importance of this aesthetic process. The image has an edge over tangible goods since it is immediately responsive to turnover and can be mass-marketed instantaneously over a global space. Indeed, the accelerated speed of newness makes tangible products into a liability. The cumbersomeness of physical property is manifest in the time-lags required to transport and store goods in real space. The other major obstacle is in consumption. The use value of a tangible product is specific and defined, thus it is finite in its functionality. The durability of items previously sold becomes congestion to the next fresh wave of same-but-different things. Automated production, which has actualized this problem by its very efficiency, also provides the solution. The anonymity and uniformity of mass consumer goods create a deficiency in look and feel which advertisers can exploit. The stimulus from consuming comes to a great extent from novelty, which, in mass-produced goods, is used up much sooner than the comfort they yield.[11]

In other words, the pleasure from consumption derives in large part from factors external to the characteristics of the object in question. Wolfgang Haug sensed this seismological shift when he located the 'place' of the use value to outside the product itself: "The balance will shift from an unmediated, materially purposeful use-value to thoughts, feelings, and associations, which one links to the commodity or assumes that others must associate with it. [. . .] Thus it becomes ever more important to see what points beyond the commodity itself, for example, positive and negative relationships to other commodities, its 'meaning' and 'sense' being based on determinants outside it." (Haug, 97–8) The shift of focus from actual use to the appearance of use, and from the commodity to that which points beyond the commodity, has seminal consequences for Marxist theory. Wolfgang Haug stopped short at the remarks cited above. After having witnessed the aesthetisation of the economy for another thirty years, we are in the position to expand on his preliminary observations. In the classical definition given by Karl Marx, use value is an objective relation between the person and her needs, a relation that is valid irrespectively of the existence of comparable use values. He contrasted it to exchange value which only exists as a measure. The absoluteness which he ascribed to use value must be rethought when the image becomes the hegemonic form of the commodity. This is because image is essentially the same thing as language. In language, meaning exists as a difference between signs. Hence, the image necessarily relates to a constellation of other images as a difference. Positional goods derive at least part of their use value from their positions vis-à-vis comparable goods. In this sense, there is some merit to Jean Baudrillard's well-known catch phrase: 'the sign has no referent'. By that he expressed the idea that there is no function or concrete use which a product ultimately refers to. He claimed that the use value of a product derives from its relation to other signs in a never-ending, self-referring circle.[12] Insights from feminist, Marxist theory can be useful in our search for the mechanisms that codify a consumer product-image as desirable. The objectification of the female body is very much part of the same complex of problems. To illustrate what could be meant by saying that the commodity points beyond itself, a quote from Naomi Wolf's *The Beauty Myth* on what makes a face look beautiful gives direction to the mind: "Its power is not far-reaching because of anything innately special about the face: Why that one? Its only power is that it has been designated as 'the face'—and that hence millions and millions of women are looking at it together, and know it."[13] The last sentence is the key to the puzzle. It is the knowledge of other people knowing. It is the desire created by other people desiring. And what goes for a beautiful face goes for any other object deemed as attractive, a slick car or a fashionable dress. In other words, both the use value and the production process of the image are located in communication, which necessarily points beyond both the product itself and the factory in which the product was made. This provides another facet of the labour of audiences, as was discussed at length in chapter two. Audiences have become a labour force on a parity with employees and the decoding process emerges as a source of surplus value in its own right. Youth subcultures that actively take part in defining tastes and promoting consumption is only the furthest exponent of a labour process that is generic and spread out among audiences, users, and consumers.

CONSUMPTION AS PRODUCTION

The idea that the distance between producers and consumers is closing is often voiced by critics of intellectual property law. That claim is one of their main reproaches against the policies of the culture industry. In their opinion, business models based on the delivery of information content to paying customers are hopelessly outdated, at least as far as the Internet is concerned. Instead these critics like to highlight the example set by FOSS ventures and underground record labels that experiment with alternative licenses. In such forward-thinking business models, customers and users are invited to participate in the development process. Their argument resonates with a claim first made by the futurist Alvin Toffler in the early 1980s. He too predicted a merger between the producer and the consumer and invented the neologism 'the prosumer' for his new creature.[14] Both Toffler and contemporary critics of intellectual property law give credit to digital technology as the agent behind this transformation. Typically, the interactivity of videogames is contrasted with the passivity of watching television, and a vague optimism is attached to the surge of new media.

A glance at any of Karl Marx's extensive writings on political economy clarifies that production is consumption and consumption is production, and this always was the case. For instance, the consumption of a loaf of bread is simultaneously the reproduction of human labour power. It is the reified relation in bourgeois society that makes production and consumption appear as two distinct spheres of activities. From this standpoint the productive consumer does not look like such a curiosity or novelty. This is not to say that we should rule out that there are changes in the economy moving in the direction suggested by the critics of intellectual property. But these changes cannot be adequately explained with a reference to information technology. Digital media is not the best end to start an inquiry into the merger of the consumer and the producer. The retailing industry might seem like an odd place to depart from, but hopefully it will make more sense as the discussion proceeds. Paul du Gay has examined how the work situation in retailing is reformed by the ambition of firms to stay close to its customers. Anticipating the next wish of the consumer and giving her an out-of-the-ordinary experience has broadly been recognised by managers as the king road to profits. The margins in this segment of the market are higher than when competing with low prices. Furthermore, leading on from the previous discussion, consumer satisfaction exists to some degree in the moment of buying a product, rather than in anything innate belonging to the product. Providing that sensation at the point of sale can be worth more to the customer than the object itself. A dilemma for managers, however, is that the experience that customers have of the company derives from their contact with the front-line staff. It is hard for managers to monitor the subtleties of person-to-person interactions. Commanding the personnel to act pleasantly towards customers tends to be counterproductive. Hence, it becomes crucial to get the clerks at the bottom of the corporate hierarchy to identify themselves with the goals of the company. This requirement goes some way to explain the emphasis on culture in business organisations in the last decades. The firm tries to pass itself off to its employees as if the organisation was about some core value above and beyond making money. Of course, those corporate values always hinge on serving the customer in the right way. The customer is the norm for ethical behaviour in corporate cultures. The hypocrisy is not lost on employees, and, as Paul du Gay readily acknowledges, there is a big rift between what corporate cultures look like on paper and how they come out on the shop-floor. Among low-paid and expendable personnel, cynicism is a common response to management talk about corporate values.[15]

The warring interests between workers and owners make it tricky for a company to give customers the cosy welcoming that will induce them to spend money. And now, finally, we return to the question of the so-called prosumer. The people that are closest to the customers, thus best placed to persuade them, are the customers themselves. Retailers on the Internet have explored this opportunity to the fullest. A well-known example is the book reviews on Amazon that are submitted by previous customers. The rationale for this policy is evident. First and foremost, the company could not afford to pay a staff to review and keep up-to-date with every new book release. Secondly, the book reviews are credible precisely because they are written by another disinterested reader and not by a company employee with the incentive of getting the book sold. While Amazon might not sell one particular book due to an angry reviewer, on average the book store will benefit from the input of readers. More cases supporting the observation can be found outside the retailing industry. Video games have from the start been the parade example of interactive media. It is logical then that the gaming industry has gone the furthest in engaging their customers in game development. In computer games played over the Internet, almost all interaction in the game world is between players/customers. Not only are the in-game experiences delivered by fellow players, the administration, marketing, even coding of the games, are increasingly outsourced to the players.[16] When scratching the surface, it turns out that interactive media comes down to little more than intensified exploitation. It must be stressed, nonetheless, that the benefits from enrolling customers instead of workers in the provision of services cannot be reduced to simply a matter of cutting costs. Equally important is that customers do a better job. The benefits from enlisting consumers as opposed to employees is that the former have a high degree of voluntariness in going about doing what they are doing. Voluntariness is a chief competitive asset to firms that are in the business of selling concepts. And, if we are to believe management gurus, selling concepts is the lead tune in the weightless and aestheticised economy. It follows that the reformed post-Fordist labour market pivots around convincing employees to act as if they had volunteered to do the job. Drawing from the experience of fashion designers, Angela McRobbie examines how work has been stylised as a way of self-enrichment. In the majority of cases the rhetoric about personal development on the job is little more than a cover-up. But it is in those occupations where self-enrichment is experienced as real that the rhetoric becomes truly effective. In a key remark, McRobbie notes that where individuals are most free to chase their dreams of self-expression, they are most effectively controlled.[17] That FOSS development fits into this larger picture is evident from Pekka Himanen's endorsement of the hacker spirit, 'the work ethos of the information age', as opposed to the protestant ethic of industrial times. Corporations such as IBM do not have to invent an internal, corporate culture to lure employees into extended cooperation and identification with the firm; an undertaking frustrated by class antagonism and entrenched bureaucracy. They only have to take onboard the FOSS development community.

It would be erroneous of us, however, to explain the current trend with a capitalist master plan. The chain of events has been set off by working class defection from alienated labour. In order to see the full ramifications of this defection, we must look beyond overt cases of workers' resistance. Part of the resistance is carried out in the passivity of non-employees. That is, in the strategies of working class people to avoid entering the labour market in the first place. Another sizeable factor is employees that hang on to their means of income but expend a minimum of effort while doing so. Capital has to improvise to cope with these kinds of furtive refusals. It is telling, as Paul Heeles notices in an article about the 'softening of capitalism', that interest in company cultures began in the 1960s and 1970s. He suggests that it was rising labour militancy that convinced commentators and academics that there was a problem with work. The monotony of factory and office work had to be softened to 'win over' labour. From then onwards a stream of psychologist reports have been produced that argue that rewarding work assignments can be reconciled with capitalist relations.[18] Of course, with the exception of the most privileged workers in the upper tier of the labour market, capital fails to deliver. But capital has found another way to get what it wants. When workers try to escape from alienated existence they deflect their time and/or energy away towards family, friends, lifestyles and hobbies. This individualised form of flight is for the most part caught up in expanded consumer markets. The next logical step is to transform these consumer activities so that they become productive to capital once again. It is thus we can make sense of the rise of the so-called prosumer. Capital counters the resistance of employees (and non-employees) by dissolving the line between the producer and the consumer. The 'hacker spirit' is pitched against the 'refusal of work'. Digital media technology has certainly facilitated this development but is by no means the root cause of it.

RESISTANCE IN CONSUMER-DRIVEN CAPITALISM

We are thus led back to the starting question: What kind of resistance is conceivable in a semiotic-based, consumer-driven accumulation regime? Criticism against consumerism has primarily been articulated either by conservatives or by environmentalist and lifestyle movements. Left to them, the criticism has targeted over-consumption. There are ascetic, moralist, and self-righteous currents in these traditions of thought. Labour theory, with its heritage from unions and the struggle for a larger slice of corporate profits, are wary against claims that the level of consumption among Western workers could be adequate, or even excessive. Such views are too close to the position of employers. It is worth keeping in mind that Karl Marx saw the multiplication of needs as a civilising force of expanded human richness; and he even congratulated capitalism for it. His criticism was levelled against the bias of the growth of needs fostered under capitalism. It always swelled those needs most profitable to capitalist valorisation, and always at the expense of the whole range of other human needs and desires that are not readily exploitable. In the communist society, a need is limited only by other needs—i.e. all needs are free to grow and will balance each other out in an expanding universe.[19]

The conditioned objection to consumerism offered by Marx avoids falling into the self-righteous and ascetic trap of alternative life-style movements. Conversely, however, the impulse to own and consume infinitely more is certainly not a privilege of the bourgeoisie anymore. Abstract hedonism belongs to the sphere of exchange value, where possession is detached from use. It is the essence of money that there are no 'diminishing marginal returns' to ownership. The same can be said about the image. The image exists as a quantity in relation to other images. Progressive thinkers have shunned such a proposition, while conservatives have endorsed it, no doubt for much the same reason; it renders familiar forms of struggle ineffective. If semiotic consumption is truly without boundaries, then the increases of productivity in the industry make little difference. Shattered are the hopes for a future of post-scarcity and the unfolding of democratic leisure. Furthermore, the demand of workers for increased purchasing power is emptied of some of its emancipating potential, and thus its legitimacy, if redistribution of wealth only serves to grease the wheels of the system. It is on this ground that Jean Baudrillard wrote his obituary notice over anti-capitalist resistance. He failed to see, however, that struggle has not ended but is finding new outlets. Just as the use value of the image is external to the object, struggle too is external to the commodity. Production and resistance are both located in the coding of images as desirable, i.e. in the production of consumption, or, we might also say, it exists in communication.

Feminists, queers, and minority rights campaigners have long fought on this terrain, that is, from points of reference outside the wage relation.

Consumption is indirectly targeted by their protest against the hierarchies that are hard-wired in the consumer market. At least some of them maintain that by challenging chauvinism and racism, i.e. the micro-political setting of everyday life, consumerism is attacked too. Social stratifications have proved, however, to be very resilient to educational campaigns. Indeed, political correctness and cosmopolitan values often result in little more than another display of distinction and a new niche market. Another, closely related, practice is the 'judo strategy' of adbusting. Though the familiarity of a brand becomes a leveller to 'name and shame' a corporation, activists quickly discovered that the judo strategy cuts both ways. Companies themselves adapted the chic look of adbusting to market their brands, while the adbusters became brands and started companies. The focus of these left-of-the-centre movements on contesting representations has a precedent in academia. Studies of consumption and the resistance by consumers have been in vogue in universities since the 1980s. The topic of consumption replaced the emphasis on production that went before. Many of the scholars in culture studies came from a leftist political tradition and continued the themes of struggle, though this time a struggle between the broadcaster and the viewer, the retailer and the shopper, and so on. Priority was given to conflicts over representation. In hindsight, it must be said that the scope of audiences and consumers to resist domination by reinterpreting commercial messages was vastly overrated. Television audiences have had little say over the global consolidation of media ownership, for instance. The influence that media corporations exercise over public opinion, repeatedly demonstrated during general elections in country after country, suggests that the subversion of meaning by audiences is marginal and inadequate to counter biased reporting. Labour theoreticians have rightly been critical of postmodern, identity-based, left-of-the-centre movements and the assertions of media scholars, insisting on the centrality of hitting capital where it hurts, i.e. in the production of surplus value.

It is when we mingle the perspectives of labour theory with the subject of culture studies that interesting things start to happen. Such an approach follows from the claim above that consumers have become directly involved in production. The stage of consumption is an inception of a new cycle of production, not merely reproduction. Putting this statement in Marx's classic scheme, it would look something like this: means of use—consumption/production—enhanced means of use. Or, in abbreviation: MU-C/P-MU'. Because the starting point in this cycle is consumer goods, that is, means that have been purchased with a wage and not by spent surplus value, capital is out of the loop. Of course, the cycle of consumption/production does not take place independently of capital. The consumer bought the goods from a corporation and he paid with money earned from a second corporation. The nicety here is that the transaction was conducted with money and not with capital. Money and capital is not the same thing according to Marxist theory. Money becomes capital when it is set in motion in the accumulation process. It is in this restricted sense that we can speak of a cycle of consumption/production by users that does not involve capital. The metamorphosis of the consumer goods does not take place inside a firm but in a community of users. And though a firm was involved at the outset by selling the original product to the users, that might not be the case the second time that the cycle repeats itself. This is aptly illustrated by the development of FOSS applications by user groups. Computer firms have got involved in the process at a later date and are merely adding to an activity that is centred on the user community.

With these remarks at the back of our mind, and, with hacking as our touchstone, we can find valuable insights in the discipline of culture studies. It might even help us to correct labour theory on a few points. A central theme in the genre is that consumer products are not sealed off at the point of sale. Functions and meanings of the product are continuously negotiated between the user and the manufacturer. This indeterminacy is what creates a potential for resistance in the act of consumption. The statement is of minor consequence when applied to the intervention of commercial broadcasts and everyday consumer goods. There is only so much that 'semiotic poaching' can achieve. The matter gains in gravity when users intervene in consumer electronics, i.e. the praxis of hacking. We have concrete, political outcomes to show for the poaching of computer networks. Another hallmark in culture studies is to stress the subjective experience of the consumer instead of his objective position versus the retailer. Since consumption is a source of pleasure for the individual, a certain ambivalence appears in his sentiments towards the company. Though he is in a subjugated position vis-à-vis the company, as much as the employee is, the crisp, bi-polar antagonism between labour and capital doesn't cut here. Not even when the consumer is turned into a producer of surplus value for capital does it cancel the fact that the consumer, at least in a restricted sense, is volunteering to do the job. This is reflected in the ambiguous attitude towards big business in the FOSS community. Hackers are usually fine with firms making money out of their software as long as the free license is respected. In all this the labour theoretician will only see naivety on the part of the consumer or hacker. It should be taken under consideration, however, that if hackers had adopted a trade union consciousness, they would be stuck at defending their own copyright claims, and, by extension, strengthening the intellectual property regime as a whole. A case in point is the many cultural workers that front for the intellectual property lobby. There is something to be said for the playful mentality of hackers. The same observation holds true about their passion for computer technology. Marx laid down in *Capital* that machinery is capital's material mode of existence. The worker revolts against machinery because it embodies the material foundation of the capitalist mode of production. It is a hostile force that confronts the worker as deskilling, layoffs, and management control, and he responds to it by rejection and sabotage. The same technology reveals itself to hackers as a stimulus. It might then sound odd to say that hackers are part of the same revolt as workers are. Nonetheless, in their affirmation of computers the hacker movement has achieved something that could hardly be done from the trenches of the worker's movement, namely: They have invented a technology of their own.

Arguably, something similar might be said about the most enthusiastic devotees of popular culture. The culture industry is typically denounced for pacifying the audience and regimenting their tastes and opinions. Conversely, however, standardisation of narratives and references creates a protocol for communication between peers. In the fan fiction subculture, the commonness of popular culture is taken as a starting point for creativity among the participants. Their excursions into collective storytelling defy bourgeois, individual authorship and copyright law.[20] Without question, as an independent producer of culture or as a challenger of hegemony, the fan subculture is of marginal importance. Isolated and besieged by market relations, the role of the fan subculture is primarily as a laboratory feeding the culture industry with fresh ideas, as a training camp for a prospecting media workforce, and as a cohort of credible and cheap promoters. But then again, the significance of their activity is not in the products they make. Just as with the wage labourer, the real importance of their activity lies in the making of themselves as makers. In the fan subculture and in the hacker community, new models for organising labour are being rehearsed. It is thus we can take Michel de Certeau's emphasis on appropriation and subversion of consumer culture and go beyond it. To de Certeau, such practices by ordinary people are tactics to cope inside the 'belly of the beast'. The argument here is that these tactics can bootstrap a counter-logic and threaten the operation of the dominant system. When people play they produce both needs and the satisfaction of those needs for themselves and for everyone around them. Play expands the boundaries of social needs that are incompatible with market exchange. Those needs are advanced against and on top of the territory now occupied by individual, marketable needs. While individual needs are rivalrous and subject to crowding, social needs are reciprocal and strengthened by additional users. The dictum "the more the merrier" expresses this point succinctly.

It is thus scarcity can be overcome. A comparison between the two models for resolving rising demand for radio frequencies gives guidance to our thought. The state/market model is premised on portioning a limited resource in radio frequencies by drawing borders and licensing ownership rights to the highest bidder. Seen from a purely technical standpoint, segmenting the airwaves in this way prevents any two signals from interfering with each other. The auctioning of frequencies is intended to counter the stress on the transmission capacity imposed from including additional senders. A secondary consequence, however, is that as crowding builds up, both a market in frequencies and a mechanism of centralised control are established. It is social constraints, rather than technological feasibility, that favour this model for administrating radio frequencies. Technically speaking, there are many other ways to share the space in order to avoid any two signals from colliding. That is proven by 'mesh networks' where users are simultaneously senders. The signals jump from one sender to another without passing through a central transmitter. In the mesh network, additional users/senders strengthen the power and the range of the network as a whole. By meshing the sender with the receiver, or, the producer with the consumer, the terrain on which scarcity operates can be broken down. In markets in radio frequencies, or, for that matter, in intellectual property markets, scarcity exists only for as long as people abide to the rules. The mass defection from copyright law in filesharing networks demonstrates how the *sine qua non* property logic of markets can be cancelled out. It might be objected that pirate sharing is a dubious example since filesharers generally do not produce the material which they are handing out. Though labour has been invested in cracking and uploading the files, the sceptic would be justified in insisting that filesharing does not offer a sustainable model for providing new music and new films. But there are people who create the cultural and aesthetic content, fan fiction writers among others, just as resolutely as community activists labour on mesh networks, hackers write filesharing applications and crackers unlock and release encrypted information on the network.

Each of these subcultures are producers of use values within a specific field, hardware, software, culture, etc. In common to all of them is that they are at the same time producers of social needs. In this pursuit, they are not only contributing to the infrastructure on which the commodity form of information can be dissolved. They are themselves in flight from commodified life. The commodity form of need satisfaction, coupled with the wage form of labour, means that to the degree that individual needs are satisfied, they are frustrated as social needs. Indeed, this imbalance in the satisfaction of needs is the background setting from which the hacker movement, like so many other subcultures, has grown out of. While it is true that the option to devote time to hacking owes to a certain abundance in Western societies, the motivation to be a hacker comes from the one-dimensional poverty of that affluence. Frustrated with the hollowness of individual, commodified forms of gratification, people self-organise playful production-consumption of culture and technology outside the intellectual property regime and market exchanges.[21] People only have to take the needs on offer and run with them. The haste, by which image-relations accelerate and evolve in the many hands of an anonymous crowd, might just run off faster than the capitalists, who set them in motion, can cope with. Like series of pictures that replace each other faster and faster, at a certain pace the separate images melt into the motion of a single image. The closed end-product becomes an open-ended process. Or, as the hacker saying goes, 'release fast, release often'. In contrast, the commodity form and the point of sale become a seal and a stoppage in the perpetual development process. Thus we are led over to the theme of the next chapter, that is, production.

5   Production of Information

ORGANISATION OF PRODUCTIVE RELATIONS

There is an extensive amount of literature critical of the current intellectual property regime. Many of the writers make a point of the fact that intellectual property often falls short of one of its stated aims, to advance the progress of science and useful arts. Typically, this observation is a centrepiece in their case against strengthened intellectual property rights. However, the wider implications of this failure have not been given much attention. In this chapter we will attempt to relate the intellectual property regime and its shortcomings to a theoretical understanding of capitalism. We put forth the proposition that the market failures of intellectual property reflect the failure of the capitalist relation as an organising principle of labour. The capitalist relation consists of private property, market exchange, and wage labour. In the informational sector, these aspects of the capitalist relation take the form of intellectual property, markets in information, and individual authorship. All of these components are required for the reproduction of capital, and, as will be argued later on, each one bears a toll upon the productivity of labour. Our reasoning is only one step short from the well-known forecast by Karl Marx: "Beyond a certain point, the development of the powers of production becomes a barrier for capital; hence the capital relation a barrier for the development of the productive powers of labour. When it has reached this point, capital, i.e. wage labour, enters into the same relation towards the development of social wealth and of the forces of production as the guild system, serfdom, slavery, and is necessarily stripped off as a fetter." (*Grundrisse*, 749). Marx believed that living labour at this point would gain an edge over capital. A socialist relation of production would be discovered by the proletariat and would overcome the capitalist ditto. He considered this to be a necessary precondition for transcending capitalism. If the proletariat lacked an economic model of its own it could not hold on to power. In a chilling anticipation of later events, Karl Marx warned that a political revolution without an economic revolution would just result in a bloody coup.

While reviewing these claims, Michael Howard and John King stress the significance attached to efficiency by early socialists: "The materialist conception of history relates the feasibility of socialism to the question of efficiency, measured by the ability to operate the productive forces optimally. For Marx and Engels, socialist relations of production would be sustained only if they could on this criterion out-compete those of capitalism."[1] The reason for the grave importance attributed to efficiency was that if socialism fell behind capitalism in terms of productivity, individuals in the socialist society would have to make sacrifices, willingly or not, for the economy to float. Such stern measures were not consistent with the freedoms that socialism promised. Michael Howard and John King carefully examine the attempts by Marxists to defend the claim above. Their conclusion is that no plausible evidence has been presented supporting a scenario of the kind. With no indication that socialism could ever measure up to capitalism, the criteria laid down by Marx ends up pointing in the opposite direction, towards the longevity of the capitalist mode of production. Perhaps this bleak fact has contributed to the fact that these parts in Marx's thinking are seen as outdated by many contemporary socialists. The proposition here is that the idea should be re-examined in light of the highly successful FOSS development model. In the software sector, self-organised labour is outdoing capital in its own game of technological development. We have to be careful, though, not to invent a definite opposition between proprietary software and capitalism on one side, and FOSS and anti-capitalism on the other side. From the discussions in the first chapter, it should be clear that FOSS developers are deeply embedded in the capitalist society, that individual capitalists make good use of the volunteer labour of the hacker community, and that FOSS applications have become serious competitors thanks to the backing of the computer industry. For the sake of clarity, FOSS development will be discussed as an ideal model, though in reality it functions as a hybrid. The hacker community is ridden with contradicting potentialities that are constantly being fought out between rivalling fractions and external forces.

We must be equally careful when contemplating over the possibility that software technology can be reclaimed from capital. The first generation of Marxists was optimistic about the possibility that scientific discoveries could be isolated from capitalist relations. They assumed that once private ownership over machinery had been disbanded, technology would come to serve all of humanity. Advancement of the forces of production was seen as a promise of liberating humans from the realm of necessity. An extreme example is Lenin's well-known endorsement of Taylorism as a model for the Soviet industry. Karl Marx's position is harder to pin down. In some of his writings he welcomed the advancement of science, at other times he saw machinery as an instrument for disciplining workers. The latter theme was picked up by labour theoreticians in the 1970s. They argued that the growth of industry is inseparable from a deepened technical division of labour, and that the forces of production developed under capitalism are intimately tied up with the capitalist relation of production. On a more general note, disbelief is by now the common response to the modernist notion of historical progress. Herbert Marcuse is iconic for formulating a pessimistic, leftist position on technology. His reproach was not directed against any technology in particular but against technological rationality as such. In Marcuse's view, the master-servant perspective is embedded in the instrumentality of the scientific method. It mirrors the domination of humans in the capitalist, patriarchal society.

These remarks ought to caution us against an overly optimistic assessment of current trends within the FOSS movement. In the second half of the chapter, it will be argued that the seizure of the means of production is no longer a philosopher's stone that could dissolve capitalism once and for all. Quite the opposite, dissemination of productive tools is consistent with a post-Fordist labour process that has been displaced to the whole of society. Capital tries to make itself independent of unionised labour and, as a side-effect, the conditions are established for a FOSS production line relatively independent of capital. The significance of this fact, however, is overdetermined by other kinds of constraints in the capitalist society. Though the liberation of the tools and skills for writing software code is an important step, it is not in itself a sufficient condition, as early socialists believed, for stripping off the capitalist fetter.

MARKET RELATIONS AND SCIENTIFIC LABOUR

The historical record of intellectual property in hampering scientific research and technological development is a good place to start our inquiry. It is telling that the innovation iconic of the industrial age and capitalism, the steam engine, fell victim to patent disputes. James Watt's refusal to license his innovation kept others from improving the design until the patent expired in year 1800. The introduction of locomotives and steamboats was delayed because of it.[2] Watt's patent had a stifling impact on the Cornish mining district where the machine was used to pump water from the underground. A period of rapid improvements followed shortly after the patent had expired. The engineers in the area shared their discoveries with each other in a publication while aspiring to outdo each other in achieving the best performance. Rarely did these engineers protect their discoveries with patents.[3] Many key areas of the industrial revolution, such as mining, engineering, and chemistry, were advanced entirely or partially outside the patent system through processes of incremental and cumulative invention by anonymous workers and engineers.[4] In the history of patent rights, in contrast, innovations have often been held back because of conflicting ownership claims and legal uncertainties.

The early development of radio technology is a case in point. Marconi's Wireless Telegraph Company and AT&T ended up owning different components that were critical for radio transmissions. Military concerns during the First World War compelled the American government to demand that the two companies cooperated. For a brief period the patent stalemate was suspended which resulted in a rapid development of radio technology. With the end of the war and of government emergency powers, research was once more boggled down in the old patent dispute.[5] Patent stalemates of the sort are escalating because patents are systematically used in anti-competitive strategies. A colourful example is the patent filed by Romanoff Caviar Company on synthetic caviar. The artificial version of caviar would have sold for an estimated one-fourth of the price of natural caviar. Consequently, Romanoff Caviar Company held the patent in order to prevent cheap substitutes from entering the market. (*Scherer*) The list of examples making the same point could be extended to fill the whole book. And then ordinary patents look rational in comparison to the havoc that the patent system causes when it is extended to the area of information processes, i.e. software patents. Software development, like the pursuit of abstract knowledge in general, is particularly affected by patents since computer programming builds on many disparate sources of information. The writing of software is at heart a cumulative, and therefore a collective, process.[6]

Economists defending the patent system believe that, in spite of its known shortcomings, on average it contributes to the progress of science and technology. Often patents are described as a necessary evil for creating market incentives. The underlying assumption is that the market economy is the most efficient method for allocating resources. From such a perspective, the drawbacks with patent monopolies are seen as tradeoffs for setting free the productivity of market forces. The thrust of this reasoning can easily be cast around. It is precisely because such an awkward and counter-productive system as intellectual property is needed for a market economy in information to function, that we can estimate the full magnitude of failure of the market relation itself. At a closer look, the defence of property-based research turns out to be oxymoronic. It claims that by preventing the diffusion of scientific discoveries there will be more science and technology to diffuse. The paradox is reflected in neoclassical economic theory which actually advises against pricing information. Goods with zero marginal costs, such as information, should be treated as public goods and not sold as commodities. James Boyle, a long-time critic of intellectual property law, succinctly formulated the contradiction of 'informed markets in information': "The analytical structure of microeconomics includes 'perfect information'—meaning free, complete, instantaneous, and universally available—as one of the defining features of the perfect market. At the same time, both the perfect and the *actual* market structure of contemporary society depend on information being a commodity—that is to say being costly, partial, and deliberately restricted in its availability." (*Boyle*, 35) Economists are aware of these inconsistencies in their theory. Their support for intellectual property fall back on the assertion that the costs for providing the first copy must be recovered by charging for all subsequent copies made. If the price of knowledge was zero, they argue, investors would be left without any return on their investments. Research is costly so clearly investors are needed. But then again, we must retort, why is it that research is so costly?

According to a study by the *National Research Council* in America, the average cost for filing a U.S. patent is between $10 000–30 000. Most of the expense is fees for legal advice. But a patent is worthless unless the patentee also has a 'war chest' sufficient to defend his patent claim. Each part involved in a patent dispute can expect to spend in-between $500 000–$4 million. The sum depends on the complexity and the stakes involved in the court case.[7] The outlay for a patent portfolio mounts up to equal the investments in an old-time 'Fordist' machine park. To some degree, thus, it is the patent system that creates the costs that patent rights are to make up for. Or, in more general terms, research is expensive because information has been highly priced. With a zero legal price for knowledge, research and development activities could take place without large investments, thus without investors, which is to say, independently of capital and capitalists. Knowledge has to be kept costly and inaccessible to sustain market relations in the informational sector. Ideally, for information to be productively engaged, it ought to take resources on a scale of spent surplus value. Or, to phrase it differently, safely out of reach from wage earners. Science must be privatised for the very reasons foreseen by Karl Marx: "[. . .] It is, firstly, the analysis and application of mechanical and chemical laws, arising directly out of science, which enables the machine to perform the same labour as that previously performed by the worker [. . .] Innovation then becomes a business, and the application of science to direct production itself becomes a prospect which determines and solicits it." (*Grundrisse*, 704). Since the sphere of production is overtaken by science, capital must overtake the scientific process. Of course, universities have always been integrated with and contributed to the development of capital. What is happening now is that higher education and scientific research is passing from a state of formal subsumption to a state of real subsumption under capital. The composition of what we might call, for lack of better words, 'scientific labour', is reformed to better suit the needs of capital. The situation is analogous to how craft work once was transformed into factory work. The privatisation of scientific research goes beyond a strengthened patent law. Funding is shifted from the public to the corporate sector, the norm system within the scientific community is weakened, and economic incentives become more important as a motivating and disciplining factor. Given that science is advanced in a collaborative and cumulative process, stretching across institutions, national borders, and generations, the decline of the academic cudos has alarmed many scholars. Corporate backers often demand that discoveries are kept secret. Sharing of information, the lifeblood of academic research and learning, is obstructed because of it. At risk is the role of the university as a dissenting voice in society. Of no less concern is that the priorities of scientific research will be guided by short-term commercial interests. In addition to changing the direction of science, which might be welcomed by some, there are indications that the research becomes less robust, which no-one reasonably can be in favour of. The demand for secrecy and the vested interests among corporate backers make scientists doubt the validity of their colleagues' work. Instead of building upon former data they are inclined to duplicate the experiments and surveys on their own.[8]

The many chain effects from making knowledge expensive are demonstrated in the privatisation of the Landsat system during the Reagan administration. The Landsat program provides satellite images of the earth for commercial and academic use. As long as the satellites were managed by the public sector, images from Landsat were made available at the marginal cost of reproduction. When the operation was privatised, the price for Landsat images rose from $400 to $4 400 per image. Increased expenses did not merely result in a dramatic cut in research projects utilising the Landsat system. Privatisation tilted the power balance between well-funded research facilities and poorer universities and it strengthened internal hierarchies. Individual scientists became more dependent on funding and hence on decisions made by university boards and heritage funds. Correspondingly, senior researchers fared better than less merited, or maverick, researchers and students. In addition to steering research into commercial avenues and favouring projects by established scientists, the reliability of the scientific results was called in question. The shortage of satellite images hindered researchers from taking long series of images over an extended period of time and discouraged them from double-checking data.[9]

The ineffectiveness of enclosing information can also be argued by pointing at the fact that capital itself, from within, is developing enclaves free from property claims. Patent pools and collective rights organisations are set up to reduce the transaction costs of intellectual property. Members aggregate their patents or copyrights in a common pool and enjoy the freedom to draw from it without asking for permission.[10] At first sight it might appear as if the partial suspension of property rights is against the grain of the intellectual property regime. Such estimation rests on the misunderstanding that patents and copyrights are simply about enclosing information. The intellectual property regime works by oscillating between expanded privatisation of knowledge and the disbandment of private rights within 'gated commons'. Commons are needed for setting free the productivity of labour power; gates are required to uphold capitalist relations. In fact, capitalism often advances by incorporating elements on one level are antithetical to its own logic. An early parallel to patent pools can be found in the joint-stock system, which Karl Marx considered to be an abolition of the capitalist mode of production on the basis of the capitalist system itself. On one hand, the existence of patent pools confirms the inadequacy of intellectual property based research; on the other hand, it demonstrates the flexibility of capital to adapt. We might therefore doubt if the loss in productivity caused by the intellectual property regime makes any difference. Capitalism has in any case never worked optimally even when measured by its own narrow benchmark. Despite the notion of capitalism as a hothouse for the development of the forces of production, new technologies have often been suppressed by corporations, with or without patents, to entrench resource dependency and protect market shares.[11]

The argument here is that the frictions caused by market relations in higher education, scientific research, and product development weigh more heavily the more central these activities become in the perpetual innovation economy. This reasoning could have ended up in a new crisis theory of capitalism, had we not learned by now that capital feeds on crisis—even its own. Capital is not about to tumble into aggravated crisis because of falling profitability and aggravated contradictions. But capital is constrained to reinvent itself. The response of capital is to 'turn the friction into the machine', or, phrasing it differently, to make a positive, productive model out of anti-production.[12] The somewhat abstract claim can be illustrated with a reference to an optical illusion from cinematic graphics. The illusion occurs in black-and-white movies when a horse wagon is set in motion. At a certain point the speed of the cart and the frequency of the film clips will reverberate. The spokes of the wheel of the cart now appear to run in the opposite direction to the movement of the cart. Though the spokes revolves backwards, the wheels carry the cart in a forward motion. This mirage gives an accurate description of capitalist growth through anti-production. A concrete example of the claim is the research on the terminator gene. American seed corporations craved a fix to protect their genetically modified crops from infinite reproducibility of seeds. The U.S. Department of Agriculture collaborated with a subsidiary of Monsanto in developing a 'technology protection system'.[13] Preventing crops from growing was productive for capital since it strengthened market incentives for seed companies, generated lucrative patents, created jobs and made Monsanto's shareholders wealthier. The equivalent of the terminator gene on the Internet is Digital Rights Management technology. Judged from the standpoint of use value, terminating the self-reproductiveness of seeds and binaries is hampering productivity, but as far as the valorisation of capital is concerned, it is a boon.

The statement above is at variance with a postulate in scientific Marxism, namely that whatever is *productive for capital* is at the same time *productive in general*. Activities are considered to be productive for capital if they generate surplus value. According to this notion, production of surplus value is the current historical form of organising activities that are productive for the human species in general. The chief advantage of capital over the proletariat lies in that this mode of organisation is, for the time being, superior in advancing the forces of production. This assumption does not square with post-modern, late capitalism where circulating capital has surmounted productive capital. The terminator gene is hardly a neutral addition to the cumulative build-up of the forces of production. It is rather an example of how science and technology are developed to entrench the capitalist relations of production. Those things that could reasonably be called productive in general (infinite reproducibility, zero priced public goods, free access to knowledge, sustainability of resources, life) are in conflict with the creation of surplus value. Concurrently, however, it is plausible that a productive relation that does not suppress these energies has an edge over capitalist relations of production. The success of the FOSS development model can be interpreted against this backdrop.

THE PIRATE AS A WORKER

The wage relation appears to be the sole form for organising labour. At a closer look, however, it becomes evident that wage labour coexists with a range of different forms of labour relations. While marginalised and oblique, it is nevertheless true that the market society depends on the reproductive work taking place in the family, friendship circles, the voluntary sector, etc. These economies are needed as a complement to the waged economy, solving problems that the market, for one reason or another, fails to address. The FOSS development community could be added to this list, but with one crucial addition: It does not merely complement the market but rivals it. As we have seen, a number of FOSS applications compete with equivalent products developed in the corporate sector. Hence, it is at least conceivable that the FOSS development model could challenge the wage relation as the dominating principle for organising labour.

The first chapter discussed how the strengths of FOSS applications are accounted for by voices within the hacker movement. Three major advantages were identified: Free software development is not hampered by conflicting property claims, hackers have a higher motivation to do a good job than hired programmers, and more people can contribute to a project when the source code is freely accessible. These advantages all refer back to the inferiority of capitalist relations of production in organising labour in the informational sector. The discussion in the first chapter will here be complemented by looking outside the computer underground and the technicians directly involved in writing free code. As was argued in chapter two, the labour process does not end with the product passing from the producer to the consumer. Consumers work on information products when they learn about it and when they adopt their surroundings to the requirements of the product. The usefulness and value of an information product relies on this cognitive and emotional investment by audiences. The claim is clarified by thinking of how software standards are established. Each and every user of a software application contributes to the standardisation of that particular computer program. This highly distributed labour process stretches the organisational limits of the firm. Too many people have to be involved in setting a standard for them all to fit on a payroll. Corporations enlarge the labour pool beyond the in-house staff by involving their customers in the development process. But the price mechanism acts yet again as a limitation on the productivity of labour. Elementary economic theory tells us that a positive price on information reduces the number of buyers. That becomes a real constraint when the same people are the main developers of the service. It is for this reason that companies are experimenting with alternative business models that circumvent the direct point of sale. There are many ways to parcel out and fence in a knowledge commons. Perhaps only commercial uses are charged for, or revenue comes from advertising, or additional pay-per services are annexed to the free offer, or the company tries out a combination of FOSS licenses. A major drawback with all of these options is that the company gives up control over the consumer market when it suspends its right to exclude non-paying users.

There is a way for corporations to have it both ways, i.e. to stay in control while expanding the pool of developers beyond the limits of the price mechanism. Corporations can take advantage of non-paying, illicit uses of their service. This helps to explain how the software-, music- and film-industries sometimes benefit from pirate sharing.[14] The economist Oz Shy comes up with some interesting results from his study of the software sector. His point of departure is that illicit, non-paying software users, or so-called 'freeriders', expand the total pool of users of a particular software, with the outcome that the utility of the program is enhanced for paying software users. The increased utility of the computer program manifests itself in a number of ways. The computer program is more likely to be interoperable with other applications, a larger group of employees will be familiar with the graphical interface, it gives an assurance of a path dependency so that skills invested in the software are less likely to become obsolete in the near future, and the size of the potential consumer market is expanded. These are some concrete gains for the network (the software application) when it includes additional nodes (paying and non-paying users). Excluding a node bears a corresponding penalty upon the use value of the network. And yet, exclusion is the *sine qua non* of property rights. Oz Shy's conclusion is counter-intuitive: A software company can increase profits by permitting unauthorised uses of its product. The reason is that paying customers are willing to pay a higher price for the product if it is widely used. For sure, failure to enforce copyright will result in that a large number of paying customers turns into non-paying users. But the loss is compensated for by major companies and government agencies that do not have the option to use illicit copies of the software.[15] Shy's reasoning is confirmed in a study by Stan Liebowitz on the illicit copying of academic journals. Liebowitz starts with the assumption that publishers are not necessarily harmed by illicit photocopying of articles. Indirect revenue can be appropriated by charging a higher price for library subscriptions. University libraries are willing to pay more due to increased circulation of the journal among non-paying readers. Since the money that individual subscribers can spend is marginal compared to what a university can pay, a reader might contribute more to the financial standing of the publisher by reading the journal than by paying for his own copy. Hence, Liebowitz avows that publishers can, under right circumstances, be better off not charging individual subscribers.[16]

The 'pirate' now looks more like a franchised vendor than a criminal. In fact, non-paying users are better thought of as unpaid developers of the network. Leading on from this statement, intellectual property can be described as a 'labour contract of the outlaw'. This is no marginal occurrence since, under current copyright statutes; millions of computer users are being outlawed. We can safely assume that most of them will never be tried for pirate sharing—they are, after all, providing companies with free beer. However, by the same token, it is predictable that a handful will be persecuted from time to time, if only so that the work of audiences stays within the discourse of illegality. This amounts to the same thing as a state of exception, though limited to a small segment of the population. The uncertain legal status of non-paying/non-paid developers gives some leverage to firms over a development process which has escaped the direct supervision at the workplace, does not respond to the corporate command chain, and is not stratified by a technical division of labour. The need for influencing this labour becomes more pressing when users self-organise their activity in communities.

DEVELOPMENT COMMUNITIES AT WORK

The work of audiences and users includes everything from extremely disparate, haphazard user collectives with no horizontal communication, the users of Windows for example, to tight groups of developers with mailing lists, conferences, and a shared sense of purpose. The Debian-GNU/Linux user community could be an example of the later. Work with FOSS projects demands commitment, advanced skills, and collaboration from its participants. Their sustained efforts give rise to what might be called a 'community-for-itself'. With a norm system, a common identity, and a political profile, the FOSS development community gains some degree of independence vis-à-vis external forces, companies and governments in particular. This independence is demonstrated when the interests of the hacker movement and capital diverges, such as in the design of filesharing applications. Filesharing has mostly been debated from the standpoint of the alleged losses of the media industry. It is not pirate sharing that makes peer-to-peer networks subversive, though, but the peer-to-peer labour relations of which this technology is an example of. The application would never have seen the light of the day had software development been confined to the social division of labour, i.e. to professional researchers working in corporate laboratories or government institutions. It is this loss of control that is destabilising to *status quo*. The intellectual property regime does not merely address the flow of information, but, in doing so, influences the terms under which users can develop (filesharing) technologies. In other words, as much as the intellectual property law aims to prevent unauthorised sharing of information, it seeks to regulate the productive energy of peer labour communities.

Peer-to-peer became a concept with the Napster case in 1999–2001. The inventor of Napster was a young student, Shawn Fanning. He dubbed his creation Napster as it was his nick-name when addressing other hackers. The idea behind Napster was to enable people to access music stored on the computers of other users. Thereby the application opened up a vast pool of music to everyone involved. Napster was not a pure peer-to-peer system. It minimised the required storage space by having the end users storing music files on their own hard drives instead of on a central server, but the search mechanism was centralised. The central index on available music files permitted Shawn Fanning to start a business venture around the service, and, on the downside, for the Record Industry Association of Americas (RIAA) to sue him. From the outset, Shawn Fanning and his associates aimed at drawing the greatest possible number of users into the Napster system. The audience would be their bargain chip when negotiating the price for the service with RIAA at a later stage. In the heydays of the New Economy, this was a good enough business proposal to attract venture capital. Even one of the media giants and a prominent member of the RIAA, the German company Bertelsmann, invested in Napster. And the audience size was impressive. At its peak Napster had more than 70 million registered users. Almost every single one of them swapped copyrighted files in violation of the law. The 'David and Goliath' court case against Napster helped to raise sympathy, publicity, and attract even more users to the service. For a while, and for some, Shawn Fanning appeared as a hero taking on the media giants on behalf of music fans and exploited musicians. In truth, the court case was a test of strength to settle the price for the brand, the audience, and the technology of Napster.[17] It could have paid off, had Napster not been undercut in the same way it had emerged itself. As soon as the intent of the company became known to hackers they started making clones of the program. OpenNap provided the same service but was licensed under General Public License which guaranteed that the system would stay free. Several more initiatives were taken to sidestep the control of Napster over the audience. To generate revenue and thus to become an attractive partner for record companies, Napster had either to convert into an enclosed subscription service or sell advertising space. The step could not be taken since Napster's engineers knew full well that any restrictive measure would kill off the user base as fast as it had been built up. Quite right, when Napster was forced by court order to shut down its service until it had developed a feature that enabled subscription fees, users quickly switched to other peer-to-peer filesharing systems. The audience, Napster's trump card, vaporised at a second's notice.

One challenger inspired by Napster was Gnutella. Behind it stood Justin Frankel, the inventor of Winamp, an application used for listening to music, and a friend of Shawn Fanning. Gnutella took a decisive step towards a pure peer-to-peer system. It decentralised both the storing and indexing of files. When a user of Gnutella wants to listen to a particular song, she sends out a request to adjacent Gnutella nodes. If the file is not found on these machines, the request is passed on to the next circle of nodes. The request is radiated outwards until the file in question is found. The process is slower than when working through a central server, but the design was a considerate response to RIAA's lawsuit against Napster. The fact that the Napster team had the option but chose not to develop a monitoring feature within the central indexing system became a liability in the court case. With Gnutella, it was impossible for the authors to survey the activity of the users even if they had wanted to.[18] The making of Gnutella is worth expanding on since it comes with an interesting twist. Justin Frankel had started a firm based on the Winamp application. He sold the firm, Nullsoft, to America On-Line, but kept working in the firm. Gnutella was devised by him and other employees at Nullsoft. Technically speaking, America On-Line owned Gnutella. At the time when Nullsoft made Gnutella available on the Internet in 2000, America On-Line was about to merge with Time Warner—one of the largest players involved in the lawsuit against Napster. Nullsoft's employees were briskly told to take Gnutella down, which they reluctantly did. Instantly, hackers began to reverse-engineer Gnutella and improve on it, most probably with some covert assistance from the employees at Nullsoft. Three years later Justin Frankel did the same thing all over again. For a few hours the Nullsoft server hosted WASTE, a third generation peer-to-peer file sharing program. WASTE was designed to thwart RIAA's new strategy of suing individual filesharers. In WASTE the connections are established between a small circle of people who trust each other from the start and the communication, in most cases consisting of illegally copied files, is heavily encrypted. The law authorities have a very hard time to find out about the infringements taking place in the private network. In the short time that WASTE was made available by Nullsoft the code spread like wildfire in the FOSS community. The whereabouts of the application was put out of reach of AOL Time Warner. After that the plug was finally pulled on Nullsoft.

The story about OpenNap, Gnutella and WASTE gives a flavour of what can happen when the means to write algorithms are dispersed among the proletariat. FOSS licenses works in a way similar to the architecture of Gnutella. By decentralising the running of the technology, Gnutella's authors gave up their control over their creation. Thus no legal or economic pressure could be applied on them in order to influence how the technology was used, as had previously been done to Shawn Fanning and Napster. In the same way, FOSS licenses place the development of software applications out of reach of any single individual, group or company. FOSS licenses set loose the productive energies of an anonymous, ambulant crowd, and, while doing so, it offsets the concentration of power and control that follows with individual authorship. We could almost go as far as to say that the politics of the hacker movement is the sum of this mode of disorganising power.

Not only does free source code undermine the intellectual property rights of content providers. It is also destabilising to other sorts of authorities. This was clearly demonstrated when Netscape decided to release the source code of their web browser under an open license. Up till then, Netscape's web browser had been firmly controlled by the company and only in-house programmers could access the code. Ownership over the code had led to a number of design choices. Among them was the absence of advanced cryptographic features within the browser. Robert Young tells of the consequences of Netscape's decision to let the code free: "In a move that surprised everyone, including Netscape engineers who had carefully removed cryptographic code from the software, less than a month after the source code was released, an Anglo-Australian group of software engineers known as the Mozilla Crypto Group, did what the U.S. government told Netscape it could not do. The group added full-strength encryption to an international version of Netscape's Web browser, and made available Linux and Windows versions of this browser." (*Young*, 98) Though Netscape didn't intend it, the influence which the U.S. government could exercise over the web browser was cancelled out when the source code was made public.

The same principle of peer-to-peer production has found outlets outside the FOSS development community. The most politically aware experiments with user-created content are found in the movement for citizen media. Grassroots news reporting became a concept with the birth of the Independent Media Centre. It was a brainchild of the WTO demonstrations in Seattle in 1999. Indymedia consists of regional centres from which activist-reporters can access a global audience with local news. It is concerned with documenting demonstrations and political events and is meant as a corrective to the biased reporting in mainstream media. The slogan "don't blame the media, become the media" captures the philosophy of Indymedias' activists. Such ambitions have a long-standing tradition within the left. Indymedia differs from political fanzines and pirate radio broadcasts in its global reach and real-time reporting.[19] On the other hand, the political profile of Indymedia causes a constraint and lopsidedness among the readers that are contributing to the project. Arguably, the blogsphere has been more successful in 'becoming media' than Indymedia. Bloggers are stitched together in the loosest possible sense, relying on Internet search engines instead of an editor for sorting out noise from information. The loose way of organising their activity has contributed to the rapid growth of the bloggsphere. Once a critical mass of contributors has been built up, grass-root reporting is at an advantage over traditional news reporting. Eben Moglen, a prominent member of the Free Software Foundation, identified this mechanism when noticing that the broadcasting networks, with their over-paid celebrities and expensive equipment, are about the only organisations that cannot afford to be everywhere in the world at the same time. With a digital camera ready-at-hand and an Internet connection close by, the anarchistic mode of news reporting turns any passer-by into a potential journalist for a moment, just as the FOSS model turns every computer-user into a potential bug reporter. Lack of capital and abundance of living labour are here made into competitive assets.[20] The apolitical outlook of most bloggers does not disqualify the importance of a distributed organisation of news reporting. That was amply shown during America's second invasion of Iraq. In the first invasion by the senior Bush administration, the control over the journalists was so tight that it sent Jean Baudrillard pondering over if the war had really happened. The control over news media was even stricter the last time around. In spite of that journalists were embedded with the invasion forces, the junior Bush administration could not prevent damaging information from leaking out. Soldiers-becoming-journalists published home videos disclosing the abuses that they had committed themselves. Coverage of the war came from places where no professional journalist would be let within sight. This suggests the political ramifications when the means of news production spreads beyond the journalist profession.

More areas open up to peer production as the principle of peer-to-peer is applied not only to reduce costs for variable capital (i.e. living labour), but also to cheapen constant capital (infrastructure, machineries etc.). That could be the deeper implication of the SETI@home project. SETI@home is a favourite example in hacker literature, mingling high technology with fascination for science fiction. SETI stands for: Search for Extraterrestrial Intelligence. SETI searches for intelligent alien life by scanning for radio signals from outer space. The huge task of analysing the data received is distributed to volunteers who lend spare capacity on their personal computers. For a succession of years the project has out-performed state-of-the-art supercomputers at a fraction of the cost.[21] The SETI@home project is not as dramatic as the controversies surrounding filesharing networks, nor does it have the zeal of grassroots journalism. Nonetheless, peer-to-peer computing could lower the threshold for the public to engage in various forms of computer-aided tasks. A qualified guess is that hackers will have an easier time in the near future when running simulations of hardware devices. That would take them a bit closer towards the goal of building a free computer machine. Cash-strapped laboratories in the Third World might find distributed computing practical for side-stepping pharmaceutical companies and develop generic drugs. And fans could make films with the same graphical sophistication and featuring the same computer-rendered stars as in Hollywood productions, leaving the movie studios without any edge over the amateurs. In short, peer-to-peer computing lessens the need for constant capital and lowers the requirements for the public to enter various productive activities.

When amateur collectives move on from producing fan fiction to producing news, facts, source code, etc., it calls into question the credibility of that material. Installing trustworthiness in a publication is part of the labour process of readers. It can be as important to the success of a journal as the work by the writers. The stories uncovered by citizen reporters are of little consequence unless it is perceived as reliable by the public. The same goes for software code. The performance of FOSS applications is inseparable from the confidence that computer users have in these solutions. While pondering over the future of amateur production, Mark Poster recalls that the credibility of individual authorship is a cultural invention. He notes that in the seventeenth century publishers fought an uphill battle to establish a market in books and newspapers, since readers were suspicious of claims made in print. People trusted information from persons they knew and met face-to-face. It required an educational feat of publishers and newspaper editors to change social norms so that trust was placed in the gatekeepers.[22] Nowadays, a source of information is credible if it has been approved by a publisher, a talk-show host, a software company, or a certificate issued by an educational institution. In this model of expertise, a large amount of knowledge about a subject matter must converge in the single author. The accuracy of individualised sources of information relies on the past record of, and future repercussions to, the expert. In other words, accuracy of information is guaranteed by the labour market in experts, or, to be precise, by the employers of experts. We do not need to evoke Michel Foucault or Ivan Illich to recognise the power relations behind authorising texts in this way.

Mechanisms for authorisation of texts are seemingly absent in anonymous, collective authorship. Some hints about where to look for other sources of credibility are given by Wikipedia, by far the most well-known case of a peer labour project outside the FOSS scene. Wikipedia is an Internet encyclopaedia edited by the readers. It began with a vision by Jimmy Wales and Larry Sanger to create Nupedia, a freely accessible encyclopaedia on the Internet. They set out with a traditional approach, employing editors and demanding educational qualifications from writers. The project had only gathered a few hundred articles when it ran out of funding. The articles were published on a separate website named Wikipedia, and, since Jimmy Wales and Larry Sanger had abandoned their aspirations for credibility, they invited visitors to edit the texts. Volunteers joined and the content grew exponentially. In a few years the size of the English-language version of Wikipedia exceeded Encyclopaedia Britannica and it continues to grow all the time. Wikipedia expands also in regards to the languages in which it is represented. Contrary to expectations, much of the text is of fairly high quality. The Nature made a comparison between entries from the websites of Wikipedia and Encyclopaedia Britannica on a broad range of scientific disciplines. Statistically speaking, an article in Wikipedia contains four factual errors, omissions or misleading statements, while articles in Britannica contain three mistakes of the same gravity.[23] Admittedly, vandalism and biased accounts are more of a problem in entries covering social sciences and controversial topics. In addition, the risk of libelling is a major concern in the openly edited encyclopaedia. A survey by IBM in 2002 discovered that, on one hand, most high-profile articles had been attacked at some point, and, on the other hand, that vandalised articles were on average restored within five minutes.[24] Presumably, facts gone obsolete are corrected at the same speed. This observation could prove decisive to our search for sources of credibility outside the mechanisms of individual authorship. In an environment that changes so fast that no individual can stay up-to-date with her field of expertise, collectively edited texts are likely to gain in credibility over individual authorship. Arguably, this could be taken as a late confirmation of Peter Kropotkin's assertion of the superiority of anarchism: "The rate of scientific progress would have been tenfold; and if the individual would not have the same claims on posterity's gratitude as he has now, the unknown mass would have done the work with more speed and with more prospect for ulterior advance than the individual could do in his lifetime."[25]

The example of Wikipedia repeats a theme known from FOSS development. Security, stability, and relevance of data depend on the number and heterogeneity of the co-authors attracted to a project. Reliable data can be collected by a group of amateurs, each with a patchy awareness of the subject field, since the group makes up for lapses in knowledge of individuals. It is the size and the diversity of the user base that authorises collectively edited texts. Those two factors mandate openness as a principle. Commons allow a maximum of developers, users and audiences of various degrees of involvement to contribute to a development project. Conversely, as is suggested by proprietary software, secrecy and monopolisation of knowledge fails to provide security and stability. Intellectual property rights prevent feedback cycles between successive stages of uses. The development flow is ruptured by costs, uncertainty, litigations, and design incompatibilities and the production process is slowed down at a time when speed, not scale, is king. In a GPL production line, unshackled from the individual claims on posterity's gratitude, information costs are near zero and design stays open. The stages where information metamorphoses from means of production to use value and back flow more cheaply, more easily and faster. The end result is not just use values at cut-rate prices; the products are technically more up-to-date. This is, in a nutshell, the economic rationality behind voluntarily entered, peer-to-peer labour relations organised in a commons/community.

APPROPRIATION OF TOOLS AND SKILLS

Access to tools is at the heart of the Marxist critique of capitalism. The proletariat was created when it was deprived of the means of production. The enclosure movement was a decisive episode for establishing this condition. To the first generation of Marxists, reclaiming the means of production necessitated a seizure of the factories and land held by the bourgeoisie. Their revolution could hardly be anything but violent. A takeover of this kind looks highly improbable today, but, then again, perhaps such a step is not called for any longer. User-centred development models suggest that the proletariat is already in possession of the means of production, at least in a restricted sense and limited to some sectors of the economy.

The instruments of labour break down into tools and skills. As far as tools are concerned, these have effectively been put out of reach from living labour for hundreds of years by the large-scale organisation of industrial capitalism. In the flexible accumulation regime, however, both the labour force and the machinery are rapidly being downsized. An illustration hereof is the computer which over a period of thirty years has gone from mainframes to palm devices, and from being a major investment barely affordable to elite institutions to a mass-market consumer product. It is as consumer goods that the means of production are trickling down to the masses, spreading in wider circles with the expansion of markets and with every fresh wave of same-but-different items. Productive tools (computers, communication networks, software algorithms, and information content) are available in such quantities that they become a common standard instead of being a competitive edge against other proprietors (capitalists) and a threshold towards non-possessors (labourers). Once the infrastructure is in place and common to all, additional input must come in the form of more brains/people. Evidence of such a trend has been debated by management writers, industrial sociologists, and Marxists since the early 1980s. In the FOSS industry this anomaly is the rule. Glyn Moody attests to it in his study of the FOSS development model. Businesses based on free and open licenses rely more heavily on the skills and motivation of its staff than firms selling proprietary software: "Because the 'product' is open source, and freely available, businesses must necessarily be based around a different kind of scarcity: the skills of the people who write and service that software." (*Moody*, 248). Glyn Moody's observation implies that labour power is multiplied faster by the number of people pooling their capacity to a given project than by improving the equipment. This feature is likely to be in consistency with most pre-capitalist societies. Up until the breakthrough of the industrial revolution, the product of human labour probably increased much more in return to the worker's skill than to the perfection of tools.[26]

The lessons from the computer underground bring into relief a debate on capitalism and deskilling that raged in the 1970s and 1980s. The controversy took place against the backdrop of the post-industrial vision that capitalism had advanced beyond class conflicts and monotonous work assignments. Harry Braverman targeted one of its assumptions, that the skills of workers had automatically been upgraded when blue-collar jobs were replaced by white-collar jobs. He insisted that the logic of capital is to deskill the workforce, irrespectively if they are employed in a factory or in an office: "By far the most important in modern production is the breakdown of complex processes into simple tasks that are performed by workers whose knowledge is virtually nil, whose so-called training is brief, and who may thereby be treated as interchangeable parts."[27] Braverman's contribution to the debate was very influential. In hindsight, however, the rise of new professions, in computer programming for instance, seems to have proven his critics right. They replied that though deskilling of work is present in mature industries, this trend is counterpoised by the establishment of new job positions with higher qualifications elsewhere in the economy. One of them, Stephen Wood, reproached Braverman for idealising the nineteenth century craft worker. Idealisation was ill-advised, not the least since the artisans had constituted a minority of the working class. Wood pointed at the spread of literacy to suggest that skills have also increased in modern society.[28] His comment is intriguing since it brings our attention to a subtlety that was lost in the heated exchange. It is not deskilling *per se* that is the object of capital, but to make workers exchangeable. When tasks and qualifications are standardised, labour will be in cheap supply and politically weak. From this point of view, it does not really matter if skills level out at a lower or higher equilibrium. Universal literacy is an example of the latter. One of its consequences was that labour power became more abstract and more interchangeable. Literacy is in this regard quite analogous to present-day campaigns for 'computer literacy'. These reflections on the Braverman-debate give us perspective on the current, much talked about, empowerment of consumers and computer users. Displacement of organised labour from strongholds within the capitalist production apparatus, through a combination of deskilling and reskilling, has prepared the ground for computer-aided, user-centred innovation schemes.

As was expected in the debate in the 1970s, computerisation has spearheaded these tendencies. The reason is that the computer, unlike ordinary 'dumb' machinery, is universal in its applications. This feature of computers has not come about by chance, as can be seen from the introduction of computer programming in the industry in the 1950s and 1960s. Managers invested heavily in numerical control machines with the hope of becoming independent from all-round skilled labourers. Special-purpose machinery had failed to replace these workers, since incentives had still to be taken at the shop floor to integrate the separate stages of specialised production. Another drawback with single-purpose machinery was that it locked production into a single, high-volume production line, which created other vulnerabilities to capital in face of workers' resistance. In contrast, general-purpose machinery simulated the versatility of a human being, thus it was better fit to replace her. In the words of David Noble: "Essentially, this was a problem of programmable automation, of temporarily transforming a universal machine into a special purpose machine through the use of variable 'programs,' sets of instructions stored in a permanent medium and used to control the machine. With programmable automation, a change in product required only a switch in programs rather than reliance upon machinists to retool or readjust the configuration of the machine itself [. . .]" (*Noble*, 1984, 81–82). This universality of computers is directly related to the overall specialisation and lock-in of human knowledge in the capitalist labour process. Software mediation allows the single skill of using a computer program (for example Photoshop) to translate into other skills (operating the machine-language of the computer, the crafts of printmaking and type-setting). Thus computer literacy lessens some of the inertia of human train-ing. It gives an edge to firms and individuals in flexible labour markets ruled by the imperative of 'life-long learning'. And, of course, it undermines the position of skilled and organised labour. A case often referred to in labour theory is the union struggle in the printing industry during the mid twenti-eth century. Typographers had traditionally had a strong position based on their knowledge monopoly over the trade. Computerisation of the labour process was decisive for breaking their strength.[29] No doubt, the importance of software algorithms in the so-called new economy owes to its expediency in this regard. Programmable automation, i.e. computers, has accelerated the logic of automation to a breaking point, both in its despotism and in its emancipatory potential. Previously, human knowledge was objectified in cogs and wheels, now it is objectified in binaries. The need for living labour is sharply reduced by the fact that electronic texts can be repro-duced infinitely, what we know as the 'information exceptionalism' dictum. However, as was argued in chapter two, digitalisation comes with a catch. The electronic text cannot alter itself in a novel and meaningful way. The game changes so that living labour must be deployed to produce a perpetual stream of novelty, meaning, affects, and context. To combine abstract cues in novel ways (innovation) or integrate them with lived experience (construct meaning), requires cognitive and analytical efforts of living labour, based on holistic understanding and personal engagement. Labour theoreticians and management consultants concur that Taylorism tends to lay waste to these capabilities.[30] What's more, these qualifications are generic. Anyone born a human is able to conceptualise, communicate, write, perform, etc., which makes the technical division of labour harder to sustain.

Contrary to popular belief, Harry Braverman was not oblivious to these possibilities, though he had no illusions that the emancipatory potential could be realised under capitalist work relations. Approvingly he notified a tendency in the general development of machinery: "The re-unified process in which the execution of all the steps is built into the working mecha-nism of a single machine would seem now to render it suitable for a col-lective of associated producers, none of whom need spend all of their lives at any single function and all of whom can participate in the engineering, design, improvement, repair and operation of these ever more productive machines." (*Braverman*, 320). His divination is quite similar to what we are witnessing in the computer underground today. Knowledge monopolies are flattened so that larger sections of the proletariat can engage in any (and several) productive activities. Because Photoshop is substituting traditional forms of typesetting and printmaking, crafts that took many years to master and that required major investments in printmaking facilities, a broader public can produce posters and pamphlets that are instantly applicable to their local struggles. The dissemination of productive skills and tools make it much harder to control the productive use of these capabilities than was the case when the means were concentrated in the hands of a few, though organised and relatively powerful, employees. What is true of graphical design equally applies to the writing of software code. An indication hereof is the difficulties of the state and capital to suppress the free development of filesharing and encryption technologies. We would be mistaken, however, to jump to the conclusion that these productive forces are mushrooming independently of capital. The perspective of another of Harry Braverman's critics, Andrew Friedman, might be more applicable when we move on to look at how capital reintegrates user-centred development communities in the capitalist valorisation process once again. Friedman stressed that in addition to overt coercion and control of workers, managers win over employees by building consensus and giving them leeway.[31] The approach of 'responsible autonomy', as he called it, becomes the lead tune when firms set out to manage communities of volunteer developers. Needless to say, carrots and sticks are not polar opposites but are part of one and the same strategy. Inside firms, cooperation between employees and managers takes place under the unspoken threat of downsizing and outsourcing. Such tacit pressures are voided when the other part is a volunteer development community. Instead, firms have to fall back on copyright law, patent suits, and various acts on computer decency and cyber-terrorism. Law enforcement authorities are the necessary companion to the soft approach of the corporate allies of the FOSS movement.

INSIDE THE SOFTWARE MACHINE

We have worked ourselves towards the conclusion that, if the critical inputs in post-Fordist production are the aesthetic and cognitive processes of workers and audiences, then the proletariat is in possession of the means of production. But doubt lingers if the proletariat can be said to be in charge of the instruments of labour, even if it is their own brains. The ambiguity can be reformulated as a question and set in the context of the FOSS community. Is free software a tool reclaimed from capital, or is it a cog integrated into a larger software-capitalist machine? Harry Braverman followed Karl Marx in differentiating between tools that extend the powers of the human body, and machinery which turn workers into human appendages. The distinction was straightforward in the industrial conflicts which he studied and where machines consisted of mechanical parts. The components of the software machine, in contrast, are made out of signs. In important respects the software machine is identical to human language. In this case, it is the unconsciousness that acts as a human appendage to the machine, rather than the fingers, muscles and eyeballs of the worker. In computer science there is even a word for the human component, the 'wetware'. The task of formulating an emancipatory project is complicated by the fact that the species being can barely be told apart from the matrix which he is integrated and subordinated to.[32] Liberation from this machine can neither be had by claiming legal ownership over it, as in 'expropriating the expropriators', nor is it clear how it could ever be smashed, as is advocated by self-described neo-Luddites. Hackers hold out the possibility of a third way. Since the software/wetware machine is omnipresent there can be no external points from which to confront it. Struggle is carried out from inside the enemy host and must therefore be subversive rather than confrontational in character.

To carry this thought any further, we need to examine in more detail what constitutes the machine as opposed to its human limbs. The problematic demands a philosophical line of attack. Humberto Maturana and Francisco Varela have presented a distinction between two forms of organisation, that of the living system and that of the man-made system. The criterion for an organisation to count as a living system is as follows: "[. . .] they transform matter into themselves in a manner such that the product of their operation is their own organisation"[33] Maturana and Varela call these systems autopoietic because they are, not in an absolute sense, but in a number of important aspects, autonomous within their unity. They produce a plenitude of qualities all referring back to their regeneration (for example, a plant that grows seed, strong smell, pure colour, etc). This condition fundamentally set them apart from non-living, man-made systems: "Other machines, henceforth called allopoietic machines, have as the product of their functioning something different from themselves (as in the car for example)." (*Maturana*, 80) The product of allopoietic systems is their output, which is the sole rationale for their existence. A car that is built without motion would not qualify as a car. The operation of an allopoietic system is defined, and the output is decided over, by an observer—an alien power—not by the organisation itself. In addition, the lack of autonomy of allopoietic systems is established by that they have inputs. That is, they depend on an alien power outside their own reach for acquiring and digesting supplies that are required by their central operations. For a car to function as a car, access to fuel is mission critical.

Maturana and Varela acknowledge that autopoietic systems can be integrated as a component in a larger allopoietic system. Plants grown in industrial agriculture is a case in point. Such corps are breaded to produce not according to their own plenitude of needs, but according to a one-dimensional requirement as determined by an alien power. All the plants in a field are streamlined to duplicate the plant with the highest output of them all, so that diversity is replaced with monoculture. By extension, regulation over a plant's inputs and outputs translates into control over the farmer tending the plant. Men themselves are grouped into allopoietic 'social machines'. The first example coming to mind is the factory. Subsumed under capital, living labour has outputs (surplus value) and inputs (commodified needs). Historian of technology Lewis Mumford dated this wretchedness back to Pharaohs' Egypt. The orchestration of slaves and free men on a grand scale, crowned by the erection of the pyramids, exemplified to him a gigantic, allopoietic system. He labelled it the mega machine. Here the concept of the machine is extended beyond a narrow focus on any single device, giving due credit to the social machine which organises and confines the operation and scope of the technical machine.

Gilles Deleuze and Felix Guattari have gone the furthest in broadening our understanding of what defines a machine, to the point of denying any substantial difference between the living organism and the technical apparatus. They argue that there are always intersecting flows at some sublevel which blurs the notion of a definable, molar object.[34] The wasp and the orchid is their favourite example. The fact that the orchid can't reproduce itself without mediation from the wasp does not disqualify the flower as a living organism. The symbiosis between the flower and the insect forms an assemblage. Thus the plant and the animal qualify as a machine, in the terminology of Deleuze and Guattari. If their reasoning is accepted, the distinction between allopoietic and autopoietic systems cannot be found in that one of them is self-reliant within its unity towards an Outside. But if the definition is modified just slightly, the two systems can be differentiated by the presence or absence of mutual reciprocities in the flows. The central question becomes if a dependency is asymmetrical to the point that one part has the power to define one-sidedly the relationship and the internal composition of the other part. We might say that an allopoietic system is a system that has fallen prey to 'real subsumption'. In plain language, the distinction between a living system and a man-made system boils down to power relations.

Thus we are brought back to the question of how emancipation is possible inside the software/wetware machine, or, to be more specific, how the proletariat can take charge of the instruments of labour that they already are in possession of. The appropriation of the means of production has proved to be an insufficient condition for achieving freedom. The reason is that the productive tools are framed within a social machine of unfreedom. The post-Fordist labour process has always-already anticipated the independent worker capable of administrating his own labour power. He is held in place by a network of economical, social and ideological constraints that extends far beyond the work situation. Maintaining these conditions is the object of the workfare state. Planned insecurity persuades the worker to willingly take the form of the commodity. Even though the instruments of labour are now at her disposal, her newfound freedom is nonetheless put to the service of production for exchange. Leading on from the discussion above, emancipation would require a reversal of the process previously referred to, whereby allopoietic systems are regrouped into autopoietic systems. Gilles Deleuze and Felix Guattari would have phrased the same thing as the forming of a nomadic war machine. Such airy proclamations tend to create more confusion than they explain. We are left wondering what an autopoietic system would be if it is not a living organism in the commonsensical meaning. Drawing from Maturana's and Varela's description, it could mean an organisation where the product of its operation is an end in itself. A concrete example of such an organisational form, to be discussed in the next chapter, is the reputation-based, gift/library economies that stratifies FOSS development projects. The desire and logistics of the market economy are here reprogrammed into an economy of play and excess. Inside these constellations the conditions are provided for employing productive tools and skills for non-instrumental, convivial ends.

6 Markets and Gift in the Networked Economy

NETWORK THEORY

Dreams of an alternative to capitalism have often stranded on the question of how to allocate resources. The chief historical alternative to markets has presented itself as central planning. With the moral and economical bankruptcy of really existing socialism, most people have come to accept markets as a fact of life. One attempt to steer a path between the Scylla of markets and the Charybdis of planning has been to point at worker councils and other, more participatory, forms of organisation.[1] Though these experiments suggest the possibility of an alternative, they are effectively under siege by the world market. The Free and Open Source Software (FOSS) movement is an exception in that it outdoes proprietary software firms in open competition. The FOSS development model is neither a market nor a firm, but might be characterised as a network. This chapter is devoted to the question, with an eye on the computer underground, if reputation-based gift economies organised in networks could offer a pathway between market exchange and state planning. Filesharing networks demonstrate one instance where markets in information are outflanked by gift exchanges. It remains to be investigated if these clusters of economic activity could overtake market relations in other walks of life. A serious impediment to markets in information is that they can only allocate information resources if these resources are scarce. In other words, markets precondition exclusive ownership rights over information. Exclusion is antithetical to standards, and standards are the life-blood of networks. This, in a nutshell, is why a networked mode of production is better organised in gift-exchanges and commons as opposed to through market transactions and private property. At the outset it should be clear though that the high-tech gift economy we are talking about looks nothing like its anthropological forerunner. In fact, it is by crossing elements of gift and market that the filesharing networks have become a serious rival to markets in information.

Talk about networks is a staple ware in the post-industrial, 'information age' literature. The idea is typically labelled the 'network society', the 'network industry', or the 'network firm'. Despite the ideological air that is coupled with these terms, labour theory can benefit from a closer look at networks. Indeed, Marxists will be familiar with some of the thinking in network science since the discipline, just like Marxism, stresses relational characteristics over inherent and absolute properties. Many unwarranted hopes have been attached to networks, though, and a clarification of the concept is needed for the sake of orientation.[2] A network emerges when individual nodes are in communication with each other through a common protocol. Nodes cannot be defined in-themselves, as individual, atomistic units. Nodes exist as a relation, a relation vis-à-vis neighbouring nodes. Thus, concepts such as reciprocity, feedback cycles, and complexity are central to the discipline. A crucial aspect of network theory, with implications for our further discussion, is the assumption that the network as a whole is strengthened by including an additional node. This straightforward description fails to capture the multiplicity of the concept, since the network now appears as if it was a solid structure frozen in time. A network comes to life in processes, in the flows running between its nodes, and the network is perpetually recreated and restructured by these flows. It does not spring fully-fledged from a single source of authorship whose origin can be pinpointed in space and time. This brief presentation of networks is in danger of falling pray to yet another misconception. It is at risk of appearing as a novel feature in history and to be placed in a binary opposition with an 'obsolete' structure—the Pyramid. There is no shortage of celebrations about the new, non-hierarchical, and networked way to organise. Both management writers and anti-globalisation campaigners claim that the network has replaced the 'old', monopolistic and monolithic model of organisation (be it the corporation or the political party). The objection here is not against the claim of 'newness' but against the sloppy use of the network concept. Networks are not homogeneous and undifferentiated spaces. Some nodes are more equal than others. Nodes differ in the number of connections they have with neighbouring nodes. Nodes with many connections are called 'hubs'. The ideal network, as it comes across in popular culture, is portrayed without hubs. The distribution of linkages is evenly shared between the nodes. It portrays a chart corresponding to an early, mathematical model known as a 'random network'. But only occasionally is this kind of network encountered in real life. The road system would be one example. More common are networks that consist of a few hubs with many links and a large number of nodes with few links. From this perspective the Pyramid looks more like a gigantic hub connected to all the other nodes. It thus becomes clear that we are not concerned with two diametrically opposed categories, the Network versus the Pyramid. Rather, we face a question of proportions. It is therefore an error to equate the absence of a centre in the network with the absence of power relations. More often than not, network organisation proves how control can profitably be combined with decentralisation.[3] Asymmetries continue to be reproduced in the relative connectedness or isolation of a node, and, crucially, power resides in the protocol that enables communication between the nodes. The part defining the protocol is in some sense in control over the network. The pain of computer firms to influence the setting of communication standards in the industry gives a hint. With this knowledge, the custom of associating networks with egalitarianism looks wrongheaded. It is particularly unfortunate since the network increasingly stands as a model for post-Fordist, capitalist restructuring.

NETWORKED MARKET OR MONOPOLIES

Our aim is to assess whether the network is a renaissance for the free market economy or possibly an alternative that could replace the market. The debate on how networks, markets and monopolies hang together goes back to an older dispute between liberals and socialists about the existence, or absence, of a free market. In opposition to the liberal economists of his day, Karl Marx maintained that free markets, even if they exist momentarily, always tend towards monopoly.[4] He identified a number of factors endogenous to the market economy that encourage concentration of capital and, by extension, the cancelling out of free markets. Corporations benefit greatly from economies of scale. This bias is tilted yet further by cyclical punctuations of crises and recessions, which provide the opportunity for big players to consolidate their position against smaller rivals. Years later, Rudolf Hilferding observed how the growth of oligarchies was catalysed by the advance of finance capital. Individual industries were tied together under the wings of conglomerates. The trend towards larger corporations carried on for the better half of the twentieth century. In the late 1970s and early 1980s, however, established theory and solid data were contradicted by odd anecdotes, multiplying into a stream of anomalies. The tendency towards bigger and bigger corporations was seemingly reversed into downsizing and outsourcing. Liberals quickly put a post-industrial, end-to-big-business spin to these figures. During the 1990s, for instance, it was proposed that a 'high-tech cottage industry' would blossom in connection to the information highway. Garage firms and freelancers were said to be ganging up in a network that could tilt old monopolies and reinstate a truly free market.[5] Though the hype was temporarily cooled down with the burst of the dot.com bubble, a distant echo of that promise can still be heard in the computer underground. The free marketeer spirit is here blended with opposition to intellectual property law. Monopolies built up around proprietary software are believed to be axed soon by FOSS start-ups. The advantage of FOSS businesses is partly that they are closely allied with free market forces, partly that they are integrated into a network that includes the hacker community.

In recent years, the law professor Yochai Benkler has come forward as the chief interpreter of the FOSS development model in terms of a networked mode of production. In his view the network is distinct from both the market and firm. Benkler's argument builds on the theories of the economist

Ronald Coase. In 1937, Coase put his finger on the fact that the agents operating on the free market were firms. The existence of firms contradicts the market principle since the firm has internally dissolved the price mechanism. It runs counter to the assumption in economic theory that markets are prevalent because they are the most efficient method to organise economic interactions. Coase's response was that firms emerge when the transaction cost from coordinating buyers and seller are higher than the cost of a hierarchic organisation.[6] Benkler adds to Coase's reasoning by saying that falling costs of communication technology have given rise to networks of volunteer developers. Transaction costs can at times be lower in the network than in both the market and in the firm. Furthermore, the strengths of the network model are accentuated in the creative economy. The individual has superior knowledge of his own capabilities and interests, and how to apply them in a project. Economic incentives (market) and bosses (hierarchy) will always fall short in allocating the creative labour of individuals.[7] Benkler's contribution consists in having drawn the connection between FOSS development and an earlier discussion about networked management of firms. The idea that networks is a novel mode of organising businesses and that it is distinct from markets has been in vogue since the 1990s. According to the argument, networks are supposed to be superior for sharing tacit know-how, in adapting to a volatile environment, and for perpetual learning processes.[8]

Unfortunately, Yochai Benkler's decision to follow Ronald Coase and confine himself to an analysis of transaction costs puts a limitation on his thinking. The observations on networks ought instead to be framed in the debate about markets versus central planning that was waged between neoclassical and socialist economists in the first half of the twentieth century. In the 1930s, the great depression gave socialists wind in their sails when advocating the rationality of central planning against the anarchy of markets. The classic liberal defence of free markets was developed by the Austrian School, Ludwig von Mises and Friedrich von Hayek being its two most prominent members, in direct polemic against the socialist critique. With the collapse of planned economies in most parts of the world, the case for markets looks stronger than ever and few would line up behind central planning today.[9] The left have largely retracted from expectations of ever transcending the market economy. It is against this background that it is intriguing to elaborate on the idea about a third, networked mode of organisation, different from both market exchange and state planning, and exemplified in the FOSS development model. Such a take on the matter, however, is in jeopardy of adding uncritically to the hype already surrounding the concept. We ought to keep in mind that the surge of networks originates in post-Fordist capitalism. The claim can be substantiated by a closer look at how the restructured, precarious labour market is fashioned after the network model.

The statement that monopolies are giving way to networks of entrepreneurs has been scrutinised by Bennett Harrison. After examining the empirical data, he confirms that the number of small firms is on the increase. This observation does not, however, mean that the power of multinational corporations is dwindling.[10] Many small firms recognised as *de jure* independent firms, are *de facto* bound up in an intricate chain of dependencies to a major corporation, to the point that for most purposes and practices the subcontractors are mere satellites of the core corporation. Harrison calls this process '*concentration without centralization*', since power remains concentrated even when production is decentralised. The dependency of subsidiaries is most formally codified in the franchise contract.[11] In franchised operations, small units of self-owning producers run most of the supply chain, from the farm to the fast-food outlet. Capital does not own the installations *per se*, still it reaps the lion's share. The fact that the franchisee has invested his lifesavings to become a legal owner of the facilities in which he works does not translate into more independence. On the contrary, the financial risk is disproportionally carried by the franchisee and makes him all the more industrious and submissive. Karl Marx once noted how the merchant could benefit from leaving the producer as an owner of sham property: "He buys their labour and takes their property first in the form of the product, and soon after that the instrument as well, or he leaves it to them as *sham property* in order to reduce his own production costs." (*Grundrisse*, 510) Karl Marx was talking about the original cottage industry when he made the remark. In its high-tech version, the reasons for leaving behind sham property are even more compelling. Product diversification, rapid turnovers and short life-cycles have made the management of physical assets risky. The burden of ownership is pushed down onto smaller entities while corporations stay in control by gate-keeping finances, marketing, distribution channels, and intellectual property. Labour is reinvented into working micro-capital, and subsequently, micro-capital is subjugated under networked, monopoly capital. The multiplication of small firms, franchisees and freelance workers goes hand in hand with the deepening of a dual labour market. Stable and well-paid employment is reserved for core workers in the major corporations while employees in smaller firms and self-employed labour are plagued with insecurity and poor working conditions. Ultimately, it is these peripheral workers that provide flexibility in 'distributed production networks'. Union leaders interviewed by Bennett Harrison tell about the difficulty of organising the demands of employees in the 'ring firms' against the actual sovereign, the core corporation. Working conditions and targets on productivity, previously dictated in a formal hierarchy that could be confronted face-to-face, is here mediated through fixed market exchanges.[12]

In conclusion, the rise of the 'networked firm' should be seen as part of a strategy to weaken the strength of organised labour. The statement can be illustrated by adding a small twist to an example given by Duncan Watt. In his presentation of network science, Watt spans many subjects, biology, mathematics, sociology, and towards the end he has a bite at management theory too. He retells a story from Toyota, the icon of a corporation that has reinvented itself as a business network. Aisin Seiki, a subcontractor in the Toyota ring, happened to be the only manufacturer of a component critical to the whole Toyota network. The factory site was destroyed in a fire. The whole conglomerate was in jeopardy of grinding to halt. In two months Toyota would run out of supplies of the parts produced by Aisin Seiki. Faced with looming disaster, the network of subcontractors fervently cooperated and created provisory means for substituting the factory. In a stunningly short time, Toyota subsidiaries had restructured themselves and could carry on unaffected by the incident. Duncan Watt attributes the swift response by the Toyota conglomerate to its networked mode of organisation. The relevance of this story for labour theory becomes apparent if we stipulate that the factory was not destroyed in an accident but was held-up in a labour conflict. Networked capital turns every point of production, from the firm down to the individual work assignment, into a node subject to circumvention. The 'network society' and the 'network firm' has for too long been discussed as if it was ad hoc to capitalism, or, even more absurd, antithetical to the hierarchies and bureaucracy of monopoly capital. Quite to the contrary, it is capital's ambition to route around labour strongholds that has brought capitalism into network production. The network is the logical endpoint of capital's efforts to homogenise the workforce into an abstract, standardised labour supply. Nations, factories, natural resources, and positions within the social and technical division of labour, are all made subject to redundancy. Thus has capital annulled the threat of blockages against necks in the capitalist production chain, upon which the negotiation power of unions is based. The fading strength of unions will continue for as long as organised labour is entrenched in past victories and outdated forms of resistance. But the networked mode of production opens up a 'window of opportunity' for a renewed cycle of struggle, this time, however, of a different kind. *Since all points in production have been transformed into potentially redundant nodes of a network, capital as a factor of production in the network has itself become a node subject to redundancy.* The central dilemma for capital in managing a networked mode of production is simply to stay relevant. In the context of the computer underground, corporate backers ensure their continued relevance to the FOSS development community by amassing legal powers over developers. That goes a long way to explain the corporate push for software patents. A patent assigns exclusive ownership over an idea, while copyright is narrowed down to the ownership over a single expression of an idea. A very broad field of activities is thus made subject to the legal powers of a patentee. The contradictory policies of IBM towards software patents are suggestive. One branch is lobbying for the introduction of software patents in EU, while another branch of the corporation promises not to use software patents against FOSS developers. In this way, hackers end up working under a condition of suspended illegality where they depend on the goodwill of IBM. Hence, capital can stay relevant in a networked mode of production through a deepened symbiosis with the capitalist state.

THE SCHUMPETERIAN COMPETITION STATE
AND THE NETWORK MODE OF PRODUCTION

Heavy involvement of the state in the economy is far from a novel feature. The bureaucratisation of capitalism was discussed already back in the 1940s by the Johnson-Forrest Tendency, a group of former Trotskyites. They argued that central planning in the Soviet Union and growing technocracy in the west were both expressions of worldwide pressures converging in state capitalism.[13] In those days the state policy was characterised by Keynesianism. The common impression is that the state since the Reagan and Thatcher era has withdrawn and given free reins to the market. In fact, the spontaneous, laissez-faire market depends heavily on state planning and an authoritarian form of Keynesianism. The changes that have taken place in the involvement of the state in the economy are described by Bob Jessop by contrasting the 'Keynesian Welfare National State' of yesterday with the 'Schumpeterian Competition State' of today. The Keynesian state addressed overproduction. It ensured full employment and sought political stability at the national level. The Schumpeterian state, in contrast, is geared towards fostering innovation and advancing the national economy in fierce international competition. Market success in knowledge-intensive sectors is decided by extra-economical factors, such as collective learning processes, institutional knowledge, and socio-cultural practices. Creating the right milieu for knowledge production is above and beyond the scope of any individual firm. These provisions can only be secured if the whole of society is turned into an incubator for 'sunrise industries'. Moreover, the defence of the commodity form of information requires extensive surveillance of citizens and users. Only a state has the resources to do so.[14]

The inadequacy of firms in organising and policing the distributed production chain is underscored by the fact that audiences, consumers and illicit users have become major contributors in the production process. We might explore this statement in more detail in order to get some additional clues as to how the Schumpeterian Competition State relates to a networked mode of production. As was mentioned in the previous chapter, the economist Oz Shy has demonstrated that software firms can benefit from allowing unauthorised copying of their software products. Unlike reformist critics of intellectual property, who have drawn similar conclusions, Oz Shy does not argue that it is therefore in the best interest of companies to disband intellectual property rights. While he never enters into this discussion, the implication of his reasoning is that firms should just look in a different direction when their rights are violated by private users. What the reformist critics fail to recognise, and the economists prefer not to spell out, is that firms need the copyright law to be in existence even if they are better off not enforcing it. For as long as their property rights are officially recognised, some users will have to remain paying customers. Government institutions and multinational companies do not have the option to bypass the legal distribution channels. It is thus software firms compensate for the loss of private customers. The individual who is let off using illegal copies of the software product, will end up paying indirectly through taxes or higher prices on goods sold by corporate customers of the software firm. Stan Liebowitz bears witness to the same mechanism in his analysis of unauthorised copying of academic journals. The university library, acting as an arm of the state, is basically administrating the revenue streams from individual readers that the firm itself is incapable of handling. The heavy-handed reaction from proprietary software firms when FOSS applications make inroads into government clients confirms this suspicion. An early encounter came with the legislative proposal in Peru in 2001 by Congressman Edgar Villanueva. The bill, dubbed proposition 1609, mandated the use of FOSS solutions in public administrations. Microsoft's general manager in Peru declared that the bill threatened the nation's security. The warning was underlined by a letter from the U.S. ambassador to the congress flagging that U.S.-Peru relations would be harmed by the bill. After intense lobbying by Microsoft, a watered-down version of the proposal was passed in October 2005. Similar legal procedures have begun in Brazil, Venezuela, Spain, Vietnam, and many other places. This trend is considerably more troubling to proprietary software vendors than violations against their intellectual property rights by individual users.

From the discussion above we can deduce that the state is the sole body left that can collect and distribute revenue without destroying the productivity of the network. Charging individual customers of network services/products will deplete the use value of the service for which the customers are willing to pay. Or, to put it differently, the exchange value of a commodity increases if the commodity form is abolished. For sure, this paradox is not a short-cut for the self-destruction of market relations and private property. The network externality touched upon by Oz Shy and Stan Liebowitz translates into a greater first-mover advantage and a vicious cycle of 'winner-takes-all', fuelling the tendency towards monopolies yet further. Nonetheless, the economy of networks causes a restriction upon capital. When the option of selling directly to clients is ruled out, two opportunities remain: Either advertising or tax subsidies. Advertising is the earliest example of market relations clashing with the productivity of language. The diffusion of an advert is a direct measure of its success. Restricting access to an advert by applying a price mechanism would be irrational. The cost for marketing is instead covered by raising the price of the advertised product. As is the case with advertising, individual customers will pay for networked services/products through higher prices on non-networked products. This solution cannot last in the long run if we are to believe the advocates of the New Economy. The network firm is hailed as the 'sun-rise industry' of the future, or, borrowing a phrase from Karl Marx, it will be the general illumination that bathes all the other sectors of the economy in its light and particularities. In plain language, all products will be networked products, which begs the question: Where can rent then be taken from? Most of it will have to take the form of taxation, collected and distributed through the state. The endpoint of this reasoning is: State as opposed to market is the sole agent left that is able to allocate information resources and steer the flow of profits in the networked economy. This conclusion runs contrary to a popular explanation of the collapse of the Soviet Union. Manuell Castells, for one, argues that capitalism won out over socialism because free markets are better equipped than political hierarchies in handling a networked mode of production.[15] It seems more plausible that the deepened bureaucratisation of state capitalism, making market societies look more like the Soviet Union by the day, owes in no small part to the economic clout of information and networks. The similarity between how photocopiers were monitored in the Soviet Union for political reasons and the state surveillance of copying facilities today for economic reasons is suggestive. A wide range of leftist thinkers have described how the state gets increasingly involved in administrating markets. We might elect to call these state-administrated, laissez-faire constructions for 'make-believe markets'. Of course, the existence of markets has always required state protection of property rights and contractual agreement, as well as an element of fiction. A make-believe market is defined by the fact that the equilibrium is determined by political means. Trade in carbon emissions, the auctioning of wave-frequency rights, the privatisation of the public sector, imaginary gold exchanged in on-line computer games, and, above all else, intellectual property rights, fulfils this criteria. Intellectual property turns out to be just one instance out of a more generalised pattern in post-modern capitalism. Conclusive of this pattern is that the state is expropriating social production and distributes it among private entities. It appears at face value as if wealth is created in these markets 'as with the stroke of an enchanter's wand', to borrow an expression from Karl Marx. With that phrase he was referring to the role of the public debt in boosting circulating capital. The private wealth created in this way, Marx assured his readers, in spite of appearance, is in fact nothing but primitive accumulation. The statutes on intellectual property and the make-believe markets amounts to the same thing as a second enclosure of the commons.

TRAGEDY OF EXCLUSION, COMEDY OF COMPATIBILITY

At the heart of the topic under discussion is the incompatibility between private property and the productivity of language. This contradiction arises out of the fact that language can exist only as a standard, or, in other words, in a commons. The same goes for networks. Commons in information are paramount to networks since a shared body of knowledge is a prerequisite for enabling communication between nodes. We can choose to read Garrett Hardin's classic paper, *Tragedy of the Commons* in the light of this collision between language and private property.[16] Referring to medieval commons, Garrett famously claims that free access to land leads to disaster, since the individual herdsman collects full gains from increasing his herd, but the reprisals for doing so, land depletion, is shared evenly by everyone. His solution to the tragedy of the commons is private property. Owners will then be inclined to use their resources responsibly. Better still, the individual has now an incentive to develop his property and increase productivity for the greater benefit of everyone. These words are familiar enough as are the objections. To start with, peasants have organised their labour in some kind of commons for most of human existence, which suggests that commons can be a stable form of organisation. The behaviour of individuals tends to be checked by community norms.[17] Overuse of resources became acute when community norms were eroded by the general exchange relation. As long as production was oriented towards self-subsistence, as opposed to producing for a market, the peasants had little reason to squeeze more out of the commons than they could consume. Surpluses in grain and meat could not be stored for an endless period of time and could not be transported to remote markets. Neither were there incentives to infinitely hoard livestock infinitely as there is to accumulate abstract wealth (money). Security for the future was seen to, not by saving money, but by ensuring that the land would produce a harvest the next year too.[18] The back-and-front argumentation of Hardin is not very convincing, and yet his influence is still being felt. The same argumentation underpins present-day beliefs in that the environment can be saved from capitalist exploitation with an intensified property regime and by enacting make-believe markets in carbon emissions and waste disposal.

The merit of Garrett Hardin's paper is not his case in favour of private property over commons. It is worthwhile to bring him up since he is the first mainstream economist to have touched upon the subject of externalities. In his argumentation he focuses on the classic example of an externality, land depletion. Pollution illustrates how some of the burden from the transaction between buyer and seller is carried by third parties. Occasionally, those effects are life-threatening, as when toxic waste is dumped in a poverty-stricken neighbourhood or when floods and tropic storms lay waste to coastal areas in the south. The working class, minorities, women, and Third World populations are proportionally worse off because of the collateral damage of market circulation. In those cases, from an economist point of view, expenses have been externalised and are no longer a major, theoretical concern. Externalities are not acknowledged in neoclassic economic theory until they 'boomerang'. That is, when the effect on the third party bounces back on the decisions made by the seller and the buyer. An example of a 'boomerang externality' is the software pirate who makes a computer program more valuable to paying customers simply by using the software application. Another example is the photocopied article that contributes to the subscription fee of an academic journal. In the cultural sector, the buzz that accompanies a film release could be described as a boomerang externality. A wider public is exposed to a commercial release through private conversations taking place outside the regular distribution channels.

Those who learn about the film without intending to watch it, or watch it without paying, count as third parties. However, by just being aware of the film, the position of the 'buyer' (advertisers) and the 'seller' (movie studio) is modified. A wider diffusion of the product increases the revenue from advertising, merchandising, and secondary market sales. As has previously been argued, value added in this circumstantial way, the labour of audiences, can make up the biggest share of the total labour invested in a media production. At this point, externalities enter the calculation of buyers and sellers from the outset. It is now that the phenomenon is discovered and studied in the economist discipline. However, externalities are still placed in a residual category and include all beneficial and detrimental side-effects from market transactions. This is a cart-before-the-horse approach to understanding the concept. Instead of making externalities the odd one out, Ockham's razor suggests that we scrutinize the private property regime. Errors multiply when property rights are straitjacketted onto an increasingly socialised way of making and living. A 'John Locke'-virtuality of ownership turfs is projected on top of the common standard that is language. The process is already under way when we speak of information in terms of information. In our thinking we have made the perpetual flux of reciprocities into manageable, delimited units of information content. Were we instead to use the word 'communication', it would be hard even to think what 'enclosure' would mean. Privatisation of communication is a contradiction in terms. Language can only exist in a commons. This is true whether the language in question consists of words, software code, or brands. Signs acquire their use value when they are diffused to the point of becoming a standard, in which case the product is pushed to the edge where the commodity form dissolves. Historian of technology, Lewis Mumford, grasped this as a potentiality many years ago: "[. . .] the production of words introduced the first real economy of abundance [. . .]"[19] For as long as words were little more than the building blocks of prose, Mumford's observation was of limited relevance. When signs become components in software machines, and start to intervene directly in economic reality, his remark carries a lot more weight.

Both neoclassic economic theory and Marxist literature leaves us in the dark at this point. The chief resource for understanding postmodern capitalism in general, and so-called attention economy markets in particular, is Georges Bataille.[20] He turned the economist's preoccupation with scarcity on its feet, arguing that the economic principle of the universe is excess. Bataille called the biosphere the *general economy* and opposed it to the *restrictive economy* that is studied in economic science. From the perspective of general economy, the fact of life is a surplus of energy. The individual organism processes some of the energy it receives from the sun. Energy is metamorphosed into growth. But the flow of energy exceeds by far the needs of the life form.[21] Most of it slips away as heat emission, or, in the context of our discussion, it becomes an externality. Life forms organise their existence in niches created by the expenditure of excess by other life forms. For instance, the air turbulence accidentally caused by a bird in flight is taken advantage of by the bird flying immediately after. Aerodynamic externalities are an important boon for migratory birds enabling them to cover very long distances. Indeed, the utilisation of excess capacity in this way is paramount to the health of all ecosystems. With knowledge of this fact, the restricted economy of capitalism shows up as a mirror world of anti-production where the principle of life has been inverted. If the first bird was a bourgeois, he would sue the second bird for piracy. At each and every instant, private property acts as a stoppage. It could rightly be described as a 'Tragedy of the Anti-Commons'. The term was made up by Michael Heller in his criticism of Garrett Hardin's essay.[22] Heller argues from a conventional economist's perspective, but he reaches an unorthodox conclusion: An overly strong private property regime can cause under-use of resources. Conflicting ownership claims might prevent two parties from developing a resource. Additionally, resources might go undeveloped because high prices hinder people from accessing and improving the resource in question. The most striking example of an anti-common with tragic consequences is found in countries where landless peasants starve while most of the land lies idle in the hands of the upper classes. The criticism by Michael Heller is insufficient, however, in so forth that he only identifies anti-commons where the thickness of private property claims stands out. Hence, he ends up advocating a more balanced property regime to solve the tragedy of anti-commons. But the problem of anti-commons is part and parcel of exclusive ownership rights wherever it is encountered. A market society cannot organise itself on the principle of excess and life and this is the full magnitude of the tragedy. It is thus that the gift economy emerges as a real alternative to state administrated make-believe markets.

GIFT ECONOMIES IN THE ARCHAIC SOCIETY

The term 'gift economy' originates in the pioneering anthropological works by Bonislaw Malinowski and Marcel Mauss. The word 'gift' is used in this context to describe the organisation of tribal societies. The gift economy sets the archaic society apart from the modern, capitalist society. No doubt, the concept is problematic since it applies to cultures spanning the whole globe and includes most of human existence. The merit of talking about gift economies, at least in the case of this book, is that it makes us aware of the fact that the market economy is not an/a historical and universal principle of life. Saying that, it must also be clear that class rule is much older than capitalism, and, as much as we would like to think otherwise, gift economies are not antithetical to hierarchies and domination. Endorsement of pre-capitalist customs is constantly in peril of ending up with a pastoral idealisation of outdated forms of oppression. Slavery and gift economy, for example, has not only co-existed, but could turn into a particularly noxious breed. Georges Bataille described an Indian tribe called Tlingit where prestige was gained by destroying property in public, rather than by giving it away. Sometimes that property was other human beings. According to Bataille, chieftains could slice the throat of a vast number of slaves only to outdo their rivals in the destruction of property. Likewise, Marcel Mauss understood the gift economy as a method of stratifying hierarchies in the tribe. He stressed that the acceptance of a gift makes the receiver morally indebted towards the giver. If possible, the debt is repaid with interest, i.e. with an even finer gift. In Mauss' opinion, the gift economy is not fundamentally different from the modern credit system. In fact, giving is the original version of market exchange, still underpinning it.[23] When the topic is discussed in the computer underground, gift economies are usually understood in alignment with Mauss' concept. Contending interpretations have been put forward, however, and need to be taken under consideration. The French philosopher Jacques Derrida reproached Mauss for interpreting giving as a direct negation of the logic of capitalist accumulation.[24] Derrida stated that the act of giving must not be recognised as such if it is to be a true gift. In agreement with Derrida, gift economy is here understood as something essentially different from the credit system. Even the kind of gifts that Mauss had in mind, that is, a gift recognised as a gift, are not a perfect inversion of the domination established in market exchanges. Unlike the closed loop between a buyer and a seller, giving is not confined to the transaction taking place between the giver and the receiver, with one part gaining what is lost to the opposite part. The part loosing out from a gift exchange is the third part not involved in it. The subjugated position established in tribal societies is reserved for the individual/family/clan that is the least successful in building alliances through gift giving, rather than any part that has accumulated most fictious 'moral debt'.

The main difference between a gift economy and a market economy is that power relations in the gift economy are mediated through prestige and person-to-person relations. In a society dominated by general commodity exchange, power relations between members of a group take the social form of relations between objects. The significance of objects in a market society is intimately connected with how those objects are made. In other words, it hangs together with the social division of labour. A prerequisite of general commodity exchange is that the population has been deprived of the means to provide for their own subsistence. Instead they depend on a market for satisfying both vital and superfluous needs. Obviously, the situation is very different in an archaic society. Gift economies tend to discriminate between different classes of items. Primary goods and household tools are in most cases not subject to exchange at all. People in archaic societies have the means to provide for these needs when they so require. Items subject to gift swapping are things like necklaces, clams, pearls and other ceremonial, symbolic items. The objects are of secondary importance compared to the meanings they convey. Gifts institute a 'morality of social exchange' that extends beyond the individuals directly involved in the transaction.[25] Scholars are therefore obliged to examine the whole society in which the individual transaction takes place if they are to understand the meaning of that transaction. It is a lesson well worth keeping in mind when the discussion is shifted to the gift economy in the modern society.

Before the notion surfaced about a high-tech gift economy on the Internet, it was commonly believed that the gift economy had been marginalised in modern society to the point of near extinction. Igor Kopytoff recounted a short list of goods that never enters into commodity circulation, not even in neo-liberal capitalism. Norms and law are mobilised to exempt these unique objects. Atomic bombs, crown jewelleries, body parts, child pornography, and endangered species, are rare examples where legal markets have been withdrawn. Even with an official decree not to trade in a certain kind of goods, however, the pull from generalised exchange is always-already present. Indeed, illegalisation of some goods can end up in making those goods even more attractive on the black market.[26] Previous to the emergence of filesharing networks, there has only been one case of decommodification that went beyond the limited examples given by Kopytoff. That is the abolition of slavery. Admittedly, slavery was phased out at the same time as waged labour became the dominant labour relation. Though the decommodification process was incomplete, the abolition of slavery did significantly delimit the terms under which humans could be owned and traded. This observation reflects directly upon the central claim of the book that the FOSS movement is essentially a struggle against the wage relation. The resilience of information commons in repelling market expansion is an index of the degree to which human labour has been decommodified.

INTERNET AS A HIGH-TECH-GIFT ECONOMY

The idea about a 'high-tech gift economy' has most compellingly been articulated by Richard Barbrook. In the midst of the market hype surrounding the Internet in the 1990s, Barbrook exclaimed that Americans were superseding capitalism in cyberspace. The possibility of evading both the market exchange and state planning through gift giving had first occurred to the Situationists in the 1960s. Barbrook argued that this route was now taken by Internet's users *en masse*. He made a point of the fact that people chose to give away their time and creativity to peers without the ideological zealousness of the New Left protagonists.[27] It goes without saying that the high-tech gift economy and archaic gift economies are more different than they are similar. It is only in respect to the market economy that a common denominator between the two can be traced. While elements of archaic gift are present in the exchanges taking place on the Internet, characteristics of market exchange are just as prevalent. The high-tech gift economy is not a polar opposite of market exchange and/or state planning. It is a hybrid that incorporates aspects from the market and cuts it 'diagonally'. For instance, software firms hire programmers to customise source code released by the FOSS development community. By doing so, employed labour fills up the gaps that have been left behind where no-one volunteered to do the job. This pragmatic course of action would not have been possible if hackers had shared the ideological fervour of the New Left advocates of gift giving. It is by drawing on the strengths of rivalling systems that the shortcomings of the gift model can be compensated for. John Frow suggests the term 'library economy' instead of 'gift economy' to describe accurately the hybrid economic activity taking place on the Internet:

> In this sense, [library models] partake of the impersonality and the abstractness of the commodity form; unlike commodities, however, they have also been largely free of the forms of coercion (the constraints on access and use) that tend to flow from the price mechanism. While the 'library model' thus tends to collapse rather than dichotomize the categories of gift and commodity, it does nevertheless represent a genuine alternative to the privatisation of the commons in information.[28]

The library analogy seems appropriate when referring to filesharing networks. Peer-to-peer networks involve users with even less personal ties than those bringing together two parts on the market. Indeed, the political relevance of filesharing rests on the fact that it can attract a mass of outsiders without asking them to commit to community bonding. Only then will the crowd grow to a size whose actions have an impact on the real world. A central feature of the gift economy in an archaic society, in contrast, is the mutual and personal obligation it inspires. But the indifference between persons that is characteristic of filesharing networks does not apply throughout the register. The situation is quite different when we turn to FOSS development groups or teams of crackers. They invest a lot more effort into their gifts than a computer user who merely lets other users access his files on the hard drive. The endeavours of hackers/crackers are marked by intense collaboration as well as fierce competition. 'Flame wars' are instrumental in keeping tabs on rivals. Hierarchies based on prestige, the building and breaking of alliances, and the will to outdo peers by contributing the neatest code, is consistent with how a traditional gift economy is thought to work. The heterodox economic activity on the Internet hinges on the cross-over between the gift and library model. While the reputation-based gift model is crucial to sustain efforts among a committed few over longer periods of time, the impersonal library model diffuses those efforts to a significant number of recipients. Some guidance about how to think of this relationship is offered by Peter Wayner in his review of the Free Software Movement:

> The code circulates for everyone to grab, and only those who need it dig in. There's no great connection between programmer and user. People

grab software and take it without really knowing to whom they owe any debt. [. . .] This vast mass of contributors often negates the value and prestige that comes from writing neat code. Since no one can keep track of it all, *people tend to treat all requests from unknown people equally*.[29]

Wayner's last sentence is intriguing. One would expect that chances for mutual aid to thrive in the 'virtual community' would be ruled out by its size and anonymity.[30] What Wayner attests to is that the anonymity of the computer interface can be beneficial to the group since mutual aid stretches out and embraces even those who have not 'earned it'. His observation runs counter to the common wisdom that charity and a code of conduct can only be upheld in delimited, stable and close-knit groups.[31] These conditions seem next to obligatory in kinship societies, as is suggested by anthropologist Claude Lévi-Strauss' distinction between restricted exchange and general exchange. In restricted exchange, the part giving something expects to receive something back from the benefiting part. In general exchange, on the other hand, giving and taking involves more than two parties. The giver still expects to receive something back, but not necessarily from the part to which he gave. Hence, while discussing Lévi-Strauss' work, Peter Ekeh emphasises trust as a key feature for enabling generalised exchange: "This implies, above all, that there is enough trust that the giver will be reciprocated from someone and somewhere else in the future. This means that univocal reciprocity can only operate in an atmosphere of generalized morality and trust that the system will work."[32] In order to preserve trust the gift economy must raise borders between the inner and the outer circle. The reactionary element of gift and community boils down to this border. The author Lewis Hyde even recognises an emancipatory potential in commodity exchange insofar as it takes place at the border and lessens this divide. His reproach against the market economy is, as he puts it, that gift giving has been retracted to the point were it only encircles the single individual. To ask if commodity exchange can be surpassed without falling back on tribal allegiances is partly to ask if a gift economy can exist without a separation of an inner from an outer. The interplay between the gift economy of hackers and the library economy of filesharers points at such a possibility.

The fact that the virtual community sustains an atmosphere of generalized morality and trust in an open, fluid environment is indeed one of the enigmas of the movement. Law scholar Jacob Strahilevitz is puzzled by the absence of misbehaviour and the high level of trust in these networks despite the ease by which havoc could be brought into the system. His attempt at shedding light on this mystery is instructive, especially in those places where he goes wrong. According to Strahilevitz, the explanation is 'charismatic code'. The interface in peer-to-peer systems is built to distort the picture of reality, he says, so that participatory behaviour is magnified and freeriding is veiled. Though only thirty percent of the filesharers using Gnutella make files available for their peers, the other two-thirds who do not upload files are invisible in the network. While some people will share irrespectively of the behaviour of others, most people will share on the condition that they think others are sharing too. The ingenuity of charismatic code is that it portrays the reality so that users only can see those users who are sharing. Thus the norm of univocal reciprocity is continuously reinforced in the virtual community.[33] Strahilevitz advice to the RIAA is telling. He urges the record companies not to litigate users but to attack the 'morality of social exchange' within the peer-to-peer movement. The underlying assumption is that if the 'freeriders' are exposed; well-behaved users will stop sharing too.

Strahilevitz sees with the eyes of the robbed content provider. Blinded by the objects shared in the network and the loss of value which it represents to the rightful owners, he fails to recognise that these gifts are vehicles for realities of a different order.[34] The bulk of copyrighted material released on the Internet is not cracked by people urging to use the utilities in question. The warez scene is driven by reputation-games within small circles of crackers. These people keep a close tally on the achievements and status of rivalling groups.[35] Reputability is the incentive for devoting time and effort to writing software code and cracking encryptions. An economist would call it 'opportunity cost', though if a cracker thought of cracking in terms of loss, he would not start doing it in the first place. Economists are so deeply entrenched in the market perspective that they take for granted that cracking is a privation engaged in to access consumable information. That assumption, and all the theoretical constructs that builds upon it, is annulled by the motivations of the cracker. To him, it is the challenge of picking the electronic lock that provides the highest entertainment value. The biggest crack of them all is that copyright infringement has been made into a sport. The reputation-game between crackers results in mass releases of encrypted information goods. But this is of secondary importance to them. Their disinterest in consuming the information goods points at a rejection of commodified forms of entertainment. Instead it is the commodity form as such that has become their playground. As far as the cracker is concerned, information warez is an excess and surplus. What is heat emission to him, however, is a desirable use value to someone else. Ordinary computer users with no stakes in the reputation-game encounter warez as 'free lunch'. But crackers do not look upon them as 'freeriders'. On the contrary, these people are known as 'lamers', the word for computer users that have not distinguished themselves in the warez scene.

It is thus the border between the gift and the library model can be redrawn. Play, the most non-instrumental of human actions, is short-circuiting the *quid pro quo* logic of markets *and* gift economies. In the filesharing network, the act of giving is not recognised by the parties involved in it as a gift. Therefore giving qualifies as a true gift in Derrida's sense of the word. The expenditure of excess in the warez scene and in filesharing networks is a showcase of giving without reciprocity. It corresponds to the principles which George Bataille meant was basic to life, and exemplified by the sun that radiates energy without asking for anything in return. In fact, play and gift are closely related concepts. When we read the eighteenth century poet Friedrich Schiller's musings about play, of which much more will be said in the next chapter, the connection between the two is made explicit. Play emerges spontaneously wherever there is superfluous capacity. Even creatures without reason have been given by Nature more than the bare necessities of existence, Schiller wrote in one of his famous letters, and thus shed a glimmer of freedom in the darkness of animal life. He exemplified the statement with an image of the lion. When a lion is not tormented by hunger or faces an immediate threat, the unemployed strength of the animal creates an object for himself. He lets his terrible roars echo through the desert out of pure joy. Excess capacity becomes play and display.

In the final analysis, this is how the private property regime is undermined by hacking. The more obvious candidate, mass violations of copyright law on the Internet, is not in itself a threat to markets in information. On the contrary, increased exposure of information goods due to filesharing activities tends to improve corporate revenues. Neither is it free and/or open license schemes that will overthrow the intellectual property regime. These licenses are based upon copyright law and re-negotiate rather than disband individual authorship. For sure, the capacity to mass distribute files in peer-to-peer networks and the protection that alternative license schemes offers against private appropriations are not unimportant. But what sustains the importance of these technical and legal innovations is the instinct that Schiller once identified as the play drive. The play of hackers mounts a challenge to the philosophical foundations of private property. As was mentioned in the third chapter, the justification for intellectual property rests heavily on John Locke's notion that the individual has a right to the fruits of her labour. These fruits take the form of a wage or property rights. Not only liberals, but labour organisations too, are contribute to this moral investment in the property regime. Indeed, the left has built much of its politics around the demand for equal reciprocation, thereby confirming the logic of exchange value with every victory they have scored. A case in point is the cultural workers who equate their own rights against employers with expanded intellectual property rights. The indignation by which many cultural workers put forward their demands calls our attention to a weakness in Lockean claims for compensation. It stipulates that the labour activity is a privation to the individual. If the activity is engaged in for its own sake and is freely chosen by the individual, in other words, if it is play and not work, the individual has no reason to ask for retribution. We can see this in that hackers tend to be perfectly happy for others to use their software code without receiving anything in return. Most of them do not even mind if corporations make money from software code that they have developed. It might sound strange that such an attitude threatens the private property regime when the immediate outcome from volunteer labour is increased corporate profits. Nevertheless, this is the mindset it takes to invent new exchange relations free from reciprocity.

Referring back to the discussion in the last chapter, it is on the principle of excess, rather than through inputs and outputs, that an autopoietic machine can be assembled. This machine operates through a paradox. The cracker and the lamer must be ignorant of the other part's needs. If they relate to each other in a common interest they will engage in a market transaction, and, if they are tied together by a personal relation, they will fall back to a gift exchange. Still, even though they are not in touch with the desires of the opposite part, the information good must end up as a use value to the receiver. Otherwise the expenditure of excess is without any social consequences. The same thing could be phrased as a familiar question, by what mechanisms do supply and demand meet up in a playful gift/library economy? Among the ranks of crackers and hackers, the answer is given by the partial suspension of the technical division of labour. FOSS developers coordinate their labour power to the equilibrium of user demand by the most direct and rational manner conceivable, the programmer and the user being one and the same person. Or, with an allusion to hacker speak, the allocation of programming resources is no more difficult than to know when and where to scratch an itch. It is the need itself that provides the incentive to do the job, because a solution to the problem is craved by the person undertaking the task. This is possible since the hacker is in possession of the necessary instruments of labour. When hackers join together in larger, cooperative projects, the direction of community efforts is guided by prestige. The magnitude of a problem stands in relation to the number of people that have encountered the difficulty/scarcity. Equilibrium is found between the urgency of a problem to be solved and the peer recognition attained from solving it. Inside a community, where the opinion of others counts, coordination of volunteer efforts is hard but manageable. Less convincing is the record of development communities in response to outside demand. Here the paradox referred to above comes to the fore. Recipients of digital gifts, unlike consumers on the market, are not in the position of calling the shots. In practice, however, the sheer abundance of cracked information means that most desires can be satisfied. What gift economies lack in precision they compensate for in their excess of dispenses. It is thus a third path between market exchange and state planning, or, really, an alternative to state planned make-believe markets, can be conceived. This potentiality has been revealed in the play of hackers and crackers. The task ahead of us is to examine how political subjects are constituted in play.

7   Play Struggle of Hackers

MARX ON LABOUR, ART, AND PLAY

In this chapter the hacker movement is taken as a showcase of the concept
of play struggle. Previously in the book it has been argued that play stands
on equal terms with work. Both activities are enrolled by capital as sources
of surplus value and are therefore contested points of struggle. Needless
to say, the conflicts surrounding play activities diverge greatly from the
conflicts centred on the workplace. The axis of labour struggle is the wage
relation, and clashes erupt on pay levels, working hours, and the like. Play
struggle pivots around the same axis, with the difference that its chosen
strategy is to withdraw from the wage relation. In collaborative and institutionalised forms of play, such as in FOSS projects, the labour market is no
longer the chief principle for organising labour power. Needs are produced
and satisfied in ways not directly submitted to the commodity form. The
motor of this development is a gut reaction against alienated labour. Karl
Marx's critique of alienation is the beginning and end of an understanding
of the hacker movement. Of course, with few exceptions, the propagators
of play struggle do not frame their activity in such terms. Their engagement
is spontaneous and they are largely unaware of the forces that confront
them. A major problematic of the chapter is how the hacker movement
can constitute itself as a political subject in spite of a general lack of class
consciousness. It is proposed that a radicalisation of the hacker movement
will be inspired by two factors. Firstly, the play-activity is in itself a source
of knowledge. Collective forms of play strengthen solidarity among players
and foster viewpoints that are at odds with dominant ideology. Secondly,
for the very reason that play is destabilising to the *status quo*, it becomes a
target of repression. At the same time as municipalities and firms are enlisting FOSS developers, a legal and technical infrastructure is advanced by
state and capital that threatens to destroy the hacker community. Hackers
are forced to mobilise politically in order to defend the foundations of their
way of life. It is in these unfamiliar terms that the politics of play struggle is
acted out. The principal goals of the hacker movement, free access to information and an open computer architecture, are not primarily desired out

of ideological conviction. These aims are prerequisites for the community to continue to flourish. Their approach to politics set play struggles apart from, and, occasionally in conflict with, the priorities of traditional, leftist movements. While an activist might be tempted to describe the bias of hackers as a lack of political awareness, there is also a merit to the hacker's brand of politics. Like most New Left movements emerging after 1968, the hacker movement exists to the side of the workplace and debates issues not overtly concerned with work. Unlike most of its political siblings, however, the question about work is at the heart of hacking. It relates to wage labour as a negation. Thus, just like the labour movement before, hackers challenge the forms of creation and production in society. It is for this reason that the hacker movement both actualises Marxism and causes interesting problems to Marxist theory.

A central theme running through Karl Marx's *oeuvre* is his critique of alienated labour. We will give a thorough account on this matter since it provides a key piece of the puzzle to our further discussion on hackers. Readers that feel they are familiar with Marx's theory of alienation might choose to jump ahead to the next paragraph. It was in his earlier writings that Marx referred directly to the concept of alienation. Most of his thoughts on alienation can be found in the *Economic and Philosophic Manuscripts of 1844*. Nonetheless, the same concerns and viewpoints informed the economic-political studies that he conducted later in life. The term alienation originates from the history of philosophy. Marx borrowed the idea from Hegel and the young Hegelians, most notable of them Ludwig Feuerbach. The latter used the concept to describe how man weakens himself by projecting his virtues on an imaginary God. The divinity becomes an alien force not recognisable to man as his creation. Marx continued the atheist critique in his own inquiry into alienation. He drew parallels between the religious belief system and the ideological mirror world that bourgeoisie society veils itself in. The touching stone of Marx's alienation theory was the capitalist labour process. Under capitalism the worker is forced to sell herself as a commodity on the labour market. The products that she produces are subsequently claimed by her employer. Only as commodities can the worker take possession again of some of her objectified labour. Just as with God, the worker doesn't recognise the object as her own creation. The object gains an existence independent of its creator. And since the worker depends on the item for satisfying her vital needs, the object becomes an alien power confronting her. Hence, because of the abstraction of commodity exchange, power relations between humans take the appearance of relations between things. The worker, who is alienated from the result of her labour, is by the same token alienated during the labour process. When work is subdued under capitalist relations, the sole purpose of her endeavours is to produce commodities for the market. The imperative of market competition comes to define every moment of her operations. Even if the labourer is more privileged than the coal miners of Marx's days or the maquiladora workers of our time, even if some concessions have been made for her comfort, she is alienated by the very principle for which she is set to work, namely: the expansion of capital. Alienation is present because she does not experience her work as a need in itself, but merely as a means to satisfy needs external to her work. And, Marx inserted, that which applies to a person's relation to her work also applies to her relation to other people. The other human being is not any longer an end, but, just like work, a means for something else. The outcome can be witnessed in the strife and fragmentation of bourgeoisie society. Possessive individualism is the trait of an era dominated by alienated labour, and, subsequently, private property. The ramifications of the injustice of alienation become clear when we consider the role that Marx assigned to work. It is in labour that humans stand apart from other animals. Of interest to our later discussion is that among the short list of criteria that distinguishes humans from animals, Marx added that humans form objects in accordance with the laws of beauty. When those objects are taken away from her, she is not merely robbed in a narrow, economical sense. She is denied her very existence as a human species being.

The indignation that Marx expressed over alienation presumes an idea about what positive, unalienated labour would be like. He was scant on this, just as he refused to speculate about the details of the communist society. Some vague pointers can be salvaged from his extensive writings; the most significant being that labour ought to be in such a way that it is experienced by the individual as a need in itself. This state of things cannot be reached inside the confines of capitalism. The species being which Marx compared his contemporaries with is located in the communist future. As of yet, there has never been an unalienated human, since every society in history as far we know has been founded on the division of labour. Thus he declined to concretise his vision of unalienated labour by pointing at any example in his surroundings. There could not be pockets of unalienated activity in the midst of a society ruled by abstractions. In spite of Marx's reluctance in this regard, we will try to articulate the idea of what positive labour might be like. The discussion will assist us when arguing that the FOSS development model is a germ form for such a positive labour relation of the future. If we are to pinpoint any sphere of activity that might be close to what Marx had in mind, two strong candidates stand out, play and art. In both cases the activity is an end in itself rather than a means for something else. Play, and, to a lesser extent, artistic creativity, are spontaneous, freely entered, and self-realising, qualities that Marx deplored alienated labour for not being. In an examination of Marx's theory of alienation, Kostas Axelos makes feelers in the same direction. He brings attention to Marx's lifelong and ambiguous engagement with art and poetry. On a personal level Marx took pleasure in classic literature. Occasionally he summoned up Dante, Shakespeare or Goethe for piercing into the secrets of bourgeoisie society. When approaching the subject of art as a theoretician, however, Marx placed art together with other ideological reflections of alienated life, such as religion, philosophy and morality. He assured his readers that art had no history that stood apart from the history of class struggle and political economy. And as far as the artists were concerned, they were petty commodity traders making objects for sale like everybody else. A factor that might have contributed to Marx's position on art was his hostility towards romanticist notions. Romanticism, with its adoration of chivalry, pastoralism, and the idea of the genius-artist, had surged in response to the French revolution and the ideals of modernity and equality. Marx, in contrast, had his eyes fixed on the future. In the communist society, he wrote in the *German Ideology*, there will be no painters but at most people who engage in painting among other things. When the division of labour and private property, the causes of alienation, have been stripped off, the need for seeking comfort in art and religion will no longer exist. But the abolishment of art as an institution and as a profession does not necessarily invalidate the continued relevance of aesthetics and the laws of beauty. Kostas Axelos infers such a possibility from Marx's theory on alienation: "It would be quite legitimate to think that, beyond the death of poetry and art, beyond the death of the work of art and the poem, the dimension of the poetic and artistic will unfold as an 'activity' that is not directly productive or technically organized. It would not be illegitimate to think that this poetic and artistic dimension might deploy itself, then, as Play."[1] If Marx was ambiguous on art and literature, however, he was outspoken when coming down against those writers who advocated play as an alternative to work. The nineteenth century utopian socialist Charles Fourier had made such a proposal. On two places in *Grundrisse* Karl Marx dismissed Fourier and the notion that labour could become play. Marx underscored that though the human species being in the communist society would reach self-realisation through work, it did not imply that work would become 'mere amusement'. And he followed up with the statement that really free work is at the same time 'the most damned serious' thing and involving 'the most intense exertions'. These last comments throw back the question on Karl Marx and his disparaging of play. One of his many disciples, Herbert Marcuse, made an appropriate observation on the general disregard for play in modern society: "[. . .] Play is *unproductive* and *useless* precisely because it cancels the repressive and exploitative traits of labor and leisure [. . .]"[2] What makes play look unimportant, in other words, is exactly what makes it politically explosive. In spite of Karl Marx's harsh words on the topic, a disparate group of socialists have figured that play could become an alternative to alienated labour. Herbert Marcuse is the thinker that most consistently has pursued this line of inquiry.

THEORIES ON LIBERATION, AESTHETICS, AND PLAY

As the book draws to a close, the many lines of argument converge in the thinking of Herbert Marcuse. He was an idiosyncratic member of the

Marxist family. Previous to joining the Frankfurt School, he had been a student of Martin Heidegger. Though Marcuse would soon disavow himself from his tutor, he never broke entirely free from Heidegger's influence. The pessimistic view on technology in Heidegger's philosophy and the hopeful, even positivistic, outlook in the Marxist tradition made for a conflicted authorship. The assumption in scientific Marxism that the advancement of productive forces is ultimately benefiting the emancipation of the proletariat could not go unquestioned with Marcuse. One of the ideas inherited from his former master was that technology is not merely a tool but a carrier of a higher order of instrumentality. The domination of nature through the scientific principle extends seamlessly into the domination of men. Then again, with Marx, Marcuse approved of that an end had been put to the subjection of humanity under the blind forces of nature. This dilemma of how labour, the provision of necessities and domination relates to each other was a central problematic in Marcuse's thinking. Could humanity liberate itself from repression without first having rendered toil and scarcity obsolete through technological development? If the answer was no, Marcuse would come up against the counterposing question. Could human liberation be built on the same scientific rationality that was the principle of domination in the one-dimensional society? This tension is present already in the article from 1933 on the philosophical foundations of labour. The article expanded on Marx's *Economic and Philosophic Manuscripts of 1844* that had been published for the first time a year before. Marcuse disputed the narrow treatment of labour in the discipline of political economy. From the economist's point of view, labour is a privation simply engaged in to fulfil material needs. Marcuse complemented the picture by highlighting Marx's description of labour as a fulfilment of psychological and social needs. In the article, Marcuse introduced a discussion about play and opposed it to labour. He asserted that play was liberating because the player makes up her own rules when toying with an object. In contrast, the worker must submit herself to the laws of the object in order to be productive. Marcuse's reasoning resulted in a standpoint partially at odds with Marx. Labour, just like one of the products of labour, i.e. technology, was portrayed as domination for ontological rather than for historical reasons. Human emancipation could then only be sought apart from labour.[3] Later in life Marcuse would retract from some of these claims made in the article. He remained committed, nevertheless, to investigating the liberating potential in play. The irrationality of play was a precious antidote to the reign of instrumentality in the modern world. At times he hinted at the possibility that art and play could resolve the contradiction between nature's oppression and oppression in society through technological rationality. Play was here elevated to the missing piece in the dilemma of emancipation that Marcuse wrestled with throughout his life.

Marcuse inferred this idea from a re-reading of the eighteenth century poet and philosopher Friedrich Schiller. In his political-philosophical tract, *On the Aesthetic Education of Man in a Series of Letters*, Schiller had elaborated on how aesthetics related to human freedom. He built on Immanuel Kant when suggesting that beauty was a mediating, third force. Aesthetics could reconcile the particular, the individual, with the universal, society without the level of coercion otherwise deemed as necessary. If necessity forces humans into society, Schiller wrote, and reason teaches them social rules, it is beauty that can give them a social character. The political charge in his words is better appreciated when we acknowledge that his point of departure was the French revolution. Many of his contemporaries had reacted to it by disavowing the ideals of the Enlightenment. Schiller remained open-minded towards the values claimed by the revolutionaries even as he condemned the 'excesses' of the revolution itself. On the one hand, he defended the dream of human liberation against a reactionary backlash in Germany and elsewhere. On the other hand, he recognised the fallacy of entrusting human liberation to a purely rational, enlightened mind. Schiller asserted that reason alone made the human being into a barbarian enslaved under abstract thought. If man instead was subdued under nature, both his own nature and the nature of his surroundings, he was little more than a savage. He believed that this tension was present in two conflicting forces, the *form instinct* and the *sensuous* instinct. The latter term concerned material existence and everything that owes to the senses, while the first term referred to the world of concepts and abstractions. Schiller meant that humanity was tored between these two instincts. The rift in man had been caused by specialisation. A more complicated and advanced society necessitated a sundering of ranks and occupations, and, as a consequence, man had been chained to a fragment of the whole. The narrowing down of man's psyche inhibited his potential to organise a peaceful co-existence with others in a state of freedom. In order to realise the dreams of liberty, equality, and brotherhood there had to be a change in the sensibilities of people. Schiller believed that if individuals had not passed their days in self-denial and repression they would be better fit to rise to the occasion and take a point of perspective larger than their own immediate interests. This thought of Schiller was echoed in one of Marcuse's most well-known works, *Eros and Civilisation*. There Marcuse engaged with the heritage from Marx and Freud to make a case for the possibility of a new social synthesis based on the pleasure principle instead of repressed desires. Marcuse followed the poet in searching for this synthesis in art and play. Friedrich Schiller had proposed that the two rivalling instincts, the *form instinct* and the *sensuous instinct*, could be balanced by a third force, the play-drive. He declared that the object of play is beauty and its goal is freedom. Freedom had to be sought through beauty, he said, since it was the only force that could heal the fragmentation in society and in the human being. When reading Schiller's letters and his affirmation of play, the Marxist critique of alienated labour easily springs to mind. At one point in the *Manuscripts of 1844*, Marx had exclaimed that the worker only feels free in her animal functions, eating, drinking and procreating, and feels like an animal when she is at work. In words not all too different, Schiller wrote that: "[. . .] Man only plays when he is in the fullest sense of the word a human being, *and he is only fully a human being when he plays.*" (*letters,* 107, *italics in original*)

The political ambitions of *On the Aesthetic Education of Man* were toned down by its translators and interpreters. The then emerging current of Romanticism claimed Schiller as theirs, and his influence was confined to the fine arts scene. Marx and Engel expressed their preference for Goethe over Schiller and advised others to comply. Most Marxists followed suit with the notable exception of Marcuse. Georg Lukács gave voice to the scepticism generally felt in the Marxist camp towards Schiller by recapitulating that both the grandness and the limitations of German idealist philosophy are manifested in the poet.[4] That thinking belonged to a world bordering between renaissance and enlightenment, after capitalism had broken free from feudalist ties but before it had fully matured. Lukács credited Schiller for basing his dramas on the emerging contradictions of bourgeois society when his contemporaries were still caught up in the conflicts of the *ancien regime*. Schiller had glimpsed into the destructiveness of the capitalist division of labour. But since the political conflicts of the day had not yet centred on this schism, Schiller failed to trace the ills back to its social roots. Instead he located the central conflict to the two spiritual tendencies of idealism and realism, the form instinct and the sensuous instinct. With this model, where the fragmentation of humanity was caused by a one-sidedness of one drive over the other, man could be made whole again simply by an operation of thought. Lukács protested against the idealism of such notions. While his objection is warranted, it would be equally justified to stress other aspects of Schiller's thinking. Unlike many philosophers in those days, Schiller considered the human being to first and foremost be a product of her senses and not of her reason, an outlook rather consistent with the materialist understanding of human existence. Herbert Marcuse too admitted to the slant of idealism in Schiller's thinking but maintained that the poet nonetheless had been a radical. Marcuse pointed out a possible source of misunderstanding in that the meaning of aesthetics changed during the eighteenth century. Previously, the term had designated everything concerning senses and it was closely related to epistemology, while in its modern translation aesthetics has been narrowed down to being the subject of fine art. Lukács' judgement of Schiller assumes that aesthetics, just like philosophy, is the domain of a purely contemplative subject derived of action. Seeking the solution to reification in aesthetics can then only be an evasion of the real problem. At one point in the discussion, however, Lukács gives away a different interpretation of Schiller where aesthetics equals action. In this case: "[. . .] the aesthetic principle must be elevated into the principle by which objective reality is shaped [. . .]."[5] Lukács didn't elaborate on the statement any further. Presumably, he thought that the absurdity of the claim spoke for itself. Marcuse tried out the thought from time to time but was not convinced himself. In his last work, *The Aesthetic Dimension*, he admitted to the ineffectiveness of art.[6] The freedom enjoyed in imagination and poetry comes at the price that it cannot affect real outcomes in the world. Marcuse did not back down from the belief that art is of political relevance. But he relegated its importance to consist mainly in making people aware of alternatives to the present reality. Fantasy affects behaviour so that a dialectic unfolds between the world as it is, and as it could be. This aspect of play is likely to be vastly more important than we are able to appreciate. Nonetheless, the claim is too weak for us to stay content with. Play and labour are on a par in that they are both productive engagements with the world. They are differentiated solely by the meanings and circumstances under which the activity is performed. In play, the production process is guided by the aesthetic principle, and, hence, beauty is indeed a principle by which objective reality is shaped. Perhaps the significance of play was hard to discern in the heyday of work-centred industrial capitalism. In the midst of a consumer-driven capitalism, however, we have more examples to go by. It suffices to recall that the outcome from the activity of a hacker and a programmer, one of them playing, the other one working, are essentially the same. The sameness of GNU/Linux and Windows is corroborated by that both products are competing on the same market for software utilities. The FOSS development model has concretised some of the visions of Marcuse and Schiller. As we will come back to towards the end of the chapter, the hacker movement enables us to explore their utopian claims with a bit more self-assurance than before.

Herbert Marcuse is not the only anti-capitalist to deduce a liberating potential in art from Marx's critique of alienated labour. Similar thoughts surfaced among nineteenth century artists and bohemians in what Eve Chiapello has called 'artist critique'. Their strain of protest was formulated in the unique historical position of being economically marginalised while at the same time being given a voice in society. In the artist critique of capitalism, the economic system is deplored for the disenchantment it causes to goods and lives; and, secondly, for oppressing personal freedom, autonomy, and the creativity of people. The blind spot of this critique is in its individualism. The rights which are denied people by capital are rights to individual self-fulfilment. From such an angle, capitalism cannot easily be questioned in the name of solidarity or equality. In fact, artist critique has an aristocratic slant where dismay against commercial entertainment and those being entertained are not always distinguishable. At its worst, the rejection of commercialism is married with romanticism, so that the right to autonomy from market forces is thought of as a privilege of the artist-genius. Indeed, in a morbid twist of events, this on the face of it anti-capitalist rhetoric is sometimes enrolled by present-day cultural workers in support of the intellectual property regime. While the artist critique posed a valid inquiry into the ills of nineteenth and twentieth century capitalism, Chiapello fears that its edge has been lost with the advent of post-Fordist capitalism. The demand for self-fulfilment in work has been all but co-opted by management writers and life-style consultants.[7] These doubts have to be taken into consideration in the context of our discussion since we are closely following the themes first raised in artist critique. It is here argued that fan media producers, including hackers, provide a social basis from which a renewed version of artist critique can be mounted. This version of critique will have the professional artist as one of its main targets. The amateur is by definition positioned against the professional. Established artists have a vested interest in maintaining their status and earnings against the hobbyists, which is to say, to uphold the division of labour against workers positioned outside the artistic profession. This conflict of interest can be read out from the divergent stands taken by cultural workers and fan media producers on intellectual property. Elitism might still be part of an artist critique formulated from below by amateurs, but at least their critique will not be made to entrench privileges in the labour market. Furthermore, the attitude of fan media producers towards mass entertainment is likely to be more constructive since popular culture is the departing point for their playfulness. As was the case before, personal self-fulfilment remains the lead motif of this critique. But the bias of individualism will turn out differently since, unlike most bourgeois art, the artistic expressions of fans tend to have a collective quality. This owes to the fact that the labour relation of fan media producers is organised in a community as opposed to through a market. The major weakness of this strain of critique is its susceptibility to recuperation, especially since companies have tailored themselves after the rhetoric of self-fulfilment through work. The demarcation line between emancipating play and alienated labour cannot be taken as if it was straightforward and self-evident any longer. In order to separate one from the other, we need to investigate more closely the concept of play.

DEFINING PLAY FROM WORK

We have not specified what unalienated labour is by calling it 'play'. Herbert Marcuse didn't dwell on a definition but took the term as rather self-evident. The activity we know as play is familiar to everyone, and yet, at a closer look, it turns out to be very hard to categorise. In order for us to flesh out the concept of play struggle we must seek assistance in those scholars who have had play as their main subject of study. Stray comments about the topic have been made in many disparate disciplines. A lively debate erupted after Charles Darwin admitted to the existence of play among animals. His followers craved an explanation to this behaviour that didn't contradict the evolutionary theory. They found it in functionalist arguments. The play of young predators was explained by that the animal rehearsed hunting practices. Thus the seemingly pointless activity could be incorporated in the thesis about the survival-of-the-fittest. In a similar fashion, child psychologists have sometimes interpreted play as preparations for adulthood. Among sociologists, play is typically seen as a mechanism for society to reproduce itself across generations. Common to all of these explanations is that play is understood as solely or chiefly a means for some other, more practical, end. The general puzzlement about the non-instrumentality of play, and the pain many scholars have gone through to find a higher purpose in the activity, is a testimony of our *zeitgeist*. A parallel can be drawn to the academic debate on hacking, which is preoccupied with the question of motivation. What drives hackers to write code when there are no direct economic incentives for them to do so? Whatever the stance taken in the debate by individual scholars, the very problematic is defined by the market society. The normality is to act with an economic incentive and a rational purpose, and deviances from this pattern require explanation. All of that is invalidated once we start taking play seriously.

Johan Huizinga was an early ambassador of play. In 1938 he published *Homo Ludens* where he claimed that play is the wellspring of civilisation.[8] He documented elements of play in all historical cultures but complained about a marked decline of playfulness in modern society. In his mind, the turning point was the French revolution. From then onwards the grandiose expenditure of the royal courts was toned down. Huizinga disapprovingly exemplified his claim with the democratisation of the dress code of the gentry to the standard of the commoners. The industrial revolution was equally repulsive to him, and Marxism was the furthest outgrowth of its utilitarian, economistic mindset. It is not as a political thinker that Huizinga made his name, though, but as a researcher of play, and on that topic he had a lot to contribute. As might be expected, his study began with attacking those writers who had explained play as a means for something else and more useful. Play, he asserted, is an irreducible entity in itself that lies beyond value judgements. Play does not conform to wisdom or folly, neither can it be said to be true or false, and it does not answer to good or evil. The only point where Huizinga hesitated was if play can be related to the opposites 'ugly versus beauty'. In the end, he admitted to a close affinity between play and the concept of aesthetics. His assertion that play is beyond good and evil deserves an extra comment. It is clear from his discussion of play elements in war, and his esteem of aristocratic play, that the concept is neither meant to be humane nor democratic. It can be as cruel as the cat playing with the mouse. In spite of this, Huizinga insisted that play is free in some important, vague sense. This freedom is closely related to the fact that the activity takes place slightly to the side of what is understood as the reality. The players create a temporality in time and space for themselves. Inside the magic circle, as he called it, other rules count than those on the outside. Nothing implies that the laws of the game world would be any less unjust or violent than is commonplace in the real world. In fact, judging by children's play and computer games, these aspects of our world are nothing short of a treasured source of drama to players. The freedom of players consists in their freedom to enter and leave the make-believe situation at will.

The second classic researcher of play is Roger Caillois. In 1958 he complemented Huizinga's work by introducing a taxonomy of games.[9] He stipulated four broad categories. Competitive play was labelled *agon* and included both intellectual games and athletic sports. Distinctive for agon is that the outcome of the challenge is decided by the skill, strength, and nerve of the contesters. In contrast, *alea* is a group of activities organised around chance. The enjoyment of dice and card games, lotteries etc., is to surrender oneself to fate. It is common that a monetary reward is tied to the outcome in order to heighten the thrill. Agon and aela are ideal types while in real games elements of both are often combined. Quite different again is *mimicry*. This category includes role-playing and masquerades, but could also be extended to include some spectator sports. Caillois suggested that the public identifying themselves with the athletics at championships was a kind of mimicry. The pleasure exists in passing for someone else and borrowing characteristics that the individual are not normally in possession of. The last category listed by Caillois was *ilinx*. The objective of ilinx is to provoke a sensation of dizziness and chock. Rotation, speeding, and falling are examples of transports that seize the player. It is present in some dances, in car and horse racing, and in many children's games. In addition to the four classes, play can be differentiated by its degree of spontaneity. More regulated kinds of games tend to be institutionalised and are sometimes made into fundaments of a society. The ambition of Caillois was to move from a sociology of games to a sociology derived from games. It led him to a less valid attempt at grading the development of civilisations along a succession from mimicry-ilinx to what he considered to be the higher form of agon-aela.

A contemporary, interdisciplinary study on the topic of play has been presented by Gordon Burghardt. His primary concern is with the play of animals but he covers pedagogy, psychology and anthropology as well as biology in order to make his case.[10] From this extensive research, Burghardt boils down five criteria for deciding when an activity can be labelled 'play'. He agrees with the classical writers on play that the activity must be an end in itself. While that does not rule out some derivate good from a play activity, his first criteria calls for at least some elements in the activity that do not have any definable purpose. Play must also fulfil a subjective criterion, namely that the activity is experienced as pleasurable, spontaneous, and voluntary by the player. Thirdly, a playful situation should signal itself as different from a real-life situation, either by that the performance is exaggerated, that it is aborted half-way through, or modified in some other sense. A fourth criterion is that the behaviour in question is occasionally repeated but not rigidly stereotyped. Finally, we can only talk about play when the species is adequately fed, healthy, and free from stress. All five criteria must be met in at least one respect in order for any instance or behaviour to be described as play. As is repeatedly pointed out by Burghardt, however, play is a diverse and situated phenomenon that defies any absolute categorisation.

It is instructive to make a few comparisons between the scholarly definition of play and the activity of hacking. If nothing else, it draws our attention to those places where the theory of play and the hacker movement does not match up. Following Caillois' scheme, we can identify agon, mimicry, and ilinx in the computer underground. Attention might first be drawn to agon because of the flamboyant rivalries within the community. The flame wars hang together with the dissembled identities used by hackers, which suggests a strong element of mimicry. However, if we consider the state of being transfixed in front of the computer screen in a spur of coding to qualify as ilinx, then that must be the heart of hacking. Out of Burghardt's five criteria, the second one is easiest to confirm. Innumerous hackers have attested to that hacking is experienced as fun. The third point, which looks for some exaggeration or modification of standard behaviour to signal the playful intent, might be demonstrated in the subcultural dress codes and hacker jargon. Neither that criteria nor the fourth requirement, which states that a play activity must be repeated over time, are particularly problematic. It is the first and fifth conditions that are troublesome. It is on these two points that play is set apart from work, and, possibly, hackers from programmers. With corporations and governments investing heavily in FOSS development, however, hacking can hardly count as an unproductive pastime any longer. The prospects of earning a living from hacking call into question the fifth condition. If hackers are motivated by the same precariousness that compels an employer to go to work, they can not be said to be free from economic stress when deciding to hack. This is how liberal economists interpret FOSS developers in line with their model of the rational economic man. Hackers are giving away software code on the calculation that it will enhance their career opportunities in the future. While the economist does not by far provide an exhaustive explanation for hacking, his claim is correct in some cases and to some degree. Rising economic stakes in software code blur the boundary between play and work in the computer underground. In Huizinga's opinion this boundary is crucial to the definition of play. What happens inside the magic circle must not effect the real life situation of players, or else they are not playing. But the circle was provisional even to Huizinga since he also believed that play spills over and becomes the foundation of culture, law, trade, etc.

Once labour theory is consulted, we find that the separation of play from work is something of a historical parenthesis. In agrarian society, most undertakings were mingled with an element of playfulness. Work before the breakthrough of capitalism was orientated towards the solving of specific tasks. When the tasks in question had been sorted out, an extended period of celebrations followed. The plebeian culture of eighteenth century England was permeated with secular festivities and hoaxes. With industrialisation came a reorientation where work was seen as a clearly defined space separated from life in general. Mass production required that the work process was subdued under a strict factory regime. The notion of efficiency grew from a production process geared towards producing for a market. Work was no longer defined by the problem to be solved but centred on clock time. Furthermore, since most workers were hired to work for someone else, the hour of the day was cleaved between personal time and the employer's time. In the eyes of the employers, workers playing during work hours was plain idleness, or, worse still, a sign of recalcitrance. Often they were right.[11] The ruling class considered play to be a source of social unrest, since many riots began as carnivals and fairs running amok. Conversely, revolts often turned into festive occasions where restrictive norms were temporarily suspended. From the 1820s and onwards, the English bourgeoisie campaigned against the playful element in working class communities. Reduction of holidays and prohibition of popular recreations were justified with the need to protect public order. A popular icon in the middle class press was the worker who abstained from morally dubious leisure activities in favour of self-betterment and studies. The virtues of self-discipline, delayed gratification, and punctuality were taught to working class children through the education system. By the mid-nineteenth century the playfulness in working class communities had been dampened and the void was filled with commercial entertainment and expanded consumer markets. Agitation and ridiculing of the upper classes disappeared from popular songs and the subversiveness of carnivals faded. Francis Hearn recaptured this historical development and argued that the replacement of self-organised play with pre-manufactured and commodified dreams was a major political defeat for the working class. From then onwards, she suggested, workers' protests rarely transcended the horizon of industrial capitalism. In her article she called for a renewed politicisation of play. Writing in the 1970s, she pointed at a ludic revival in workers' unrest. One example she gave was factory employees sabotaging machinery in order to create free time to play.[12] Instances of outright hostility between management and workers of the kind were on the rise in the 1960s and 1970s. Since then, however, management ideology has prevailed over worker militancy. It has done so in part by a change in strategy, from repressing the play element to catering to the playfulness of workers. The historical end parenthesis has been reached with the decommissioning of the border between play and work in the post-Fordist labour market.

Capitalism has come full circle with the culture industry taking centre stage in the global economy. For as long as production was the foundation of social order and growth, play was marginalised by work. Now it is consumption that drives product-cycles and play is standing in the presence of work. But it is a managed and rationalised imitation of play that faithfully reproduces the power relations in post-modern capitalism. We know this because the escapism offered by the culture industry has an end different from escapism itself. It is a familiar end, namely: The expansion of capital. Adorno and Horkheimer correctly diagnosed the inadequacy of this form of play: "Amusement under late capitalism is the prolongation of work. It is sought after as an escape from the mechanized work process, and to recruit strength in order to be able to cope with it again. But at the same time mechanization has such power over a man's leisure and happiness, and so profoundly determines the manufacture of amusement goods, that his experiences are inevitably after-images of the work process itself."[13] Their distressing comment has proved to be very accurate. It is particularly forthcoming in the world of commercial online gaming. The first networked computer games were developed by enthusiasts in the 1970s. Over the years, companies have moved in to run most of them. More interesting, though, are the market relations that have crystallised from within the game worlds and largely independent of the companies administrating the service. In the beginning, individual players discovered that they could sell virtual items found in Internet games to other players. While some played to forget the drudgery of their workday, others played to make a living without having to go to work. As demand picked up, a secondary market in virtual items emerged that is now catered to by a full-fledged, global industry. Sweatshops are established in Mexico, Eastern Europe, and China for this purpose. The working conditions are no different from in the factory next door where consumer electronics and running shoes are put together. The only difference is that employees are here instructed to gather virtual items in the online game world. Play has in a very literal sense become work. More and more people are employed by industries mainly engaged in providing commodified forms of play. For this reason alone it is warranted that Marxists investigate play in relation to labour struggle.

FLIGHT FROM WORK IN THE WORKFARE STATE

The discussion so far has circled around the problematic of how labour and emancipation relates to each other. It is a question that has divided socialists from the very beginning. One side claims that liberation must occur in labour while the contending view holds that liberation occurs only apart from labour. Depending on which standpoint is taken, the socialist future looks different and the strategies to get there diverge a great deal. The viewpoint that liberation could be found apart from labour grew in popularity in the nineteenth century when hard and hazardous toil was reduced by the introduction of machinery. The hope was part of a general optimism about modernisation and progress that extended far beyond the socialist camp. A techno-utopian vein underpins the liberal cult of economic growth. Indeed, liberalism nourishes the same narrative, where scientific discoveries and general welfare are accumulated over time until scarcity and toil have been abolished. Of course, that day is forever postponed. The utopian goalpost turns instead into a justification for the sacrifices expected of the working class. Socialists ascribing to the same belief differ mainly from liberals in claiming that the conditions for abolishing toil have already been met but that scarcity is prolonged for political reasons. In contrast, for those socialists who argue that liberation occurs in labour, politics has always been the stumbling block. Whether labour is a curse or not depends on the social relations in which the work activity is framed. As hard toil has been scaled back in advanced capitalist societies, it has become clear that distress can be experienced in a thousand more ways than just through physical exhaustion. The subjugated position and the lack of meaning of the tasks performed are sources of grief in their own right, irrespective of what the job consists of. While this statement is obviously true, the implicit assumption, that any task therefore can be enjoyable if it is performed under the right circumstances, might not be.

Labour unions are the main champions for seeking liberation in work. There are two aspects to the strategy of advancing freedom from inside the employment situation. Firstly, it is only as an employee that the organised worker has any say over capital. She has used that power effectively in the past as a lever for improving the living conditions of the working class. Secondly, thanks to legislation pushed by unions on safety rules, coffee breaks, employment security etc., workers have enjoyed a period of greater freedom during work time. For as long as workers had a strong bargaining position it seemed reasonable to think that labour could be liberated from the inside. Since the 1980s, however, the tide has turned against the organised worker. In hindsight, it is dubious if betterments of working conditions and pay rises could ever come anywhere near an emancipation of labour. The core issue is that the expansion of capital is the purpose and determinant of human doing. This state of things has never been seriously challenged by unions since these organisations are too deeply entrenched in the wage relation. Indeed, the disciplining of the work force in the nineteenth century was as much a self-disciplining by the workers as it was taught by the bourgeois class. In order to organise effectively, unions needed to internalise the factory discipline. They have remained instrumental in cementing a work ethic in society and muffling spontaneous, ludic forms of workers' resistance. In spite of this, unions are contributing to the abolishment of the wage relation in an unexpected way. The advancement of labour saving technology is much hastened by the remaining strength of the organised worker. Paradoxically, unions come out as the main factor pushing us in the direction towards an emancipation apart from labour.

Variants of an end-of-work argument have been debated by leftist writers for several decades.[14] Those with a social democratic bent are alarmed by high unemployment rates and the threat to what is left of the Keynesian social contract. More forward-looking thinkers see an opportunity to introduce a citizen wage. The hope of theirs, that the abolition of wage labour could be realised through state policies, is far-fetched to say the least. The point of perspective of government officials is closer to how conservative writers have reacted on the prospect of a jobless future. In *The Cultural Contradictions of Capitalism*, Daniel Bell warned that consumer culture would undermine the protestant work ethic. Consumption and advertising comes with a logic of immediate needs satisfaction while work requires a suspension of gratification. Bell feared that the willingness of the working class to work was in jeopardy. Fred Hirsch was equally concerned that the market economy had run out of steam because of corrosive individualism and an excess of affluence. He remarked that as the mass of consumer goods piled up, the marginal satisfaction from working another hour to earn more purchasing power dropped in relation to spending that extra hour in leisure. This is a troubling thought to contemporary economists. It is a truism among their ranks that social security systems need to be cut back in order to restore economic incentives. In spite of appearances, these worries among conservatives and economists have not been triggered by consumer society or the welfare state. The same discussions surfaced in the English parliament prior to industrialisation, though the causes of demoralisation among the working class looked entirely different. In 1714, John Bellers noticed that: "Our Forests and great Commons (make the Poor that are upon them too much like the Indians) being a hindrance to Industry, and are Nurseries of Idleness and Insolence".[15] He wrote in a time framed by the first enclosure movement and early industrialisation. Enclosure of land created the preconditions for the industrial revolution in at least two respects. Firstly, the land grab resulted in a rapid concentration of wealth. That wealth could later be invested in scaled-up factories. Secondly, the peasantry that had been robbed of their land were now forced to seek employment in the cities. Early capitalists had difficulties in staffing their factories, however, since the proletariat avoided such work if they could. Thieving, begging, vagrancy, or hunting and gathering were possible escape routes. Michael Perelman describes how the efforts to create a reliable labour force out of the peasantry cut like a scissor into the life of the poor: "The first blade served to undermine the ability of people to provide for themselves. The other blade was a system of stern measures required to keep people from finding alternative survival strategies outside the system of wage labor". (*Perelman*, 14) It is thus Perelman construes the harsh bans on vagrancy, begging and hunting. For instance, according to a statute of 1572, begging was punishable by flagellation and mutation. The Waltham Black Acts of 1722 prescribed death penalty for 'pirate' hunting. Though the game laws were initiated by the landed gentry in an attempt to defend their eroding social positions vis-à-vis the urban bourgeoisie, the industrialists quickly recognised the expediency of the statues in speeding up proletarisation. It is the second blade of the scissor that present-day conservatives say must be sharpened. The forests and commons of our modern society are the general welfare system and the excess spilling over and trickling down from consumer markets. Preventing people from free-riding on this abundance in Western countries has become a preoccupation in public debate and state policies. The mission of the workfare state is to make alternative strategies for subsistence so unfavourable to the individual that wage labour is the least despicable option.

We can safely conclude that the abolition of wage relations will never be the product of the capitalist state. This opportunity must be seized from below. The first step is to defect from the labour market. Paulo Virno asserts that there is nothing passive in fleeing. On the contrary, by defection the rules of the game are changed. He is short, though, on concrete suggestions for how to establish means of non-waged subsistence. Going back to farming is not an option. Self-subsistence today looks more like the poor who foraged the wilderness and commons after they had been expelled from their homes. A close cousin is the urban movement of activists who live on the food thrown away by supermarkets.[16] That is a rather unappealing image of utopia to most people. Still, the urban activists demonstrate how niches for material support are opening up in the abundance of consumer society. Recycling waste might not offer a general model for subsistence but it can be of political relevance in a few, restricted cases. This is especially true in the high-tech sector where product-cycles are extremely short. The market value of consumer electronics drops to zero in three to five years. Out-dated computers can be made functional again thanks to FOSS applications with lower hardware requirements. Admittedly, a major impediment to the recycling and continued use of old electronic goods has nothing to do with functionality but hinges on the distinction of newness. In addition to producing free software code, however, the hacker community produces a cultural code that makes FOSS solutions attractive to users. Our argument might be refuted on the grounds that it is an example of self-administrated poverty. The charge is valid, but critics should keep in mind that the dissemination of old computer equipment has been crucial for the growth of the hacker movement among the Western working class and in East European and Third World countries. It has had real political consequences. On a more general note, there can be no ideologically pure method to defect from the wage relation since subsistence has still to be sought inside the capitalist system. These strategies tend to be partial, parasitic, and furtive, attitudes that sit badly with the heroic defeatism of many leftist movements today. Time freed up from work might be had at the expense of others (parents or spouses), by part-timing while self-reducing costs, by living on unemployment grants, or, of particular significance to the FOSS community, by hanging on to the educational system. A few more words have to be said about this last option.

It is as pupils and students that many hackers were first exposed to the idea of hacking. Equally important, as students they had the spare time to play around with computers for no particular reason. The oppositional self-image of the hacker movement is largely defined during these formative years. An account of the ambiguous attitude of hackers towards schooling is given in *the Hacker's Manifesto*. Its author called himself 'the Mentor', itself a reference to the educational milieu. The Mentor rebuked the piecemeal knowledge served in the classroom but made his accusations in the name of a search for fuller knowledge. Campus values set a dent in the computer underground that remains in force when hackers enter the labour market. The special work ethic of hackers is an attitude fostered during college years. We can reflect upon this sentiment more critically by looking back at a prediction made by Samuel Bowles and Herbert Gintis. They studied the educational system in the 1970s when it just began to recruit working class youth.[17] The conclusion they are known for is that higher education sanctions the liberal myth of a meritocracy where class inequalities are coded as differences in intelligence between individuals. Though negative in their persuasion, they kept the possibility open that the expansion of higher education could inflame a renewed struggle. During college years, students enjoy a degree of autonomy that they will be deprived of when becoming employees. As students' expectations of work turn sour, labour conflicts might erupt based on demands for greater autonomy. Daniel Bell dismissed Bowles and Gintis' speculation and the likeliness of a revolt from dissatisfied, former college youths. Students would conform to the system once they encountered the economic hardship of adulthood. If we count student riots and open labour militancy, then Bell has been proven right. But the work ethic of hackers signals a bigger sea-change in sentiments that is in accord with Bowles and Gintis' estimate. The 'organised man' with a safe office job in a large corporation, formerly an ideal to strive for, has become the bogeyman of a younger generation. This image is associated with all the drudgery of capitalist work that was canvassed by Karl Marx. Rarely, though, is self-understanding of the work situation sought in the critique of alienation. It is the meritocratic language of the educational system that defines people's dreams and fears. In the absence of organised and conscious resistance against alienated labour, people are left with individualised strategies of flight. When the longing for self-expression is articulated as an individual ambition rather than a collective, political demand, it verges on narcissism. These sentiments in the workforce are readily taken advantage of by capital to undermine pay levels and working conditions previously secured by unionised labour. No-one can then be surprised that the ideal of self-fulfilment through work is trumpeted in popular culture, job training courses, and management literature. Richard Florida's notion of the 'creative class' is the latest addition. His claim is that work in capitalism is being changed for the better due to the rise of creative professionals. People demand more fulfilling jobs and employers are happy to comply since it increases profits. Florida acknowledges the existence of a dual labour market and admits that the comforts of the creative class owes to the toil of a service class. This injustice is amended by the prospect that the more unfortunate workers too will join the expanding creative class. He declines to consider the reversed scenario, where more and more professionals come to join the service class as the culture industry matures and the labour process is rationalised.

The wind of change is not blowing from the creative professionals, whether that is engineers, designers, or artists. The economic system works reasonably well for these people, or, at the very least, they think that it could if they adapt to the system. In other words, they willingly take the shape of the commodity. Their desires and energies are subdued under commodity relations, individual authorship, and the intellectual property regime. What comes out of the creative class will never go beyond existing social relations. The only changes they produce are changes that keep the essentials in place. Change of a qualitatively different order will have to come from the service class. It is a stratum swelled by disappointed graduates, part-timers, the unemployed and downsized professionals. The 'ethics of the creative class', in Florida's terminology, or 'the hacker spirit' as we know it from Pekka Himanen, is rarely talked about in connection to these people. It wasn't meant for them except as a mirage. But the ideals of self-enrichment are touted for everyone to hear. When it sticks with those who on a daily basis are denied self-enrichment, we get politics. What the service class is in possession of, and the creative class lacks, is dejection in regards to individual career opportunities. Workers in the lower tier of the labour market do not count on getting to express themselves inside the confines of the social division of labour. With the framework provided by the educational system, disappointment about work is understood as a personal failure. But as their numbers grow, the feeling is generalised into a shared, collective experience. From this platform new artistic expressions can be invented. These expressions are novel in the real sense of the word since the social relation is different from the market relation. Production is based on the principle of gift and excess. Freed from the confinements of market exchange, the individual author is stripped away and replaced with a collective authorship. The longing to express oneself is directed towards a collective authorship because, as Marx pointed out long ago, true individuality can only blossom in a community. Play is by default organised in communities and these bodies constitute the cells of play struggle. We will be disappointed, however, if we look for the same determination and coherence as we know from labour organisations. The politics of play must not be judged by the same meter as we use for labour struggles. With these cautions in the back of the mind, we can begin our investigation into how the play of hackers can constitute a political subject.

THE HACKER MOVEMENT AS A CLASS STRUGGLE OR AN IDENTITY CONFLICT

Now when play struggle is established as a concept, we are confronted anew with the same old questions that have boggled labour militants for a century and more. What does the composition of the class look like? How does the subordinated class become aware of its antagonist? Where does class solidarity grow from? And what strengths and weaknesses does the class possess? To make a stab at an answer to these questions we need to re-examine the Marixst theory about the working class. It is a concept that has caused much headache for Marxist scholars. For more than half a decade they have tried to pin down the boundaries of the bourgeoisie as opposed to the workers. The basic definition of the proletariat includes everyone who does not own the means of her subsistence. Such a categorisation ends up being too broad to be of much use in an analysis of modern society. The working class and the middle class can be differentiated only by adding more clauses. When Marxists have tried to specify the working class in more detail the result has been overly narrow. Still more problematic, the objective demarcation of class positions has tended to drift very far from the subjective experience of class belonging.[18] The working class has been fragmentised and grown increasingly heterogeneous, sometimes beyond recognition. Social scientists have responded by abandoning class struggle as a topic of study. Priority is given to identity instead of class as the axis for categorising social conflicts. Specific to class as opposed to identity is that the concept of class is inherent to the concept of productive relations. Marxism holds that the position individuals come to occupy in the scheme of the productive forces forms the practical basis of their capacity for organising as a class.

The linkage between class struggle and the relations of production in classic Marxism was singled out by Ernesto Laclau and Chantal Mouffe, two self-described post-Marxists who have had great influence on changing the perspective within academia and the political left.[19] Early Marxists held on to this claim, Laclau and Mouffe reckoned, because it was a necessary condition for a homogeneous class of proletarians to emerge in the future. Karl Marx and the generation superseding him expected that as capitalism matured and the poverty of the masses worsened, capitalism would end up confronting a unified proletariat. Laclau and Mouffe, on their part, wanted to challenge this notion of a monolithic working class in Marxist theory. Conflicts over class occur when workers as individuals, not as embodiments of economic categories, experience their situation as unjust. By interpreting class as a question of identity they placed it on a par with gender issues, minority campaigns, and civil rights activism. Laclau and Mouffe's moderate vision for the future consisted of a plurality of movements working for what they called a radicalised democracy. In a reply to their reasoning, Slavoj Zizek declared that post-modern identity politics has silently withdrawn any ambitions for a theoretical understanding, much less a political confrontation, of the liberal market economy. Since the post-modern discourse avoids the issue of class, many of the burdens in a class society are excessively attributed to minority belongings. Far from rebelling against the power structure, Zizek charged, multi-culturist politics is consistent with how post-modern capitalism stratifies people in contemporary class society.[20]

Post-Marxism is not the answer to the problem of class if we still are interested in challenging the market economy. We need a theory that acknowledges the continued relevance of labour conflicts and capitalism without letting familiar kinds of class struggle overshadow emerging, unfamiliar ones. A problem with many Marxist accounts of class is that they have taken conditions that were specific to unionised forms of labour resistance as invariably true to capitalism as such. However, since capital undermines the strength of the working class by dissolving its fundaments, we should not be surprised that many assumptions in labour theory have been rendered obsolete by post-modern capitalism. This dynamic is captured in the concept of *cycles of struggle* that is central in the autonomous Marxist tradition. Cycles of struggle describes the ebbs and flows in the conflict level between labour and capital. On the one hand, capital attempts to define a class composition with a particular distribution of intra- and inter-class relations. The goal is to isolate workers from each other by creating internal divisions, such as through chauvinism, nationalism and racism. When capital is successful, the working class is reduced to mere labour power, i.e. the proletariat is subjugated under capital's command. The workers, in their turn, try to redefine internal and external relations and seek a new ground for unity. They regroup as a working class and mount a renewed challenge against their class antagonist. Capital is forced to decompose the former class composition that has now become an obstacle to the valorisation process. Thus begins a new cycle of struggle.[21] An advantage with the theory is that it provides the flexibility to reinterpret the current situation in light of past labour conflicts.

When capitalism is periodised according to cycles of struggle, three major class compositions stand out: The professional worker, the mass worker, and the social worker. Of course, this categorisation is provisional and should be seen as hegemonic but not homogenic of the working class in the given period. At the turn of the last century the class struggle was spearheaded by the professional worker. He was skilled and relatively independent towards his employer. The professional worker stood apart from the majority of the pauperised working class and often he defended his privileges at the expense of women and less fortunate male workers. Still, the small strata of skilled and militant craftsmen caused trouble to their employers. Capital made itself independent of the professional worker by developing a semi-automated production line. The Fordist factory could be run by a labour force with moderate to low skill levels. Unlike the professional worker, the mass worker had no specialist training to fall back on. Instead he learned to increase his collective strength by unionising the whole shop floor. Mass organisation was facilitated by the Fordist labour process where a large number of workers congregated in a single location and where the technical qualifications of the operators were levelled to the same low point. In the 1960s the power of the mass worker stood at its zenith. The beginning of post-Fordism could roughly be dated to the same decade. Capital attacked the power of the mass worker by removing its bastion of strength, the factory site. In post-Fordist capitalism the production process is dispersed to the whole of society. Antonio Negri proposed at one point in his intellectual career that this creates the foundation for a new subjectivity among the proletariat. The social worker is taking the place of the mass worker. Characteristic of the social worker is that her labour power exists in communication and is distributed to the whole of the social basin. Negri asserted that the categorisation of the social worker must be equally open-ended as her work process.[22]

The theory of cycles of struggle gives an explanation to the surge of information systems. Electronic networks and digitalisation have played a central part in the restructured labour market. Factory jobs are replaced with work-at-home-schemes, telecommuting, and freelance contracts. Those labour theoreticians who suspect that information systems have been advanced to weaken the working class are not entirely off the mark. Unfortunately, however, they tend to stop at condemning the current situation. But the history of resistance doesn't end at the downturn of the cycle. At the verge of completion of the techniques intended to fragmentise the working class, a new subjectivity is materialising on top of the very same infrastructure. The one merit commonly granted to the Internet by left-leaning sceptics is its usefulness for linking isolated pockets of opposition. These appraisals have mainly been confined to the mobilisation of street protests and grassroots media campaigns. For instance, the surge of the anti-globalisation movement in late 1990's, crowned by the coordinated, global demonstration against the U.S. invasion of Iraq on 15th February 2003, would be inconceivable without the Internet. The matter gains in gravity when we consider that the computer network is not just a means of communication but an instrument of labour. The unification of labour power over the computer network might provide a stepping stone for a new round of struggle. With these reflections in the back of the mind, FOSS developers appear to be a fairly good approximation of Negri's concept of the social worker.

For the sake of clarification, we better spell out how this idea differs from McKenzie Wark's proposal of a 'hacker class'.[23] He uses the word 'hacker' in a metaphorical way without directly referring to existing hackers. Our ambition is to understand the concrete movement of hackers with help of the concept of class. There will be readers, some of them hackers, who will object to such an undertaking. Is it not flawed, they will ask, to frame a movement that is organised around a subcultural identity in theories about class? Without doubt, most studies in the field have analysed hacking as an identity movement. The question merits a considerate response. Against the argument of post-Marxists and other propagators of identity politics, we contain that the multiplication of identity-based conflicts in contemporary society does not necessarily contradict the Marxist concept of class. The importance of identity movements owes to that subjectivity in post-modern capitalism has been 'put to work', to borrow an expression from Paulo Virno. Aesthetic innovations are not only made in the factory, but in the school, in the street, in the community, etc. And, of course, as concerns the FOSS community, innovation is not 'merely' aesthetical but extends into technology as well. In other words, subcultures have become sites of production in their own right. The connection between social conflicts and productive relations is still in force. It is therefore warranted to talk about class antagonism when referring to struggles within the hacker movement.

CLASS CONSCIOUSNESS AND THE PLAY STRUGGLE OF HACKERS

Framing the hacker movement in terms of class struggle leaves us with a number of practical difficulties. A major one is the limited, political outlook of hackers. The issues cherished in the computer underground, free access to information, the right to anonymity on the computer network, campaigns against state censorship, etc., are restricted in scope. At times these demands clash with broader political priorities. The tension can be read out from dwindling debates on mailing-lists between techies and hacktivists. To a techie, the supreme freedom is the freedom of the computer user. Needless to say, that freedom doesn't always coincide with freedom defined in a more general sense. For instance, during the demonstrations in Seattle in 1999, a group of hacktivists calling themselves Electro-Hippies launched a Denial-of-Service attack against WTO's servers. Techies protested that blocking access to an Internet server was a form of censorship that restricted their freedom to visit the site. The role of WTO in the world was quite beyond their horizon. To be fair, labour struggle has had its fair share of the same dilemma. It is for this reason that labour theory stresses the development of a class consciousness so that workers can rise above immediate and particularistic concerns. A universalistic approach is assumed to be necessary to match the latitude of capital. However, the concept of class consciousness is fraught with problems of its own. Various themes on false consciousness have surfaced in the century-long Marxist debate. Such statements inevitably put the spotlight on the intellectuals who claim to know what the correct point of view for the proletariat is. Post-modern scholars have reminded us of the dangers of the birds-eye perspective. It is a source of power in its own right. The warning is apt given the historical record, but it comes with dangers of a different kind. If we choose to see only what is immediately in front of our eyes we will be blind to the powers that act behind the backs of individuals. In order to unmask systematic forms of domination we need to have a provisionary idea about the totality of social relations. The trouble for Marxists has traditionally been how this theoretical knowledge is passed on to, or, spontaneously emerges, in the proletariat.

Georg Lukács' *History and Class Consciousness* is a milestone among the many attempts at resolving these matters. He objected to an empiricist approach to the problematic, asserting that the class consciousness of the proletariat is not the sum of their convictions and beliefs. Class consciousness cannot be read out of surveys, interviews, or statistics over the individuals in question. Only in its relation to the society as a totality are a class and its expressions intelligible. Lukács claimed that for the first time in history it has become possible to acquire knowledge about objective class positions. The reason was that in capitalism the economic class interests are brought to the fore as the motor of history. Unlike insurgencies by plebs and mobs in the past, the proletariat could reach a consciousness of a different order and become truly revolutionary. That is, their victory would not merely replace the ruling class but abolish class society as such. This task would demand of the proletariat the maturity to integrate their immediate interests with a total view and relate it to the final goal of overcoming capitalism. At this moment, Lukács declared, social struggle is reflected in a struggle for class consciousness. Men have a false concept of the world due to the reification taking place in market society. Specific to capitalism is that the commodity has subsumed all of society under general commodity exchange. This creates a reified point of perspective where relations between men take the appearance of relations between objects. Bourgeois minds are reared in this second nature. Indeed, the ruling class cannot see the truth about class society without abdicating from power. The proletariat, in contrast, has the advantage of looking at the class society 'from the centre'. In the commodity the worker recognises herself, that is, her status as a commodity on the labour market. While the bourgeoisie can only gain knowledge about an object from a distance, the knowledge of the proletariat is the self-consciousness of the object. It was an elegant argument presented by Lukács but not without inconsistencies. He made precautions that the working class might be led astray. The reformism of social democracy and trade unions were examples of a fraction of the working class that merely negated some aspects of capitalism without aspiring to a critique of the whole. Thus, it was still necessary to theorise ahead of the proletariat. And, in the end, Georg Lukács came down as a supporter of the idea of a vanguard party.[24]

The unified, revolutionary class imagined by Lukács is a far shot from present-day reality, and nowhere is it more remote than in the computer underground. No-one can represent the hacker community since there are no clear borders where it begins and ends. A party line is quite unthinkable. That is not to say that the hacker movement is an undifferentiated space of individuals where all have made up their own minds independently, though that thought appeals to the voluntaristic ethos of many hackers. Representative bodies exist inside the community and exercise great influence over it. The Free Software Foundation has a particularly strong position. It is the overseer over the General Public License, it has a fairly organised member base with a shared sense of purpose, and it fronts a charismatic leader in Richard Stallman. He is outspoken about the intent not only to spread free software in society but to educate hackers on the ethical and political dimension of doing so, in other words, to make hackers 'community conscious'. For this reason, the Free Software Foundation is in constant feud with another camp that seeks to minimise the political issue. Here we find the Open Source initiative, the publisher O'Reilly, various authors in the field, computer magazines like Wired, and many of the software firms. Money is an important factor but it doesn't carry all the weight. Other sources of influence are distinguished hackers and project leaders, the discussions taking place at computer clubs, hacker conferences and mailing lists, and close-knit groups with hacktivist, artistic or feminist agendas. Adding to the confusion, there are considerable regional differences in the importance of these many sources. Though the computer network is global, much of the discussions are confined to language areas. The Chaos Computer Club is an institution in Germany for more than twenty years back. In Italy there is an overlap between the anarchist left and the hacker movement due to hacklabs and media studios being set up in occupied buildings, so called social centres. And the closeness of Silicon Valley makes an imprint on hackers on the American west coast. In other words, the hacker community is extremely heterogeneous and is better thought of as a 'movement of movements', in the same way as the Internet is sometimes referred to as a 'network of networks'. Contacts with corporations, governments, and the general public are conducted through the many organisations within the hacker community. Additionally, the self-image of the hacker community is constantly being negotiated in these forums. By presenting and interpreting hackers in one or another way the organisations, ventures, discussion groups etc. seek to influence the direction of the hacker movement. Sides are taken depending on if one cares to differentiate between lawful, white-hat hackers and lawbreaking, black-hat hackers, if one speaks of free software or open source, and, more generally, if FOSS development is framed as a political concern, a moral standpoint, or a matter of sound business practice. The contest over the consciousness of the community bears little resemblance to Lukács' struggle for class consciousness though. A few hacktivist groups and discussion lists are pushing for a radicalisation of the movement. But they are not in need of building consensus and they can afford to take a fringe position. All the major players, Free Software Foundation included, converge on a liberal rhetoric when making their case. If an argument favours a reduction of private property and market relations, it is usually phrased as a defence of civil liberties or is veiled behind the notion of information exceptionalism. The politics of the hacker movement centres on a few issues that everyone agrees upon, in particular that information should be freely accessible. Support for these narrowly defined goals can be drawn from many ideological camps on the condition that other controversial topics are left out of the picture. If a more elaborate thought model is required to flesh out the argument, that model tends to be *ad hoc* and apolitical. The information age narrative fulfils this task elegantly. Internal politics in the hacker community leads away rather than towards an articulated analysis of society as a whole.

It is not primarily in debates, however, that hackers' concept of the world takes shape. The organisations are fronts of the movement, but the real momentum lies with the people who write source code, crack encryptions, and hack into computer systems. It is here that Georg Lukács has interesting things to say to us. He stressed how praxis intervenes in thought and gives rise to class consciousness. In an activity new concepts are born that challenge the norms by which those activities were previously understood. In the context of this book, we could say that the verb 'hacking' is bigger than the individuals calling themselves hackers. The statement holds true in a strict numerical sense and in relation to outcomes. Many people who hack technology do so without ascribing to the hacker identity. Employees crashing the computer system of their employer are a case in point. It must be remembered that hacking is subversive only to the extent that it overflows the confines of both professions and identity groups, opening up the possibility to interfere with technology to everyone. Hence, the politics of hacking is not identical to the viewpoints among those people identifying themselves with the hacker movement, nor can it be exhaustively summed up in a reference to their class, ethnicity, or gender bias. These two points are crucial to make in a time when political analysis has been replaced with opinion polls and quotas of identity belongings. A serious attempt to dissect the relevance of the hacker movement should first and foremost start by looking at the practice. This practice becomes intelligible when it is weighed against the social totality. In other words, hacking and the hacker movement must be examined in their relation to capitalism. Without taking account of the usefulness of software algorithms and computer networks in the global economy, for example, we can't make much sense of the computer underground. Of course, objective criteria do not go all the way in explaining the politics of hacking. The ability of hackers to make history hangs together with them becoming conscious of themselves and their class antagonist.

The central problem for Lukács was if the same overview, which Marxist theory aspires to, can grow from the experience of workers. As we saw before he answered positively, though he was not entirely convinced himself. With regard to some occupations, journalists for instance, he made concessions to the power of reification in penetrating the human soul. With Foucault, we have become more aware of the productive aspects of power, and thus, of the commodity, in shaping the human subject. Putting it simply, people adapt to a life of wage labour since the wage relation is all there is. It seems highly improbable that the proletariat would reach the same standpoint as Lukács had. He needed them to do so in order for them to shoulder their historical mission of ending class society. The requirements look quite different though if the proletariat is not motivated by the final revolution but 'just' the revolution of everyday life. Then the local knowledge gained from practice can be the most applicable. Over the years, hackers have proved themselves capable of navigating in a hostile terrain of proprietary software vendors, copyright law, and whispering campaigns. This has been possible even though the multitude of hackers are led by no headquarter and their understanding of the system which besieges them is a ragbag of information age lore, technological determinism, and high-tech libertarianism. The reason is that their struggle is one of tactics, in Michel de Certeau's sense of the term, and not strategy, as is the case with the captains of industry and the generals of the vanguard party. Certeau developed his idea about tactics versus strategy when examining consumer resistance in a consumer society. When scales are weighted so heavily against the weaker part that she appears to be voided of any power to resist, she still keeps a space open through tactic manoeuvres. By constantly being in movement, by changing directions erratically and by making decisions on the spur of the moment, her path is nondenumerable to the antagonist, and, thus, she enjoys a limited freedom in the midst of social control.[25] Hacking, that is, the bending of a pre-existing system into serving a different end than it was designed for, is the ideal example of a tactic, bottom-up act of resistance.

In their local operations, hackers draw first and foremost from intimate familiarity with programming languages and computer architecture. One might suspect that these spontaneous acts of resistance lack any sense of direction. It is true that hackers are not guided by a shared ideology with a defined goal. Nonetheless, some sort of direction emerges due to the common source of distress that they are fleeing from. The same driving force that motivated them to become hackers in the first place is providing orientation in their day-to-day activity, namely: The flight from the boredom of commodity relations. Alienation, both as a consumer and as a worker, is the motor of their struggle. The joy of a less alienated existence encourages people to have more of the same. Play therefore has a direction pointing towards the expansion of non-commodified relations. Needless to say, those attempts are captured and fed back into the capitalist machine. But commercialisation is not uncontested, and recuperation is frustrated by new escapes. Play struggle mushrooms again and again, in new and unrecognisable forms, and often without being acknowledged as a political force. Since play is picked up spontaneously, political innocence of the practitioners is a given. Indeed, ignorance towards the outside world is almost implied by the concept of play. Huizinga, Caillois, and the other students of the subject, all stressed that play must be an end in itself. If play is instead a means for ideological ends, the activity is not play at all but suspiciously akin to work. Herbert Marcuse made a similar reflection on the relation between art and revolution during the social upheavals in the early twentieth century. The role of aesthetics was an ongoing source of tension between artists and militants. When art was subjugated under political goals its power to assist the revolution was lost together with its independence. Thus, it turns out that techies have a valid case against the hacktivists.

What we are wrestling with is the old sticking point of how a universalistic perspective can emerge and become one with practice without techies having to take instructions from hacktivists and intellectuals. There is definitely a need to anticipate, if not a totality, then at least a plan of action going beyond the immediate. Francis Hearn affirmed that play can bring about emancipation but it has to be informed by critical theory. She immediately inserted that if we are to avoid the petrifaction of a vanguard party and the reproduction of old power structures in new cloths, the critical theorists must themselves become playful. Her note is very apt. She does assume, however, that critical theory must be delivered from an outside. We ought not to rule out the possibility that the hacker movement catches up with politics on its own. Playful doing, simply from being an end in itself, is destabilising to a system built on the principle that everything and everyone is a means for something else. The subversiveness of play is particularly forthcoming in the hacker movement, as opposed to, for instance, the fan fiction subculture. This owes to the importance of computer networks and software algorithms to the command structure of post-Fordist capitalism. Capital needs to maintain its control over information systems and therefore reacts with arbitrary arrests of hackers, laws forbidding pirate sharing, the introduction of Digital Rights Management technology, and the list goes on. More subtle, but no less corrosive, is corporate involvement in FOSS development which works towards the replacement of community norms with monetary incentives. Furthermore, as competition between FOSS firms hardens, we can expect to see attempts to streamline development projects in the same way as in-house labour was rationalised before. State repression and capital's micro-management of FOSS projects will radicalise parts of the hacker movement. Thus the hacker community is compelled to constitute itself as a community-for-itself. Hackers have no choice if they are to keep playing. It is this motive that ensures that their politics will be of a different order than the politics originating in ideological convictions. An indication of what such a mobilisation could look like is suggested by the method by which the warez scene organises itself against the intellectual property regime. Teams of crackers are racing each other in releasing most warez to the community. Resistance has here become a game. Politics, just like work, is subjugated under the play-drive.

HACKING CAPITALISM

The fact that a loosely knit community of tinkerers can rival the research departments of the world's largest corporations, epitomised in GNU/Linux versus Windows, is quite remarkable. The significance of this observation pivots on the expectation that the success of FOSS development can be exported to other walks of life. Ultimately, we are enticed by the thought that the FOSS model could become the dominant mode of organising labour in the future. Evidence in support of such a scenario, however, is left wanting. The scalability of FOSS projects has no comparison elsewhere in the economy. The ability to coordinate a large number of contributors is facilitated by the fact that the whole development process of software code takes place in communication networks. We are accustomed to encounter the same argument in the simplistic, but effective, language of information exceptionalism. It says that FOSS development is unique because of the unique properties of information in contrast to tangible, material resources. Our discussion on the hacker movement has stayed away from this dichotomy between virtual and real space. It is a reified perspective and subject to the errors of ideological thinking that Georg Lukács criticised so thoroughly. To the bourgeois, he charged, history stops unfolding just before the present 'now'. If they became aware of that those commonsense facts and 'general laws' that they abide to are just moments in a process, and that this process is ongoing, they would also have to admit that the class rule of the bourgeoisie is finite. In regards to our discussion, the words of Lukács highlight that the border between intangible and tangible resources is in perpetual flux and constantly negotiated. That which now appears as unique circumstances behind the success of the FOSS movement might one day encompass the whole economy. In previous chapters we have argued that there are strong economical and political interests behind making ever more of the world subject to digitalisation, and, thus, it is a trend likely to continue in the same direction in the future.

At the time when Herbert Marcuse expressed his regrets over the inability of imagination and poetry to have real outcomes in the world, the computer industry was just about to prove him wrong. A quote from *The Mythical Man Month* sets us on track. The book was written in 1975 by Fred Brooks and is still mandatory reading to students in computer science. The opening paragraphs by which Brooks introduced the subject to his readers ought to be studied with Marcuse in the back of the mind: "The programmer, like the poet, works only slightly removed from pure thought-stuff. He builds his castles in the air, from air, creating by exertion of the imagination [. . .]. Yet the program construct, unlike the poet's words, is real in the sense that it moves and works, producing visible outputs separate from the construct itself."[26] Again we must caution ourselves against fetishising computer technology. Software code is interesting to bring up only because it serves as a cursor of the general intellect. It illustrates to us how the mind has grown into a productive force in its own right. Computer languages are one of many examples underlining the observation by Ernest Mandel that the superstructure has been mechanised. Art, language, and imagination are rationalised and put to work. Conversely, however, technology is aestheticised and put to play. A hacker does not speak about a program script in terms of functionality. Neat source code is a matter of good taste. Aesthetics is the organising principle of their play, which, mostly by accident, also produces working computer applications. A paraphrase of Friedrich Schiller can underline the ramifications of what just has been said: The object of hackers' play is the beauty of the baud and its goal is software freedom. This reasoning is also consistent with how Marcuse envisioned that the instrumentality of technology could be resolved in modern society. Technology had to be returned to its origin in craftsmanship. Since the day when *techné* was split between useful arts and fine art proper, technological development has been defined by utilitarianism, while poetry has been relegated to the domain of the unreal and inconsequential. At least that is how things generally come across. A closer look will reveal that a play element has persisted throughout the history of technology. To the side of industrial and military innovations, there have also been innovations made purely for the sake of amusement. These technologies flourished in the renaissance courts. It was here that engineers of the day found their outlet since they were kept at bay from entering the industry by trade guilds. Architecture, gardens, water works, pyrotechnics, and automata are some examples. Moreover, to the list can be added cabinets, bestiaries, and scientific experiments that were as much performed as researched.[27] It is this marginal and aristocratic lineage of technological development that has been picked up, and, to some degree, democratised, by hackers, by radio amateurs, and hobbyists.

The first generation of hackers nurtured a dream of making computer resources accessible. Members in the Homebrew Computer Club envisioned a small computer 'able to run on the kitchen table'. They were in part motivated by a desire to play with those machines; in part they were aware of the political importance of democratising computer technology. Present-day hackers pursue the same mixture of play and politics within the technological platform of small computers and open-edited software handed down to them by the first generation. The passion for writing software code is contagious and easily spills over to other fields of doing. A popular sideline within the computer underground is to build mechanical replicas of classic computer games and exhibit these gadgets at hacker conferences. The step is a short one to more ambitious hardware projects, such as the OScar project. It is a collaboration between car engineers and tinkerers to design an 'open source car'. What is gradually taking shape within the hacker movement at this moment is an extension of the dream that was pioneered by the members of the Homebrew Computer Club. It is the vision of a universal factory able to run on the kitchen table. The idea is not as far-fetched as it first might seem. Development trends towards flexible production within industry are pushing in the same direction. Researchers at the MIT laboratory, for instance, have experimented with computer-aided manufacturing facilities small enough to fit into a single room and easy enough to operate by lay people after a short, introductory course. The facility can be used to cut, solder, cast, compress, etc. almost any material into a finished product.[28] Likewise, a group of engineers in Brighton try to construct a 'self-replicating rapid prototyper' that can mould everyday items out of plastic. The machine is meant to be able to make the parts out of which a second copy of the machine can be assembled. In a nod to the hacker movement, the blueprints of the self-replicating rapid prototyper have been licensed under GPL. The performance and significance of these research projects are open to dispute. In most cases, hardware designs developed from below will proceed through the novel combination of mass-produced, off-the-shelf electronic parts. More important than the individual technologies is that these dreams are now being articulated. This is not how cadres of revolutionaries visualised the 'expropriation of the expropriators'. Nonetheless, the desire for a 'desktop factory' amounts to the same thing as the reappropriation of the means of production. The seizure is unfolding as new productive relations are being invented in play.

Summary

We have finally arrived at the question that has guided our long journey through the computer underground: what is the relevance of hacking to the future of capitalism? Our reply must be the same as the one given by a minister of Mao Tsetung, when he allegedly was asked about the relevance of the French revolution. He answered that it was too early to tell. It is much too early to say anything for certain about the FOSS development movement. And yet, we wouldn't have gone through all the effort without some hunch, and, perhaps, some hope. This study has been a search for hope in a time permeated by cynicism and opportunism towards the possibility of radical social change. The peril here is not so much to become dejected as to jump at false promises of hope. For sure, optimism is plentiful in the futurist literature where utopian longings are tied to the development of information technology. Hope is cheaply had which only testifies to its high marketability. Hardly any more convincing than the futurists are the post-modern, left-of-the-centre academics, who seek to restore hope through a general disregard of power relations that are more tangible than those flowing from the interpretation of texts. The invisibility of capitalist relations in the writings of these authors is deceptive. Capitalism has become omnipresent to the point of disappearing from their horizon altogether. If we want an analysis that gives some gravity and proportion back to the world, we must insist on bringing to the fore the formative power of commodity relations, private property, and the social division of labour. The hacker movement can be of assistance in this attempt. By putting some distance between their doing and the wage relation, FOSS developers have set the contours of the capitalist relation in relief. Concurrently, however, if we are to abide to the pledge of proportionality, we better not make too much out of hacking. Placed next to the likely outcomes of global warming, the injustices committed against the global poor, or, the force of a hangar ship, the hacker movement is a very minor player indeed. The relevance of hacking to capitalism, if any, must be sought in a potentiality that points beyond the marginal existence of the hacker community and the issues debated there.

The emphasis of this book, in affinity with our mission statement above, has been on the totality of social relations that is inscribed in the practice of hacking. We have argued that facts and polls about the hacker movement can be assessed correctly only with an eye on the alienation of labour in capitalism. This claim is valid both for the cracker breaking into computers and for the hacker writing software code. Hacking, for short, ought to be understood in terms of class struggle. It is an odd proposition to make about an activity that diverges so far from what is usually considered to be political, and stranger still to hear in a time when class struggle as a concept has almost disappeared from the social sciences. The computer underground, along with the Internet, came to maturity in a decade when despair had overtaken most of the traditional left. A short breeze of May 1968 was sensed with the rise of the anti-globalisation movement. The collapse of the World Trade Organisation summit in Seattle in 1999 gave activists around the world the impression that they could put a halt to neo-liberal expansion. But the spirit was soon to be extinguished under escalated violence, even before the turning point of September 11th. The anti-globalisation movement has since been set on the defensive by a world order rewritten by War on Terror. The millions of people, who marched on the streets against the invasion of Iraq in 2003 to no avail, merely demonstrated the ineffectiveness of this kind of protest. In the old days, the threat of labour strikes put teeth into the manifestations of the left. It was a threat that could move mountains. Welfare provisions, universal suffrage and the rights of minorities are some very concrete gains of working class struggles in the past century. Nowadays, attempts by labour to create hold-ups in the flow of capital are quickly isolated and the disturbances generated by struggle give new energy to the adversary. When every point in the circulation of capital is productive to capital, it becomes hard even to see what unionised resistance could mean. We could go as far as to say that the post-modern condition of late capitalism boils down to this loss of labour's former bargaining strength.

The situation is not as novel as it first might appear. With a longer perspective, we will find that the period when the strength of organised labour could match the power of the ruling class was something of a parenthesis in history. Neither is the demise of the dominance of unionised struggle all bad. In order to contest capital's supremacy, labour organisations had to be in agreement with their opponent on the terms of conflict. The existence of the wage relation, and, thus, the prevalence of the social division of labour, were conditions taken for granted by both sides. Disputes were concentrated to decisions over the exchange rate of wage labour. The deadlock on these issues has been broken and we are therefore freer to re-conceptualise our critique of capitalism. A sign hereof is renewed scholarly interest in miscellaneous dissent that for long had been overshadowed by the pre-eminence of trade unionism. Historians are unearthing struggles that took place in class societies previous to the forming of a strong, coherent working class-for-itself. Concurrently, activists and theorists take inspiration from eighteenth and nineteenth century insurgencies of sabotage and refusal when envisioning tactics for the future. A recurring theme in this literature is studies of the mob. Since the poor lacked a foothold in the capitalist production process, their negotiation strength vis-à-vis the ruling class consisted mainly in the threat of violence. Historian Eric Hobsbawm has famously described machine breaking as a kind of 'collective bargaining by riot'. Such demands were most effectively delivered in big numbers. No less important was that the mob provided some anonymity in confrontations with the enemy. The individuals could not as easily be singled out for retaliation when they acted as a crowd. These historical reflections on anonymity versus identification are actualised once more in the debate about Internet surveillance. Dissent against intellectual property, for instance, is facilitated by that individuals can seek refuge from law authorities in the anonymity of the computer network. The politics of hacking have quite a few things in common with eighteenth century plebeian struggle. Similar to those insurgencies, campaigns by hackers against government eavesdropping, censorship and copyright law are often furtive, spontaneous and leaderless in character.

But the intent here is not to suggest a historical return to old forms of social conflict. While archaic elements have refigured in this narrative, the social bandit, the Luddite, etc., the aim of the discussion is to highlight the opportunities of a renewed cycle of struggle. These are treacherous waters to pass since so many claims for newness have been made in association with information systems. It better be stated once more, we are not expecting anything new to come from the technology. What we are looking for, the holy Grail in this day and age, is a substitute for labour's threat of blocking bottlenecks in the production process. The potency of that threat has faded as networked capital has turned every stage of production into a node subject to redundancy. It does not follow that all resistance therefore is futile, but the conditions for fighting capitalism have been radically transformed. An aspect of this new terrain is captured in the hacker proverb: "don't resist what you can circumvent". The saying suggests that the capitalist relation itself has turned into a node in the network subject to redundancy. An example of how circumvention works in practice can be found in conflicts over filesharing networks. Markets in information are not attacked directly by hackers but are rendered superfluous when the same goods are made available for free elsewhere on the Internet. In their challenge against intellectual property law, the preferred strategy is to decentralise the flow of information and leave authorities without any targets to pursue. Hackers routing around markets, private property, and the state apparatus are promising cases in themselves. What makes it all possible is something even more enticing. The hacker movement has demonstrated how to disconnect capital from the production process, at least in a restricted sense and as far as the production of computer algorithms is concerned. Of course, we are talking about a potentiality in hacking. The actually existing hacker community has neither disembodied itself from capitalist relations nor expressed a strong will to do so. Nevertheless, without necessarily intending it, they have set an example by which we can extrapolate an alternative to capitalism, and concretise some ideas about how to get there. In the theoretical sections of the book, three longstanding objections against the likelihood of a socialist society have been confronted. Chapter four responded to the notion, cherished by post-modern critics, that semiotic consumption has dashed all hopes of transcending scarcity. The following chapter spun on Marx's old prediction that the proletariat could out-perform capital in terms of productivity, a belief running contrary to the common wisdom about the superiority of the market economy. A third classic stumbling block for socialists was discussed in the chapter on circulation, namely: how to allocate resources without the guidance of neither a market price nor state planning. Our answers to these questions derived in one way or another from the social relations that organise the activity of hackers. Those relations and that activity we have elected to call 'play'.

The strategy of blockades and that of circumvention refer back to the disposition of labour struggle in contrast to play struggle. These two types of struggle differ chiefly in how the proletariat relates to its class antagonist. Labour unions build their strength on a social relation where both parts are tied together in mutual dependencies. Sit-downs and strikes are effective to the extent that capital requires the workers to work. The workers, in turn, are for economical and social reasons bound to resist capital, backs to the wall, in their function as employees. In the last few decades, capital has got the upper hand over its antagonist by fleeing into the so-called weightless economy. New methods for valorisation have been created in the circulation of capital that, though, in the final instance deriving from living labour, do not depend on any one particular site of production. Partly because of this course of events, and partly due to the flight from alienation by the working class, living labour too is distancing itself from the employment status. We have studied the FOSS development model as a showcase hereof. Labour activities organised outside the wage relations are characterised by a high degree of freedom of movement. Hackers are free to move in and out of a development project in the same way a player may enter and leave the magic circle of a game. From the perspective of traditional struggle, mobility of this sort is a weakness that undermines the collective strength of organised labour. Individual members must be discouraged from defecting from the common cause, as is typified in the stigmatisation of blackfoots. In the hacker community, on the contrary, mobility is a precondition for collective existence and is a right to be defended. Indeed, the right of any individual to leave and/or fork a development project is one of the key points of FOSS licenses. The freedom of users to vote with their feet puts a restraint on how power can be exercised inside the community, thus it helps to maintain the community as we know it. Still, one might for good reasons doubt the fortitude of a group where no economic hardship forces its members to stick together and endure. But the objection could be turned around. The fact that individual hackers take the risk of heavy fines and imprisonment when defying political and economic interests, even though they could easily walk away or sell out, tells us something about the quality of play struggles. That is not to say that hackers are exceptionally loyal to their cause. Quite the opposite, what is intriguing is that defection and opportunism is anticipated and built into the calculation from the start. The hacker movement sustains its singularity in the midst of a perpetual flux of additions and loses of individual members. Scaring individuals away or paying them off, as capital frequently do, buys no decisive advantage over the movement since the individuals in question are quickly sidestepped. The principle of mobility that organises the hacker community internally translates into a mode of dealing with external adversaries, that is, the strategy of circumvention. Rather than entering heads-on confrontations with opposing forces, hackers route around obstacles. The class antagonist is made irrelevant to the point that one acts as if no bipolar conflict existed to begin with. From the perspective of traditional labour struggle, no doubt, such radical disinterest among hackers looks no different from political naivety.

Skeptics might object that the significance of computer hobbyists has been blown out of proportion, much in the same way as some post-modern scholars have overstated the importance of consumer resistance and conflicts over representation. A few readers will have Theodor Adorno's denouncement of the radio amateur ringing in their ears: "As radio ham he becomes the discoverer of just those industrial products which are interested in being discovered by him. He brings nothing home which would not be delivered to his house"[1] The radio amateur was included in Adorno's rant against what he considered to be a consumerist attitude among music listeners. The commodity triumphs when the retarded listener attempts to revolt against fetishism only to succumb more deeply into the pseudo-activities of fandom, Adorno charged back in 1938. He was not wrong in bundling together consumers of popular culture and users of home electronics. All the suspicions that consumer politics give rise to can with some justice be thrown at the politics of the hacker movement as well. Both draw from an individualistic, liberal and commonsensical worldview, and, thus, are vulnerable to recuperation. Nonetheless, we have previously speculated in that repression and micro-management by the dominant power structure will impose a different reality upon the hacker community. The reason is the greater relevance of the dealings of the tinkerer compared to the average consumer. This claim can be illustrated by a note published by the BBC in 2003. The media network reported that a hobbyist in New Zealand, previously a member of the model air plane community, had decided to put his skills to a different end. He claimed to have built a do-it-yourself cruise missile capable of carrying a ten kilo warhead and with the range of 100 kilometers. The design was similar to a German V1 rocket but with improved accuracy due to an added gps-system. According to the hobbyist, all the components had been ordered on e-Bay and it had cost him less than $5000. The existence and performance of the weapon is not confirmed, but the threat was serious enough to alert the U.S. and New Zealand governments.[2] The anecdote provides a reality check when judging the political significance of hacking. We must decide against Adorno's debunking that tinkerers never bring home any products other than those that would have been delivered to them by the industry anyway. The alignment between the democratisation of the means of production, on one side, and the democratisation of the means of destruction, on the other, is quite evident from the example above. The distinction between production and destruction comes down to a point of perspective. Hence, the efforts by intellectual property advocates to equate pirate sharing with terrorism is not without a grain of truth, though the connection looks very different from how it is presented by them. The War on Terror signals that the state has lost its violence monopoly and that loss is analogous to capital's lost monopoly over the production process. We would have fooled ourselves to think that the means of production could be expropriated in a peaceful manner. Question is if the restraint on violence that has been upheld in developed, capitalist countries, partly due to the fact that the class antagonists are tied together by mutual dependencies, will count when the capitalist class confronts an opponent that is external to the valorisation process? Our talk about play and aesthetics should not lead anyone on to think that what is at stake in this struggle is of lesser gravity.

The tradition of labour struggle is simultaneously continued and transcended in play struggle. Labour conflicts and conflicts centred on play relate to each other in the same way as the struggle against unfreedom relates to the struggle for freedom. The two are not identical as it first might seem, and, indeed, occasionally one contradicts the other. A case in point is the conflict of interest between professional artists and fan media producers. Some of the tension between the two owes to capital's strategy of pitching volunteer labour against in-house staff. While defending their working conditions, however, professionals also defend their position vis-à-vis amateurs and, thus, they inadvertently come to brace up the division of labour in society. Putting cultural workers out of work is a step towards putting culture back into the life of everyone else. The same goes for user-centred development models where decisions over technological development are spread outside the confines of the wage relation. As a result, the influence of white-coated, Taylorist professionals and the veto of investment funds and governments over technology is rendered less important. Play struggle, while confused and weak at present, takes us a bit closer towards abolishing the social division of labour. This is, in the final analysis, the potential of hacking. In the future, perhaps we can do one thing today and another tomorrow, to fish in the afternoon and hack computers after dinner, without ever becoming fishermen or computer programmers.

Notes

NOTE TO INTRODUCTION

1. For an account of how the Jacquard loom worked, see James Essinger, *Jacquard's Web—How a Hand Loom Led to the Birth of the Information Age* (Oxford: Oxford University Press, 2004).
2. Concerning the labour issues and the Jacquard loom, see Daryl Hafter "The Programmed Brocade Loom and the Decline of the Drawgirl" in *ed.* Martha Moore Trescott, *Dynamos and Virgins Revisited: Women and Technological Change in History* (London: The Scarecrow Press, 1979).
3. Denial-of-Service is a method to close down a computer network by overloading it with requests.
4. Because of changes in fashion, free trade policies, and the high costs of the machinery, it took another thirty years till the Jaquard loom was widely used in England. Natalie Rothstein, "The Introduction of the Jacquard Loom to Great Britain, in *ed.* Veronika Gervers, *Studies in Textile History—In Memory of Harold B. Burnham* (Toronto: Alger Press, 1977).
5. For a historical account of the Luddite uprising, see Kirkpatrick Sale, *Rebels Against the Future—The Luddites and Their War on the Industrial Revolution, Lessons for the Computer Age* (Reading Mass.: Addison-Wesley Publishing Company, 1995).
6. Even if machine breaking could not stop industrial capitalism, Eric Hobsbawm estimated that the implementation of labour-saving technologies in local areas was held back due to sabotage. Furthermore, the breaking of machines was part of a more general strategy of 'collective bargaining by riot', as he called it, which could also include arsoning the employer's stock and home. If judged as a method to maintain wage rates and working conditions, it was fairly effective. Eric Hobsbawm, "The Machine Breakers", *Past and Present* 1 (February 1952).
7. The joy of writing source code is the lead motive in Linus Torvald's story about the invention of Linux. Linus Torvalds and David Diamond, *Just For Fun—The Story of an Accidental Revolutionary* (New York: HarperCollins Publisher, 2001); hereafter cited in text.
8. *ed.* Elizabeth Wilkinson & L. Willoughby, *On the Aesthetic Education of Man—In a Series of Letters/Friedrich Schiller* (Oxford: Clarendon Press 1982), 9; hereafter cited in text as *Letters*.
9. Charles Babbage, *On the Economy of Machinery and Manufactures* (New York: Augustus M Kelley Publishers, 1971), 54.
10. Jason Scott, *BBS the Documentary* (2004).
11. Andrew Sullivan, "Counter Culture: Dot-communist Manifesto", *New York Times* (Sunday 11, June 2000).

12. Slavoj Zizek, "A Cyberspace Lenin: Why Not?", *International Socialism Journal* 95, (summer 2002).
13. In "The DotCommunism Manifesto" Eben Moglen directly paraphrases Karl Marx's manifesto. emoglen.law.columbia.edu/publications/dcm.html (accessed 2007-02-08).
14. "Gates Taking a Seat in Your Den" *CNet News.com* (January 5, 2005).
15. For a less cosy account of IBM's political legacy, see Edwin Black, *IBM and the Holocaust: The Strategic Alliance Between Nazi Germany and America's Most Powerful Corporation* (London: Little, Brown & co, 2001). IBM's modern-day political stand can be read out from their donations to George Bush's presidential election campaign in 2000 and 2004, hardly an administration associated with the old hippie slogan.
16. In his essay on a socialist theory of mass media, Hans Enzensberger complained about the disinterest among progressives in the topic:

    > "If the socialist movement writes off the new productive forces of the consciousness industry and relegates work on the media to a subculture, then we have a vicious circle. For the Underground may be increasingly aware of the technical and aesthetic possibilities of the disc, of videotape, of the electronic camera, and so on, and is systematically exploring the terrain, but it has no political viewpoint of its own and therefore mostly falls a helpless victim to commercialism." Hans Enzensberger "Constituents of a Theory of the Media" in *ed.* John Hanhardt, *Video Culture—A Critical Investigation* (New York: Virtual Studies Workshop Press: 1986), 103; hereafter cited in text.

17. For an exhaustive account of the social perils with computers, see Lenny Siegel's and John Markoff's *The High Cost of High Tech—The Dark Side of the Chip* (New York: Harper & Row, 1985). On the global exploitation of workers in East-Asian and Mexican sweatshops where computers are built, see *ed.* Gerald Sussman and John Lent, *Global Productions—Labor in the Making of the Information* Society (Cresskill: Hampton Press, 1998). For a more general critique of information technology, see Kevin Robins and Frank Webster, *The Technical Fix—Education, Computers and Industry* (Basingstoke: Macmillan, 1989).
18. Michael Hardt and Antonio Negri, *Empire* (Cambridge, Mass.: Harvard University Press, 2001); hereafter cited in text as *Empire*. For a collection of essays critical of Micheal Hardt and Antonio Negri's work, see *ed.* Gopal Balakrishnan, *Debating Empire*, (London: Verso, 2003). For a summary of the key concepts and thinkers behind the autonomous Marxist tradition, see Finn Bowing, "From the Mass Worker to the Multitude: A Theoretical Contextualisation of Hardt and Negri's Empire", in *Capital & Class* 83 (2004).
19. Antonio Negri, *Revolution Retrieved—Writings on Marx, Keynes, Capitalist Crisis and New Social Subjects (1967–83)* (London: Red Notes, 1988).
20. The major work by John Holloway is Change the World Without Taking Power (London: Pluto Press, 2005). Some of the debate sparked by the book was covered in a special issue of *Capital & Class*. See for instance Alex Callinicos, "Sympathy for the Devil? John Holloway's Mephistophellan Marxism". Capital e Class 85 (spring 2005).

NOTES TO CHAPTER ONE

1. Bruce Sterling, *The Hacker Crackdown—Law and Disorder on the Electronic Frontier* (London: Penguin, 1994).

2. Claude Fischer, in *ed*. Chant, *Sources for the Study of Science, Technology and Everyday Life 1870–1950—A Secondary Reader* (London: Hodder & Stoughton, 1988).

3. For a detailed summary of the background history of the Internet, see John Naughton, *A Brief History of the Future—The Origins of the Internet* (London: Phoenix, 2000).

4. Note that this is not the Marxist writer Paul Baran.

5. Less known is Donald Davies, a British scientist who also worked on a digital communication network and even got a prototype up and running. Janet Abbate, "Cold War and White Heat: The Origins and Meanings of Packet Switching" in *ed*. Donald MacKenzie and Judy Wajcman, *The Social Shaping of Technology*, 2nd edition (Buckingham: Philadelphia, Pa: Open University Press 1999).

6. Marie Marchand, *A French Success Story: The Minitel Saga* (Paris: Larousse, 1988).

7. For a background on UNIX, see Peter Salus, *A Quarter Century of UNIX* (Reading Mass.: Addison-Wesley 1994).

8. John Naughton, *A Brief History of the Future: the Origins of the Internet* (London: Phoenix, 2000), 176, *italics in original*.

9. Cudos is an acronym used to denote principles that should guide good scientific research. It was introduced by the sociologist Robert King Merton. One of the principles of Cudos is that scientific results ought to be freely shared among colleagues.

10. John Markoff, *What the Dormouse Said: How the Sixties Counterculture Shaped the Personal Computer Industry* (New York: Viking, 2005).

11. Langdon Winner, *The Whale and the Reactor—A Search for Limits in an Age of High Technology* (Chicago: The University of Chicago Press, 1986).

12. Steven Levy, *Hackers—Heroes of the Computer Revolution* (New York: Delta, 1994), 214.

13. Paul Ceruzzi, "Inventing Personal Computing", in *ed*. Donald MacKenzie & Judy Wajcman, *The Social Shaping of Technology*, 2nd edition (Buckingham: Philadelphia, Pa: Open University Press 1999).

14. In the United States, the scope of copyright was originally limited to the protection of maps, charts, and books. When congress passed the *Copyright Act of 1976*, the general applicability of copyright was broadened so that software could arguably be said to have been included. Software was explicitly covered under copyright after the amendments made in the *Computer Software Copyright Act* of 1980. Software code had been included in national copyright law in most European countries by the end of the 1980s.

15. Peter Drahos and John Braithwaite, *Information Feudalism—Who Owns The Knowledge Economy* (London: Earthscan, 2002), 171.

16. Translating source code to binary code is called compiling. The reversed procedure is known as decompiling. It is much harder to decompile and it is often prohibited in law.

17. A collection of Richard Stallman's speeches, where he outlines the major issues within the free software movement, as well as an appendix with the GNU General Public License, the GNU Lesser General Public License, and GNU Free Documentation License, can be found in *ed*. Joshua Gay, *Free Software, Free Society: Selected Essays of Richard M. Stallman* (Boston: GNU Press, 2002). An excellent study of the FOSS movement has been made by Glyn Moody, *Rebel Code—Linux and the Open Source Revolution* (London: Penguin Press, 2001); hereafter cited in text.

18. Richard Stallman, "The GNU Operating System and the Free Software Movement", in *ed*. Chris DiBona, & Sam Ockman & Mark Stone, *Open*

Sources—Voices from the Open Source Revolution (London: O'Reilly & Associates, 1999), 59; hereafter cited in text.

19. Section five in the General Public License reads:

> "You are not required to accept this license, since you have not signed it. However, nothing else grants you permission to modify or distribute the program or its derivative works. These actions are prohibited by law if you do not accept this license." In other words, if a user fails to abide to the provisions made in the GPL agreement, normal copyright law applies. Copyleft is *not* the same thing as the public domain.

20. Later, the Free Software Foundation added a compromise, Lesser GPL. The weaker version was required since GPL had deliberately been made incompatible with propertarian licensed code. In some areas, where propertarian code has a dominant position, GPL software was effectively shut out and its usefulness was unnecessarily reduced. LGPL is intended to allow GNU software to run side-by-side with property libraries, thus opening up a wider base of uses.

21. Ira Heffran, "Copyleft: Licensing Collaborative Works in the Digital Age." *Stanford Law Review* (July 1997). On clickwrap licenses, see Julie Cohen in *ed.* Lehr & Pupillo, *Cyber Policy and Economics in an Internet Age*, 2003. Many legal scholars have speculated if GPL would stand in an American court and have for most part given a positive answer. Daniel Ravicher, "Facilitating Collaborative Software Development: The Enforceability of Mass-Market Public Software Licenses." *Virginia Journal of Law & Technology* (fall 2000), and: Stephen McJohn, "The Paradoxes of Free Software." *George Mason Law Review* (fall 2000).

22. www.netfilter.org (accessed 2007-02-08).

23. Like most things in the hacker subculture, the name (Linux or GNU/Linux) is far from innocent. The use of either name sends signals of allegiance to those in-the-know. Richard Stallman advocates the use of GNU/Linux since the GNU toolbox plays a considerable part of the operating system out of which Linux is merely the kernel. The name dispute has also political ramifications since many within the computer underground and in the industry would like to keep the outspoken Stallman and the Free Software Foundation at an arms length.

24. Peter Wayner, *Free For All—How Linux and the Free Software Movement Undercut the High-Tech Titans* (New York: HarperBusiness, 2000).

25. http://news.netcraft.com/archives/2006/01/05/january_2006_web_server_survey.html, (accessed 2007-02-08).

26. Tim Berners-Lee & Mark Fischetti, *Weaving the Web—The Past, Present and Future of the World Wide Web* (London: Texere, 2000).

27. This fact is happily admitted to by free-software entrepreneur Robert Young:

> "Quietly, since Red Hat's founding in the 1993, we had focused on an approach to software development that enabled us to tap into a worldwide software development team bigger than even the biggest industry giant could afford" Robert Young and Wendy Rohm, *Under the Radar—How Red Hat Changed the Software Business and Took Microsoft by Surprise* (Scottsdale, AZ: Coriolis, 1999), 9; hereafter cited in text.

28. Eric Raymond would certainly object to be juxtaposed with Marxism. His engagement in Open Source springs from a libertarian conviction and he is a member of National Rifle Association. On learning that China was adopting a national version of GNU/Linux, he exclaimed:

"Any 'identification' between the values of the open-source community and the repressive practices of Communism is nothing but a vicious and cynical fraud". See *Linux Today* (November 11, 1999).

29. Eric Raymond, "The Cathedral and the Bazaar." *First Monday* vol.3, no.3 (1998), 21.

30. *Halloween Document I*, www.opensource.org/halloweenl.php (accessed 2007-02-08). *Halloween Document II*, www.opensource.org/halloween/halloween2.php (accessed 2007-02-08).

31. Reported by Greg Michalec, *Free Software: History, Perspectives, and Implications*, 2002, p.29, available at greg.primate.net/sp/thesis.pdf, (accessed 2007-02-08).

32. In words akin to those just quoted from Linus Torvalds, Karl Marx once remarked:

> "In fact, of course, this 'productive' worker cares as much about the crappy shit he has to make as does the capitalist himself who employed him, and who also couldn't give a damn for the junk." Karl Marx, *Grundrisse*, (London: Penguin Books: 1993), 273; hereafter cited in text as *Grundrisse*.

33. Robert Young, "Giving It Away—How Red Hat Software Stumbled Across a New Economic Model and Helped Improve an Industry", in (*DiBona*, Ockman e Stone).

34. Carl Shapiro and Hal Varian, *Information Rules—A Strategic Guide to the Network Economy* (London: McGraw-Hill, 1998).

35. Gilberto Camara, "Open Source Software Production: Fact & Fiction." *Mute* 27 (spring 2004).

36. Rishab Ghosh and Vipul Prakash, "The Orbiten Free Software Survey", *First Monday*, vol.5, no.7 (July 2000).

37. www.phrack.org/archives/7/P07-03 (accessed 2007-02-08).

38. Rishab Ghosh, *et al.*, *Free/Libre and Open Source Software: survey and study*, part IV, 2002, available at www.infonomics.nl/FLOSS/report/ (accessed 2007-02-08).

39. Dawn Nafus, James Leach and Bernhard Krieger, *Free/Libre/Open Source Software: Policy Support* (2006), available at www.flosspols.org/deliverables/FLOSSPOLS-D16-Gender_Integrated_Report_of_Findings.pdf, (accessed 2007-02-08).

40. For an analysis as well as interviews with hackers concerning the male dominance within the hacker movement, see Paul Taylor, *Hackers—Crime in the Digital Sublime* (London: Routledge, 1999).

41. In an interview conducted for this book in 2005, a member of the feminist hacker group Haeksen observed how the subculture mirrored dominant structures with its own particular flavour. If a woman had the fastest machine among a group of developers, the men upgraded their computer equipment very quickly.

42. Donna Haraway, *Simians, Cyborgs and Women—The Reinvention of Nature* (London: Free Association Books, 2001); hereafter cited in text, Sadie Plant, *Zeros + Ones: Digital Women and the New Technoculture* (London: Fourth Estate.: Beacon Press, 1998).

43. www.osaia.org/letters/sco_hill.pdf, (accessed 2007-02-08)

44. Red Hat still abides to the GPL license, since it publishes the source code. Instead it enjoys additional protection from trademark law, which lies outside the commitments made in the GPL license, and, more controversially, it owns software patents. Red Hat could probably not have got away with

it so smoothly had they not had a close relationship with many of the FOSS chieftains. This indicates a weakness with a copyleft license. It relies heavily on community norms and public relations for its enforcement. But Red Hat's change of policy is countered in a way characteristic of the hacker movement. Several projects are under way, made possible by the terms in GPL, to side-track Red Hat's subscription service. See *White Box Enterprise Linux*, *cAos Community Linux*, and *Tao Linux* for three such projects.

45. A copy of Red Hat's annual report 2004 is available at http://phx.corporate-ir. net/phoenix.zhtml?c=67156&p=irol-reportsannual (accessed 2007-02-08)

46. "The proprietary OS [operative system] vendors, with their huge investment in the proprietary software that their products consist of, would be crazy to try and match the benefit we are offering their customers, as we generate a frac-tion of the revenue per user that the current proprietary OS vendor rely on", Robert Young, "Giving It Away—How Red Hat Software Stumbled Across a New Economic Model and Helped Improve an Industry" in (*DiBona*, 119).

47. In following chapters, I will suggest that the exploitation of 'audience power' is complementing the exploitation of labour power. The situation is not excep-tional to hacking but is a systematic trait in post-modern markets.

48. Nathan Newman, *Net Loss: Internet Prophets, Private Profits, and the Costs to Community* (University Park, Pa.: Pennsylvania State University Press, 2002); hereafter cited in text.

49. On Bill Gate's manoeuvring to take charge of the browser market, see James Wallace, *Overdrive—Bill Gates and the Race to Control Cyberspace* (New York: John Wiley & Sons, 1997).

50. The name Mozilla was the codename which Mark Andreessen's team used when hijacking the Mozaic browser—Mozilla/Mosaic-Killer. (*Newman*, 115).

51. For a comparison between the different philosophies behind Open Source and Free Software, see David Barry, "The Contestation of Code—A Preliminary Investigation into the Discourse of the Free/Libre and Open Source Move-ments", *Critical Discourse Studies*, April, 2004.

52. Robert Young makes a key observation on how intellectual property rights creates enormous losses and hold-ups in downstream industries:

> "Executives at the highest levels at the company had long recognized that proprietary operating system manufacturers were not moving their oper-ating systems forward as quickly as Intel was advancing microprocessor technology. [. . .] If it had a new technology available at the processor level that would allow computer users to do new things, it had to wait until the operating system supplier decided it was willing to build support for these features into the system." (*Young*, 6).

53. Martin Kenney "Value Creation in the Late Twentieth Century: The Rise of the Knowledge Worker" in *ed.* Jim Davis, Thomas Hirschl and Michael Stack, *Cutting Edge: Technology, Information Capitalism and Social Revolution* (London: Verso, 1997), 91; hereafter cited in text.

54. Rebecca Eisenberg, "Genes Patents and Product Development", *Science* 14 (August 1992).

55. Manuel Castells, *The Rise of the Network Society*, (Oxford: Blackwell Pub-lishers, 2000), 50; hereafter cited in text.

56. Rebecca Eisenberg, "Intellectual Property at the Public-Private Divide: The Case of Large-Scale cDNA, Sequencing", *University of Chicago Law School Roundtable* (1996).

57. "Also, the CDDB site needed this volunteer (user) labor only until the data-base got big enough that it was valuable enough for other companies to pay

for access.", Dan Bricklin, "The Cornucopia of the Commons", in *ed.* Andy Oram, *Peer-to-Peer—Harnessing the Benefits of a Disruptive Technology* (Sebastopol: O'Reilly, 2001), 61. Dan Bricklin calls this business strategy 'a common'. It appears to him as if the volunteers have not loosed out for as long as they can access the site (and thus continue to contribute to it) for free. He fails to see that the license revenues which Gracenote collects from other companies derive from higher prices on the products sold by these companies. Hence, the volunteers working for free for Gracenote have to pay more for the wares which they provide information about to Gracenote's database. The more they enhance the value of the database; the more they will have to pay for the goods.

58. RIAA (Record Industry Association of America) and MPAA (Motion Picture Association of America) would prefer if people knew DRM as 'Digital *Rights* Management Technology'. As with the coining of the term 'pirate copying', or the negative associations conveyed from the word 'hacker', part of the struggle is fought on a semantic level.

59. Pamela Samuelson, "Regulation of Technologies to Protect Copyrighted Works", *Communication of the ATM* 39 (1996), and Peter Drahos & John Braithwaite, *Information Feudalism—Who Owns The Knowledge Economy* (London: Earthscan, 2002).

60. The third chapter on commodification of information will discuss in more detail the conflict between periphery and centre on intellectual property.

61. It says: "Banning open source would have immediate, broad, and strongly negative impacts on the ability of many sensitive and security-focused DOD groups to protect themselves against cyberattacks,", quoted in *Washington Post* (May 23, 2002).

62. So far the company has come out unscratched. The final settlement with the U.S. Department of Justice in 2001 saved the company from a forced restructuring. Amanda Cohen, "Surveying the Microsoft Antitrust Universe", *Berkeley Technology Law Journal* (2004).

63. www.opensource.org/sco-vs-ibm.html (accessed 2007-02-08).

64. Kerry Goettsch, "SCO Group v. IBM: The Future of Open-Source Software", *University of Illinois Journal of Law, Technology & Policy* (fall 2003).

65. Patent number 6658642, Dec. 2, 2003.

66. Pekka Himanen uses the term 'hacker spirit' and applies it as an attitude towards work in general, the spirit of the 'information age' as opposed to the attitude towards work in the industrial society. He never considers the existence of conflicts of interest between business, employees and volunteers. For a critical view of how the blurring of work and passion, i.e. the hacker spirit, is taken advantage of by shareholders at the expense of disillusioned, burned-out employees, see Andrew Ross' study of webdesigners working in advertising bureaus. *No-Collar—The Human Workplace and its Hidden Costs* (Philadelphia: Temple University Press 2004), Pekka Himanen, *The Hacker Ethic—The Spirit of the Information Age* (London: Secker & Warburg, 2001).

67. Dennies Hayes, *Behind the Silicon Curtain—The Seduction of Work in a Lonely Era* (London: Free Association Books, 1989), 85.

68. The tendency was noticeable within the computer industry already in the 1970s when Philip Kraft examined how the computer profession was being transformed by an intensified technical division of labour. Philip Kraft, *Programmers and Managers—The Routinization of Computer Programming in the United States* (New York: Springer-Verlag, 1977).

69. Richard Sennett, *The Corrosion of Character*, (New York: Norton & Company, 1999).

70. David Noble, *Forces of Production—A Social History of Industrial Automation* (New York: Alfred A Knopf, 1984), 231, hereafter cited in text.

71. The story about how Richard Stallman came to realise the virtues of free source code is remarkably similar. A Xerox printer in Stallman's laboratory frequently malfunctioned. He knew that he could fix the problem, but he was prevented from improving the printer because of the proprietary license. *ed.* Joshua Gay *Free Software, Free Society: Selected Essays of Richard M. Stallman*, (Boston: GNU Press, 2002).

72. The existence of a white collar working class is hardly controversial anymore. For a review of the debate, see Richard Sobel, *White Collar Working Class—From Structure to Politics* (New York: Praeger, 1989).

73. *ed.* Bernadette Schell and John Dodge, *The Hacking of America—Who's Doing it. Why, and How* (London: Quorum Books, 2002), 117.

74. Andrew Ross, *Strange Weather—Culture, Science, and Technology in the Age of Limits* (London: Verso, 1991), 92, *italics in original.*

75. For a discussion on the growth of home-work and how it is related to a two-tiered labour market, see Peter Meiksins in *ed.* McChesney, Wood & Foster, *Capitalism and the Information Age—The Political Economy of the Global Communication Revolution*, (New York: Monthly Review Press, 1998).

76. Translated and quoted by Harry Cleaver, "The Inversion of Class Perspective in Marxian Theory: From Valorisation to Self-Valorisation", in *ed.* Bonefeld, Gunn & Psychopedis, *Open Marxism*, vol.2 (London: Pluto Press, 1992), 137.

77. In a sense, placing the emphasis on the struggle of the working class community as opposed to the individual labourer acknowledges an old fact. Spouses, relatives, and neighbours of workers have always played a significant role in industrial conflicts. Corporate restructuring is not only resisted because of the loss of jobs. The threat to the way of life of the working class community has also been a powerful incitement to action. See *ed.* Nancy Naples, *Community Activism and Feminist Politics—Organizing Across Race, Class, and Gender* (New York: Routledge, 1998).

78. Alan Liu, *The Laws of Cool—Knowledge Work and the Culture of Information* (Chicago: The University of Chicago Press, 2004).

79. In the last chapter we will engage closer with the notion of play and struggle.

NOTES TO CHAPTER TWO

1. Ralf Dahrendorf, *Class and Class Conflict in Industrial Society* (London: Routledge, 1959).

2. Daniel Bell, *The Coming of the Post-Industrial Society* (New York: Basic Books, 1973).

3. For a collection of essays critical of Castell's work, *ed.* Frank Webster and Basil Dimitriou, *Manuel Castells—From the Informational City to the Information Age*, vol. III (London: Sage, 2004).

4. Richard Florida, *The Rise of the Creative Class—And How it's Transforming Work, Leisure, Community & Everyday Life* (New York: Basic Books, 2002).

5. Nick Dyer-Witheford, *Cyber-Marx—Cycles and Circuits of Struggle in High-Technology Capitalism* (Chicago: University of Illinois Press, 1999), 37.

6. For an influential criticism of historical materialism by a non-Marxist, Anthony Giddens, *A Contemporary Critique of Historical Materialism* (London: Macmillan Press ltd, 1995). A problem with the theory, according to Giddens, is that it assumes a predetermined path in history where one stage

of development leads on to a 'higher' stage, eventually culminating in communism. Another serious flaw is the reduction of all aspects of life to bare motion laws of the economy. Gidden's criticism is valid for as long as it is levelled against *one* branch of Marxism, a branch which, as it happens, has most intensively been scrutinised by other Marxists. For Marxist critiques of technicist Marxism, see *ed.* Phil Slater, *Outlines of a Critique of Technology* (London: Humanities Press, 1980).

7. Frank Webster, *Theories of the Information Society* (New York: Routledge, 2002).

8. While examining the literature of a closely related subject, post-modernity, Fredric Jameson complained about the lack of Marxist alternatives to post-industrial ideology:

> "[. . .] In the meantime the new mediatic and informational social phenomena had been colonized (in our absence) by the Right, in a series of influential studies in which the first tentative Cold War notion of an 'end of ideology' finally gave birth to the full-blown concept of a 'post-industrial society' itself." Frederic Jameson, *Postmodernism, or, the Cultural Logic of Late Capitalism* (London: Verso, 1991), 400.

9. The focus will be on the fraction of thinkers associated with Antonio Negri. In recent years, Negri's work has been widely read and lively debated in English-speaking academia and many of his texts have been translated to English. Furthermore, the issues that he is concerned with relates closely to the discussion in this book. Autonomous Marxism is a much more diverse current, however, and some of the sternest critics of Antonio Negri come from within this tradition of thought. For a broader account of autonomous Marxism, see Steve Wright, *Storming Heaven—Class Composition and Struggle in Italian Autonomist Marxism* (London: Pluto Press, 2002).

10. It is the concept of totality that is such an anathema to post-modern writers. Best known is Jean-Francois Lyotard's announcement of an end to all "great narratives". Of course, as have been pointed out by many of Lyotard's critics, the end of great narratives becomes a narrative in its own right. By denouncing totality it just slips in the back door, often in less considered forms. Martin Jay, *Marxism and Totality: the Adventures of a Concept from Lukács to Habermas* (Cambridge: Polity Press, 1984).

11. Gerald Cohen, *Karl Marx's Theory of History—A Defence* (Oxford: Clarendon Press, 2000).

12. The argument of Alvin Gouldner is that the two camps, scientific Marxism and critical Marxism, reflects an inconsistency that is present already in Karl Marx's own thinking. He believes that this tension is the source of Marx's intellectual richness, and Gouldner protests against the many attempts to purge Marx of the ambiguity and positivist lapses. Alvin Gouldner, *The Two Marxism: Contradictions and Anomalies in the Development of Theory* (London: Macmillan, 1980).

13. Wiebe Bijker, *Of Bicycles, Bakelites, and Bulbs—Towards a Theory of Sociotechnical Change* (Cambridge, Mass.: MIT Press, 1995), hereafter cited in text.

14. Joel Mokyr, *The Lever of Riches: Technological Creativity and Economic Progress* (New York Oxford University Press, 1990).

15. For instance, Antonio Negri's writes:

> "In effect, capitalist innovation is always a product, a compromise or a response, in short a constraint which derives from workers' antagonism." Antonio Negri, "Twenty Theses on Marx: Interpretation of the Class

Situation Today", in *ed.* Makdisi, Casarino and Karl, *Marxism Beyond Marxism* (London: Routledge, 1996), 158.

16. To be fair, Antonio Negri is not the only one troubled by such thoughts. Though Antonio Negri and Jurgen Habermas have few things in common, the later writes in a similar tone of voice on this subject:

> "Thus technology and science become a leading productive force, rendering inoperative the conditions for Marx's labour theory of value. It is no longer meaningful to calculate the amount of capital investment in research and development on the basis of the value of unskilled (simple) labour power, when scientific-technical progress has become an independent source of surplus value, in relation to which the only source of surplus values considered by Marx, namely the labour power of the immediate producers, plays an ever smaller role." Jurgen Habermas "Technology and Science as 'Ideology'." in *ed.* Colin Chant, *Sources for the Study of Science, Technology and Everyday Life 1870–1950—A Secondary Reader*, (London: Hodder & Stoughton, 1988), 190.

17. Bruce Norton highlights, though, that Fredric Jameson silently leaves out more than he takes from Ernest Mandel. The thrust of Mandel's work was to prove that capitalism moves towards aggravated crises and a definite collapse. Jameson takes a subtext of this argument, the idea that the commodity form is expanding ever outwards to eclipse culture and aesthetics, and makes this his core claim. Fredric Jameson ends up with a capitalism that grows without internal limits and that knows no insurmountable resistance, quite the opposite argument to Ernest Mandel's idea. Bruce Norton, "Late Capitalism and Postmodernism: Jameson/Mandel", in *ed.* Antonio Callari & Stephen Cullenberg & Carole Biewener, *Marxism in the Postmodern Age—Confronting the New World Order* (New York: Guilford Press, 1994).

18. *"Late capitalism, far from representing a 'post-industrial society', thus appears as the period in which all branches of the economy are fully industrialized for the first time*; to which one could further add the increasing mechanization of the sphere of circulation [. . .] and the increasing mechanization of the superstructure." Ernest Mandel, *Late Capitalism* (London: Thetford Press limited, 1978), 191, *italics in original*; hereafter cited in text.

19. In words similar to Ernest Mandel, Manuel Castells announces that the 'chain of causality', from the material base to the superstructure, has broken down when the superstructure becomes productive in itself, in:

> "[. . .] the information age, marked by the autonomy of culture vis-a-vis the material bases of our existence"

(*Castells*, 478). Castell is typical in that he partially accepts the postulates made in the historical materialist theory and follow these up to the point of the big rupture between the industrial and the post-industrial and/or the modern and post-modern society. From then onwards, however, the informational mode of production renders historical materialism obsolete, by which it is also implied that Marxism and the very idea of a universal, emancipatory project has been invalidated. Manuel Castells echoes the French philosopher Jean Baudrillard's charge against Marxism under the banner of simulacra. In *The Mirror of Production*, were Baudrillard definitely departed from his Marxist heritage, he announced that political economy had been overturned by semiotics. At a closer look, however, it becomes clear that simulacra is mobilised exactly for the purpose of simulating the dogmas of bourgeoisie political economy. Jean Baudrillard, *The Mirror of Production* (St Lois: Telos Press, 1975); hereafter cited in text.

20. One exception is the Soviet linguistic Valentin Volosinov. Already back in the 1920s he studied language in relation to class struggle, and argued that signs must be seen in its material and social context. Valentin Volosinov, *Marxism and the Philosophy of Language* (New York: Seminar Press, 1973).

21. Paulo Virno, *A Grammar of the Multitude—For an Analysis of Contemporary Forms of Life* (New York: Semiotext, 2004), 61.

22. The impression that the Virtual has disconnected itself from real space and become autonomous and pre-eminent is highly questionable. Katherine Hayles puts it well:

> "[. . .] *The efficacy of information depends on a highly articulated material base.* Without such a base, from rapid transportation systems to fibber-optical cables, information becomes much more marginal in its ability to affect outcomes in the material world. Ironically, once this base is in place, the perceived primacy of information over materiality obscures the importance of the very infrastructure that makes information valuable." Katherine Hayles, The Condition of Virtuality" in *ed*. Peter Lunenfeld, *The Digital Dialectic—New Essays on New Media* (Cambridge, Mass: MIT Press, 1998), 72.

23. Raymond Williams, *Towards 2000* (London: Chatto & Windus, 1983), 146.

24. Wiebe Bijker describes technical artefacts as 'bundles of meanings' negotiated between relevant social groups. But Bijker also concedes that an artefact is not infinitely malleable:

> "The relevant social groups have, in building up the technological frame, invested so much in the artefact that its meaning has become quite fixed—it cannot be changed easily, and it forms part of a hardened network of practices, theories, and social institutions. From this time on it may indeed happen that, naively spoken, an artefact 'determines' social development" (*Bijker*, 282).

25. The slogan of Mitch Kapor echoes Langdon Winner's inquiry into the 'politics of the artefact'. Winner's famous example is the low bridges over the motorways going to Long Island, New York. Robert Moses, an influential city planner in New York for many decades, specified the height of the bridges so that buses would be unable to pass under them. His intention was to keep black people and the working class, who depended on public transports, from accessing the beaches and parks at Long Island. Langdon Winner, "Do Artifacts Have Politics?, *Daedalus*, vol.109, no.1 (winter 1980). Winner's case has been contested by scholars who, pointing out that nowadays the bridges are a hindrance to luxury SUV-cars, have stressed the failure of artefacts to affect political outcomes. Bernward Joerges, "Do Politics have Artefacts?" *Social Studies of Science*, vol. 29, no.3 (1999).

26. For a summary of different positions on post-Fordism, see *ed*. Ash Amin, *Post-Fordism: A Reader* (Oxford: Blackwell, 1994). Sceptics have objected to the sharp distinction drawn between Fordism and post-Fordism and questioned if there is solid empirical evidence for the periodisation. Andrew Sayer, "Post-fordism in Question", *International Journal of Urban and Regional Research* 35 (1989). The qualifications against the theory are valid. Still, that the economy has drastically changed over the last forty years is an uncontroversial statement. The need to categorise this change is suggested by the many writers abiding to the industrial age/information age dichotomy. An analysis of

contemporary capitalism is far better off starting with the concept of post-Fordism.

27. Michel Aglietta, *A Theory of Capitalist Regulation* (London: NLB, 1979). The French Regulation School has been criticised for theorising capitalism from an institutional horizon, thus failing to give due credit to the role of class struggle. see *ed.* Werner Bonefeld & John Holloway, *Post-Fordism and Social Form—A Marxist Debate on the Post-Fordist State* (Basingstoke: Macmillan, 1991).

28. For a compilation of claims about the rise of a new class, Richard Barbrook, *The Class of the New* (London: Mute, 2006).

29. "Precisely because it is placed in the centre of the most complex mechanisms of organisational capitalism, the new working class is brought to realise more quickly than the other sectors the contradictions inherent in the system. [. . .] Its objective situation places it in the position of seeing the deficiencies in modern capitalist organisation, and to arrive at a consciousness of a new way of organising productive relationships, as the only way of satisfying the human needs which cannot be expressed within the present structures." Serge Mallet, *The New Working Class*, Nottingham: Spokesman, 1975), 29.

30. Maurizio Lazzarato, "Immaterial Labour", in *ed.* Paolo Virno & Michael Hardt, *Radical Thought in Italy: A Potential Politics.* (Minneapolis: University of Minnesota Press, 1996).

31. For a critique of this tendency in Negri's thinking, see Nick-Dyer Witheford's "Cyber-Negri: General Intellect and Immaterial Labour", in *ed.* Timothy Murphy & Abdul-Karim Mustapha, *The Philosophy of Antonio Negri—Resistance in Practice* (London: Pluto Press, 2005).

32. It must be stressed that a 'necessary need' is socially defined. What is deemed as necessary depends on the time, place, and class position of the individual in question. This distinction will be further examined in chapter four.

33. George Caffentzis, "On Africa and Self-Reproducing Automata", in *New Enclosures/Midnight Notes Collective* (Jamaica Plain, Ma.: Midnight Notes, 1990). Antonio Negri is oblivious to this argument since, though he acknowledges that labour is still the basis of value, insists that scientific labour is immeasurable and that the law of value has ceased to operate.

34. Tessa Morris-Suzuki "Robots and Capitalism" in (*Davis, Hirschl & Stack* 18).

35. Walter Benjamin, *Illuminations* (New York: Schocken Books, 1969), 220.

36. Stuart Hall "Encoding/Decoding" in *ed.* Stuart Hall, Dorothy Hobson, Andrew Lowe and Paul Willis, *Culture, Media, Language* (London: Routledge, 1996).

37. Michel de Certeau, *The Practice of Everyday Life* (Los Angeles: University of California Press, 1984).

38. John Fiske, *Television Culture* (London: Routledge, 1987).

39. *ed.* Vincent Mosco and Janet Wasko, *The Political Economy of Information* (Madison, Wisc: University of Wisconsin Press, 1988).

40. To equate 'audience power' with 'labour power' of employed workers is controversial to say the least. In his exhaustive review of Marxist perspectives on the topic of communication, Vincent Mosco dodges the question if audiences can be equated with living labour as a source of surplus value for capital. Mosco grants that the relationship between audience and broadcaster, a relationship of mutual dependency and yet ripe with antagonism, can metaphorically be likened with the uneasy coexistence between workers and management. Vincent Mosco, *The Political Economy of Communication* (London: Sage Publications, 1996), 149.

41. Dallas Smythe, *Dependency Road: Communications, Capitalism, Consciousness, and Canada* (Norwood N.J.:Ablex, 1981). A similar argument has

been made by Sut Jhally, *The Codes of Advertising: Fetishism and the Political Economy of Meaning in the Consumer Society* (London: Frances Printer, 1987).

42. Mariarosa Dalla Costa & Selma James, *The Power of Women and the Subversion of the Community* (Bristol: The Falling Wall Press, 1973). Harriet Fraad, Stephen Resnick & Richard Wolff, *Bringing it all Back Home—Class, Gender and Power in the Modern Household* (London: Pluto Press, 1994).

43. Martin Kenney "Value Creation in the Late Twentieth Century: The Rise of the Knowledge Worker" in (*Davis, Hirschl & Stack* 94).

44. Eric von Hippel, professor in economics at MIT, studies how end users contribute to innovation. He is positive about the trend and stresses that users can design equipment closer to their needs than if they depend on the guesses of a manufacturer. Eric von Hippel acknowledges that the reluctance among many companies towards enrolling user-centred innovation schemes owes to the perceived threat to the social division of labour. He goes on, however, to advocate user centred business models as a matter of social welfare, failing to see the antagonism of such a scenario. Eric von Hippel, *Democratising Innovation* (Cambridge Mass.: MIT Press, 2005).

45. Tiziana Terranova, *Network Culture: Politics for the Information Age* (London: Pluto Press, 2004).

46. The culture industry has successfully established 'pirate copying' as a term in the public debate. Many hackers refuse to use the vocabulary which they find ideologically loaded. However, to replace the word 'pirate' with 'un-authorised copying' or 'illicit copying' does not suffice since everyone will fill in the word 'pirate' in their heads. It is more appropriate to replace the last word 'copying' with 'sharing'. By juxtaposing the two emotionally charged words 'pirate' and 'sharing', the agenda behind the term 'pirate copying' is brought into the limelight.

47. Stewart Brand, *The Media Lab—Inventing the Future at M.I.T.* (Harmondsworth: Penguin, 1988), 202.

48. Fritz Machlup, *Knowledge: Its Creation, Distribution and Economic Significance* (Princeton: Princeton University Press, 1984), 159.

49. John Stuart Mill, *The Principles of Political Economy* (Kitchener, Ont.: Batoche, 2001), 1129.

50. The words of Thomas Jefferson, written in a letter dated 1813, have become iconic in the computer underground. "He who receives an idea from me, receives instructions himself without lessening mine; as he who lights his taper at mine, receives light without darkening me." *ed.* Joyce Appleby & Terence Ball, *Thomas Jefferson—Political Writings* (New York: Cambridge University Press, 1999), 580.

51. Max Horkheimer & Theodor Adorno, *Dialectic of Enlightenment* (London: Verso, 1997), 161.

52. Lawrence Lessig, *The Future of Ideas—The Fate of Commons in a Connected World* (New York: Random House, 2001), 93 and 94.

53. The label has been made up by Dan Shiller, "The Information Commodity: A Preliminary View" in (*Davis*, Hirschl & Stack).

54. Marshall Sahlins, *Stone Age Economics* (Chicago: Aldine Publishing Company, 1972), 4.

55. See Michael Perelman, *The Innovation of Capitalism—Classical Political Economy and the Secret History of Primitive Accumulation* (Durham: Duke University Press, 2000).

56. Dan Shiller, "How to Think About Information" in *ed.* Vincent Mosco & Janet Wasko, *The Political Economy of Information* (Madison, Wisc: University of Wisconsin Press, 1988), 41.

57. Katherine Hayles, "The Condition of Virtuality", in *ed.* Peter Lunenfeld, *The Digital Dialectic—New Essays on New Media* (Cambridge, Mass: MIT Press, 1999).

58. The opportunity has not been missed by mainstream economists. If Fritz Machlup's sentence is modified, so that 'knowledge' is read out as 'labour', the thrust of this development becomes absolutely clear:

> "The point to grasp and to remember is that the same amount of knowledge that is used to make *m* units of output will serve to make *m + 1* units, and the same knowledge that is used by *n* persons (producers) can enable *n + 1* persons to make the same product. There might be a cost of the transfer of knowledge, of teaching it and learning it, but there is no additional cost of using it once it has been acquired." Fritz Machlup, *Knowledge: Its Creation, Distribution and Economic Significance* (Princeton: Princeton University Press, 1984), 160, *italics in original.*

59. David Noble has argued this point in a widely read article were he predicts a proletarisation of higher learning. David Noble "Digital Diploma Mills" in *ed.* Benjamin Johnson, Patrick Kavanagh and Kevin Mattson, *Steal this University—The Rise of the Corporate University and the Academic Labor Movement* (New York: Routledge, 2003).

60. Paolo Virno, "Notes on the General Intellect" in *ed.* Saree Makdisi, Cesare Casarino & Rebecca Karl, *Marxism Beyond Marxism* (London: Routledge, 1996), 271, *italics in original.*

61. The neoliberal author Ayn Rand might have sensed this possibility when making her passionate defence for intellectual property rights:

> "Patents are the heart and core of property rights, and once they are destroyed, the destruction of all other rights will follow automatically, as a brief postscript." Ayn Rand, *Capitalism: The Unknown Ideal* (New York: New American Library, 1966), 128.

NOTES TO CHAPTER THREE

1. William Fisher "Theories of intellectual property" in *ed.* Stephen Munzer, *Essays in Legal and Political Economy of Property* (Cambridge: Cambridge University Press, 2001).

2. Dragan Milovanovic recaptures the criticism directed against Pashukanis by his contemporaries in the introduction to Evgeny Pashukanis, *The General Theory of Law and Marxism* (New Brunswick, NJ: Transaction Publishers, 2002).

3. Hugh Collins, *Marxism and Law* (Oxford: Clarendon Press, 1982).

4. Eric Hobsbawm, *Bandits* (London: Ebenezer Baylis & Son, 1969).

5. *ed.* William Scheuerman, *The Rule of Law Under Siege—Selected Essays of Franz L. Neuman and Otto Kirchheimer* (Berkeley: University of California Press, 1996).

6. Jane Gaines, *Contested Culture—The Image, the Voice, and the Law* (Chapell Hill: The University of North Carolina Press, 1991), 6.

7. Bernard Edelman, *Ownership of the Image—Elements for a Marxist Theory of Law* (London: Routledge & Kegan Paul, 1979).

8. Louis Althusser, *Essays on Ideology* (London: Verso, 1984).

9. Peter Jaszi writes on how the predominance of copyright and the notion of romantic authorship foreclose alternative forms of collective creativity and 'serial collaboration'. Peter Jaszi, "On the Author Effect: Contemporary

Copyright and Collective Creativity." *Cardozo Arts & Entertainment Law Journal* 10 (1992).

10. Brendan Scott, "Copyright in a Frictionless World: Toward a Rhetoric of Responsibility", *First Monday*, vol.6, no.9 (September 2001).

11. Carla Hesse, "Enlightenment Epistemology and the Laws of Authorship in Revolutionary France, 1777–1793", *Representations* 30 (1990).

12. Makeen Fouad Makeen, *Copyright in a Global Information Society—The Scope of Copyright Protection under International, US, UK and French Law* (Hague: Kluwer Law International 2000).

13. Lyman Ray Patterson, *Copyright in Historical Perspective* (Nashville: Vanderbilt University Press, 1968).

14. Michel Foucault in *ed.* Paul Rabinow, *The Foucault Reader* (London: Penguin Books, 1991), 118–119.

15. The fact that modern copyright and trademark law is framed within utilitarian and narrowly defined economic goals does not rule out that it has a chilling effect on free speech and free thinking. Occasionally, copyright law is used directly to silence dissenting voices. George Bush's campaign staff sent a cease and desist letter to Zack Exley, the creator of <gwbush.com>, where he parodied Bush's own site. Exley was threatened with legal action because he had graft inappropriate material "onto the words, look and feel of the Exploratory Committee's site." The endnote of the story is delivered by George Bush himself, whose comment was: "There ought to be limits to freedom". Reported by Hannibal Travis in "Pirates of the Information Infrastructure: Blackstonian Copyright and the First Amendment", *Berkeley Technology Law Journal* vol.15, no.2 (spring 2000).

16. "In the same way that 'by serving the machine' the proletarian squanders his freedom through the use of his labour power, so the photographer squanders his creative freedom in putting himself at the 'service' of his apparatus" Bernard Edelman, *Ownership of the Image—Elements for a Marxist Theory of Law* (London: Routledge & Kegan Paul, 1979), 45.

17. Celia Lury, *Cultural Rights—Technology, Legality and Personality* (London: Routledge, 1993).

18. Walter Benjamin made a similar remark while investigating the film media. He noted that the film actor is selling his own persona:

    "This market, where he offers not only his labour but also his whole self, his heart and soul, [. . .]." Walter Benjamin, *Illuminations* (New York: Schocken Books, 1969), 231.

19. Eva Hemmungs Wirtén, *No Trespassing—Authorship, Intellectual Property Rights, and the Boundaries of Globalization* (Toronto: University of Toronto Press, 2004).

20. The right to own the image of oneself might sound appealing and natural. But as with all kinds of private property, it comes with a catch. After examining a number of court cases, Jane Gaines concludes:

    "What I mean is that in current legal thought a person does not have publicity rights in himself or herself unless, at one time or another in the course of her career, he or she has transferred these rights to another party." Jane Gaines, *Contested Culture—The Image, the Voice, and the Law* (Chapell Hill: The University of North Carolina Press, 1991), 190. See also Rosemary J. Coombe, "Author/izing the Celebrity: Publicity Rights, Postmodern Politics, and Unauthorized Genders," *Cardozo Arts & Entertainment Law Journal* 10 (1992).

21. See Electronic Frontier Foundation's white paper on DMCA for an exhaustive rapport of abuses: www.eff.org/IP/DRM/DMCA/unintended_consequences.pdf (accessed 2007-02-08)

22. It is explicitly stated in the European Patent Convention, article 52:2(c), that computer programs shall not be regarded as inventions but protected as literary works, i.e. under copyright law.

23. See Robert M. Kunstadt, F. Scott Kieff, and Robert G. Kramer, "Are Sports Moves Next in IP Law?" *National Law Journal* (May 20, 1996).

24. The right to patent life-forms was first introduced when the US Supreme Court decided in 1980 to uphold the microbiologist Ananda Chakrabarty's patent claim over a genetically engineered oil-eating bacterium. Ketih Aoki, "Neocolonialism, Anticommons Property, and Biopiracy in the (Not-So-Brave) New World Order of International Intellectual Property Protection, *Indiana Journal of Global Legal Studies* (1998). Of no less controversy are patents on medical methods. Physician Samuel Pallin' filed an infringement action against a fellow ophthalmologist, Jack A. Singer, for having used the patented method to cure a patient. Public outrage followed and the Federal District court invalidated the patent claim. Joel Garris, "The Case for Patenting Medical Procedures," 22 *American Journal of Law and Medicine* 85, (1996). The question of who is the rightful owner of genetic information is raised by the story about John Moore. He underwent treatment for leukaemia in 1976. The doctors recognised the commercial value of his cells and, after removing Moore's spleen, patented a cell line found in the tissue. In 1990, the supreme court of California ruled that Moore did not own the information extracted from his cells. One irony with the ruling, pointed out by James Boyle, is that while the court denied John Moore ownership rights over his body tissue because such a right would impede the progress of science, the court acknowledged the patentee's property right as a matter of scientific discovery. James Boyle, *Shamans, Software, and Spleens—Law and the Construction of the Information Society* (London: Harvard University Press, 1996), hereafter cited in text.

25. On US policy towards the Berne convention, see Vaidhyanathan, *Copyrights and Copywrongs—The Rise of Intellectual Property and How It Threatens Creativity* (New York: New York University Press, 2001).

26. Marta Pertegás, *Cross-Border Enforcement of Patent Rights* (Oxford: Oxford University Press, 2002), 45.

27. Cherif Bassiouni, "Universal Jurisdiction for International Crimes: Historical Perspectives and Contemporary Practice", *Virginia Journal of International Law*, vol.42, no.8 (2001).

28. In her study of globalisation, Saskia Sassen points out human rights codes and global capital markets as two instances that override the legitimacy of the nation state. Saskia Sassen, *Losing Control?—Sovereignity in an Age of Globalization* (New York: Columbia University Press, 1996).

29. There has been much research on the redistributive effects of the TRIPs treaty and the role of corporate interests in drafting the treaty. Keith Maskus, *Intellectual Property Rights in the Global Economy* (Washington DC: Institute for International Economics, 2000), Duncan Matthew, *Globalising Intellectual Property Rights—The TRIPs Agreement* (London: Routledge, 2002), Susan Sell, *Private Power, Public Law—The Globalization of Intellectual Property Rights* (Cambridge: Cambridge University Press, 2003).

30. Michael Perelman "The Political Economy of Intellectual Property" *Monthly Review* (January 2003), 34.

31. Julian Dibbell, "We Pledge Allegiance to the Penguin" *Wired* (November 2004).

32. http://www.osaia.org/letters/sco_hill.pdf (accessed 2007-02-08)
33. There are similarities between high-sea piracy and high-tech piracy beyond the rhetoric of the copyright industry. Like pirate sharing, high-sea piracy was perceived as a threat against sovereignty and provoked nation states to collaborate on the first 'universal' jurisdiction. Cherif Bassiouni referes to a ruling by chief Justice John Marshall in 1820 where it is stated that crews sailing under a flag acknowledging the authority of no state is subject to the penal code of all nations. Cherif Bassiouni, "Universal Jurisdiction for International Crimes: Historical Perspectives and Contemporary Practice", *Virginia Journal of International Law*, vol.42, no.8. (2001).
34. Contrary to the reports in media, Jon Johansen was not the author of the program. The naming rights for writing the DeCSS is claimed by a hacker collective to which Jon Johansen was affiliated, the Masters of Reverse Engineering (MoRE). Allegedly, they were provided with the cracked CSS files by an un-named, German hacker.
35. Richard Spinello, *Regulating Cyberspace—The Policies and Technologies of Control* (Westport, Conn.: Quorum Books, 2002).
36. The mass exposure of the DeCSS code was partly in response to a related legal case. The motion picture studios and the DVD Copy Control Association filed suit against hundreds of people under Californian trade secret law for posting DeCSS or linking to websites with the source code. This claim was overturned since the information was public and no longer a trade secret. Alex Eaton-Salners, "DVD Copy Control Association v. Bunner: Freedom of Speech and Trade Secrets", *Berkeley Technology Law Journal* (2004).
37. Lawrence Lessig, *Code and Other Laws of Cyberspace* (New York: Basic Books, 1999), 126.
38. The notion was coined by Denise Caruso, a columnist in *New York Times*. Denise Caruso, "The Legacy of Microsoft's Trial", *The New York Times* (December 6, 1999).
39. Karl Marx, *Capital*, vol.I (London: Penguin Books, 1990), 549–50.
40. Richard Edwards, *Contested Terrain* (London: Basic Books, 1979).
41. Andrew Barry, *Political Machines: Governing a Technological Society* (London: Athlone, 2001).
42. See for example many of the essays in *ed.* McChesney, Wood & Foster, *Capitalism and the Information Age—The Political Economy of the Global Communication Revolution* (New York: Monthly Review Press, 1998).
43. Gail Grant, *Understanding Digital Signatures—Establishing Trust over the Internet and Other Networks* (New York: McGraw-Hill, 1998), 14.
44. The term 'Social Taylorism' is coined by Kevin Robins and Frank Webster. They define it as follows:

> "Our argument is that this gathering of skill/knowledge/information, hitherto most apparent in the capitalist labor process, is now entering a new and more pervasive stage. [. . .] We are talking of a process of social deskilling, the depredation of knowledge and skills, which are then sold back in the form of commodities [. . .]." Robins and Webster "Cybernetic Capitalism: Information, Technology, Everyday Life" in *ed.* Vincent Mosco, & Janet Wasko, *The Political Economy of Information* (Madison, Wisc: University of Wisconsin Press, 1988), 65–66.

45. Hybridization has many parallels with the Digital Rights Management technologies now being deployed to prevent pirate sharing on the Internet. Vandana Shiva, in a study of how intellectual property affects farmers in Third World countries, remarks that:

"Processes like hybridization are the technological means that stop seed from reproducing itself. This provides capital with an eminently effective way of circumventing natural constraints on the commodification of the seed." Vandana Shiva, *Biopiracy: the plunder of nature and knowledge* (Boston: South End Press, 1997), 49.

46. Jack Kloppenburg, *First the Seed—The Political Economy of Plant Biotechnology 1492–2000* (Cambridge: Cambridge University Press, 1988).
47. Stuart Biegel, *Beyond Our Control? Confronting the Limits of Our Legal System in the Age of Cyberspace* (Cambridge Mass., MIT Press, 2003).
48. Milton Mueller, *Ruling the Root—Internet Governance and the Taming of Cyberspace* (Cambridge Mass.: MIT Press 2002).
49. The Internet is not the first technology that has become a focal point of the struggle over how to organise communications. In Hans Enzensberger's contribution to a radical theory of communication, drawing from the insights of Walter Benjamin and Bertolt Brecht, he identifies the interests behind one-way, mass communications. The radio media is a case in point:

> "Every transistor radio is, by the nature of its construction, at the same time a potential transmitter; it can interact with other receivers by circuit reversal. The development from a mere distribution medium to a communications medium is technically not a problem. [. . .] The technical distinction between receivers and transmitters reflects the social division of labour into producers and consumers [. . .]" (Hanhardt, 98).

50. Stephanie Miles & Stephen Shankland "PIII debuts amid controversy", *CNET News.com* (February 26, 1999), news.com.com/2100-1040-222256.html?legacy=cnet (accessed 2007-02-08)
51. Mark Stefik, *The Internet Edge—Social, Legal, and Technological Challenges for a Networked World* (Cambridge Mass.: MIT Press, 1999).
52. *ed.* Anil Jain, Ruud Bolle & Sarath Pankanti: *Biometrics—Personal Identification in Networked Society*, (Norwell: Kluwer Academic Publishers, 1999), p.vii.
53. David Harvey, *Spaces of Capital—Towards a Critical Geography* (Edinburgh: Edinburgh University Press, 2001), 246–7.
54. Some examples hereof are the Simputer sponsored by the Indian government and the $100-computer from MIT. In both cases the machines are intended for rural populations in developing countries. In addition to closing the so-called digital divide, these projects will help to spread free software in the South.
55. Interview with Damjan Lampret, initiator of OpenCores. The project can be found at: www.opencores.org. Another interesting free hardware project is the GNUbook. http://gnubook.org/
56. In an article in a computer magasine with the title "Can Software Replace Hardware", the journalist tells about the promises of FPGA technology.

> "In economic terms, this enables new hardware systems to be built for producers in fractions of a second at little cost."; and:

> "Our edge is that we can use easily available programming skills to do what previously required expensive and hard-to-recruit chip designers" Marcus Gibson, "Can Software Replace Hardware", *Ericsson Connexion* (June 1999), 36 and 38.

The advantage with reprogrammable hardware is, in other words, its expediency in deskilling and cheapening labour.
57. Jason Scott, *BBS the Documentary*, 2004.
58. Ellen Goodman, "Spectrum Rights in the Telecosm to Come", *San Diego Law Review* (February/March 2004).

NOTES TO CHAPTER FOUR

1. The term 'affluent society' derives from the heterodox, liberal economist Jon Galbraith's book *The Affluent Society*. The popular adoption of the term in the computer underground, however, differs from the Keynesian arguments put forward by Galbraith under the same title.
2. The schematic summary of 'hierarchy of needs' has to be amended. Maslow does not present his steps in a so straight-forward fashion, but stresses the interface of differing needs, the influence of habits on behaviour, and the overall complexity of the human brain. Abraham Maslow, *Motivation and Personality* (New York: Harper & Row Publishers, 1970).
3. Daniel Bell, *The Cultural Contradictions of Capitalism* (London: Heinemann, 1976), 26.
4. Thomas Davenport and John Beck, *The Attention Economy: Understanding the New Currency of Business* (Boston, Mass.: Harvard Business School Press, 2001).
5. This is best shown by Marx's own words: "The course of social development is by no means that because one individual has satisfied his need he then proceeds to create a superfluity for himself; but rather because one individual or class of individuals is forced to work more than required for the satisfaction of its need—because *surplus labour* is on one side, therefore not-labour and surplus wealth are posited on the other. In reality the development of wealth exists only in these opposites: in potentiality, its development is the possibility of the suspension of these opposites." (*Grundrisse*, 401, *italics in original*).
6. Fred Hirsch, *Social Limits to Growth*, (London: Routledge, 1995).
7. Of course, it is not the phenomenon that is novel, but the extent to which it applies. Already in 1899, Torsten Veblen wrote his famous remarks on the conspicuous consumption of the upper classes:

   > "If, as is sometimes assumed, the incentive to accumulation were the want of subsistence or of physical comfort, then the aggregate economic wants of a community might conceivably be satisfied at some point in the advance of industrial efficiency; but since the struggle is substantially a race for reputability on the basis of an invidious comparison, no approach to a definitive attainment is possible." Thorstein Veblen, *The Theory of the Leisure Class* (London: Compton Printing, 1970), 39.

8. Guy Debord, *The Society of the Spectacle* (New York: Zone books, 1994).
9. In *Economies of Signs & Space*, a standard reference in discussions about the aesthetisation of the economy, Scott Lash and John Urry skips over the concept of use value in two sentences and with a reference to Jean Baudrillard. Likewise, in *Consumer Culture & Postmodernism*, another milestone in the field, Mike Featherstone cites Baudrillard extensively but the name Guy Debord seems never to have crossed his mind. Scott Lash & John Urry, *Economies of Signs & Space* (London: Sage Publications, 1994), Mike Featherstone, *Consumer Culture & Postmodernism* (London: Sage Publications, 1991).
10. Wolfgang Haug, *Critique of Commodity Aesthetics: Appearance, Sexuality and Advertising in Capitalist Society* (Cambridge: Polity Press, 1986); hereafter cited in text.
11. For an early, influential critique of the inadequacy of mass-consumption in satisfying aesthetic needs, see Tibor Scitovsky, *The Joyless Economy—an Inquiry Into Human Satisfaction and Consumer Dissatisfaction*, (Oxford: Oxford University Press, 1977).
12. "The signifier becomes its own referent and the use value of the sign disappears to the benefit of its commutation and exchange value alone." (*Baudrillard*, 128).

Jean Baudrillard has rightly been criticised for theorising use value exclusively from the viewpoint of capital and for not taking account of how class struggle intervenes in the process of defining needs. Nonetheless, both Douglas Kellner and Maryn Lee concede that the early works of Baudrillard is challenging and warrant a serious discussion. Douglas Kellner, *Jean Baudrillard—From Marxism to Postmodernism and Beyond* (Cambridge: Polity Press, 1989), and, Martyn Lee, *Consumer Culture Reborn—The Cultural Politics of Consumption* (London: Routledge 1993).

13. Naomi Wolf, *The Beauty Myth—How Images of Beauty Are Used Against Women* (London: Vintage, 1991), 76. She goes on to remind the reader that the opposite concept of beauty is when the features of a person become attractive to another person because of their unique relation.

14. Alvin Toffler, *The Third Wave* (New York: Bantam Books, 1981).

15. Paul du Gay, *Consumption and Identity at Work*, (London: Sage, 1995).

16. Stephen Kline, Nick Dyer-Witheford & Greig De Peuter, *Digital Play—The Interaction of Technology, Culture, and Marketing*, London: McGill-Queen's University Press, 2003.

17. Angela McRobbie, "From Holloway to Hollywood: Happiness at Work in the New Cultural Economy?", in *ed.* Paul du Gay & Michael Pryke, *Cultural Economy: Cultural Analysis and Commercial Life* (London: Sage, 2002), hereafter cited in text.

18. Paul Heeles, "Work Ethics, Soft Capitalism and the 'Turn to Life' ", in (*du Gay*).

19. Though making few explicit references to needs, and though there are differences between the younger and the mature Marx, it is clear that 'needs' play a central role in Marx's thinking. For an account of this part of Marx's philosophy, see Agnes Heller, *The Theory of Need in Marx* (New York: St. Martin's Publisher, 1976).

20. In his conclusion, Henry Jenkins write: "The irony, of course, is that fans have found the very forces that work to isolate us from each other to be the ideal foundation for creating connections across traditional boundaries; that fans have found the very forces that transform many Americans into spectators to provide the resources for creating a more participatory culture; that fans have found the very forces that reinforce patriarchal authority to contain tools by which to critique that authority." Henry Jenkins, *Textual Poachers—Television Fans & Participatory Culture* (New York; Routledge, 1992), 284.

21. Raoul Vaneigem gave voice to a line of thinking characteristic of the Situationist International and the New Left, where capitalism was chiefly accused for the boredom and degradation of life which it causes. Raoul Vaneigem, *The Revolution of Everyday Life* (London: Left bank books, 1983).

NOTES TO CHAPTER FIVE

1. Michael Howard & John King, "Capitalism, Socialism and Historical Materialism" in *ed.* Antonio Callari, Stephen Cullenberg & Carole Biewener, *Marxism in the Postmodern Age—Confronting the New World Order* (New York: Guilford Press, 1994), 427.

2. Frederic Scherer, *Industrial Market Structure and Economic Performance* (Chicago: Rand McNally & Co., 1970), 392, hereafter cited in text.

3. It goes without saying that this practice was much preferable to the owners. Collaboration between engineers working in different mines was facilitated by a custom of cross-ownership in the mining district. Alessandro Nuvolari, "Collective Invention during the British Industrial Revolution: The Case of

the Cornish Pumping Engine", *Cambridge Journal of Economics* vol.28, no 3 (2004).

4. Chrisitne MacLeod, *Inventing the Industrial Revolution—The English Patent System*, 1660–1800, (Cambridge: Cambridge University Press, 1988).

5. Erik Barnouw, *A Tower in Babel—A History of Broadcasting in the United States* (New York: Oxford University Press, 1969).

6. Robert Allen has written a classic paper arguing the prevalence of 'collective invention'. Robert Allen, "Collective invention", *Journal of Economic Behavior and Organization* (March 1983). For a case against software patents, see Ben Klemens, *Ma+h You Can't Use—Patents, Copyright, and Software* (Washington, D.C.: Brookings Institution Press, 2006).

7. *ed.* Stephen Merrill, Richard Levin & Mark Myers, *A Patent System for the 21st Century*, 2004. www.aipla.org/Content/ContentGroups/Issues_and_Advocacy/Comments2/Patent_and_Trademark_Office/2004/PatentRpt.pdf (accessed 2007-02-08).

8. Dorothy Nelkin, *Science as Intellectual Property* (New York: McMillan Publishing Company, 1984), David Noble, *Digital Diploma Mills: The Automation of Higher Education* (New York: Monthly Review Press, 2001), *ed.* Benjamin Johnson, Patrick Kavanagh & Kevin Mattson, *Steal this University—The Rise of the Corporate University and the Academic Labor Movement* (New York: Routledge, 2003).

9. National Research Council, *Bits of Power: Issues in Global Access to Scientific Data* (Washington: National Academy Press, 1997).

10. Robert Merges, "Contracting Into Liability Rules: Intellectual Property Rights and Collective Rights Organizations", *California Law Review* (October 1996).

11. Richard Dunford, "The Suppression of Technology" *Administrative Science Quarterly* 32 (1987).

12. "The apparatus of antiproduction is no longer a transcendent instance that opposes production, limits it, or checks it; on the contrary, it insinuates itself everywhere in the productive machine and becomes firmly wedded to it in order to regulate its productivity and realize surplus value—which explains, for example, the difference between the despotic bureaucracy and the capitalist bureaucracy." Gilles Deleuze and Felix Guattari, *Anti-Oedipus—Capitalism & Schizophrenia* (London: Athlone Press, 2003), 235.

13. Ketih Aoki, "Neocolonialism, Anticommons Property, and Biopiracy in the (Not-So-Brave) New World Order of International Intellectual Property Protection, *Indiana Journal of Global Legal Studies* (1998).

14. A number of dissenting economists have come to the conclusion that the culture industry can gain from so-called piracy. If the net effect is negative or positive depends on the circumstances, but on balance, Bakos, Brynjolfsson, and Lichtman assert that media companies profits when consumers share information goods. Yannies Bakos, Erik Brynjolfsson & Douglas Lichtman, *Shared Information Goods*, Journal of Law and Economics (April 1999). For a collection of unorthodox views on illicit copying, argued from within neoclassical economic theory, see *ed.* Wendy Gordon & Richard Watt, *The Economics of Copyright—Developments in Research and Analysis* (Northampton, Mass.: Elgar, 2003).

15. Oz Shy, *The Economics of Network Industries* (Cambridge: Cambridge University Press, 2001).

16. Stan Liebowitz, "Copying and Indirect Appropriability: Photocopying of Journals.", *Journal of Political Economy* 93 (1985).

17. For a thorough investigation into the Napster case, see Joseph Menn, *All the Rave—The Rise and Fall of Shawn Fanning's Napster* (New York: Crown Business, 2003).

18. Gnutella was rapidly followed by other architectures that radicalised decentralisation and anonymity even further. Freenet, initiated by Ian Clark in 1999, is more robust against surveillance than Gnutella. Freenet stores content on the computers of its users without letting the users know what the content is. The only thing a user of Freenet knows for sure is that a space in her computer has been designated by the system to store files which other users of Freenet may access. Thus, users are guaranteed a 'plausible deniability' if those files happen to be claimed by a third party.

19. Dorothy Kidd in *ed*. McCaughey & Ayers, *Cyberactivism—Online Activism in Theory and Practice* (New York: Routledge, 2003), Dan Gillmore, *We the Media—Grassroots Journalism—By the People, For the People* (Cebastopol C.A.; O'Reilly, 2006).

20. Eben Moglen, "Anarchism Triumphant, Free Software and the Death of Copyright", *First Monday*, vol.4, no.8 (August 1999).

21. See David Anderson, "SETI@home" in Andy Oram, *Peer-to-Peer—Harnessing the Benefits of a Disruptive Technology*, (Sebastopol: O'Reilly, 2001), 2001.

22. Mark Poster, *What's the Matter With the Internet?* (Minneapolis: University of Minnesota Press, 2001), 97.

23. www.nature.com/news/2005/051212/full/438900a.html, (accessed 2007-02-08).

24. http://alumni.media.mit.edu/~fviegas/papers/history_flow.pdf, (accessed 2007-02-08).

25. Peter Kropotkin, *Fields, Factories and Workshops Tomorrow* (London: Freedom Press, 1985), 182.

26. This case has been argued by Marshall Sahlins, *Stone Age Economics*, 1972.

27. Harry Braverman, *Labor and Monopoly Capital* (New York: Monthly Review Press, 1998), 318, hereafter cited in text.

28. *ed*. Stephen Wood, "Introduction", in *The Degradation of Work?—Skill, Deskilling and the Labour Process* (London: Hutchinson, 1982).

29. *ed*. Andrew Zimbalist, "Technology and the Labour Process in the Printing Industry", in *Case Studies on the Labor Process*, (New York: Monthly Review Press, 1979).

30. A number of sociologists, management writers, and Marxists could be quoted to demonstrate this point. It will suffice with a remark by Clause Offe on service workers:

    "Here the anticipated outcome of action is often more likely to be achieved the less means and ends are specified in detail, the more there is scope for interpretation and manoeuvre, the less the personal motivation of the service worker is subject to external control and, hence, given greater opportunity to respond *ad hoc* to the particular features of a particular environment which in principle cannot be standardized without producing counterproductive consequences." Claus Offe, *Disorganized Capitalism—Contemporary Transformations of Work and Politics* (Cambridge: Polity Press, 1985), 106–7, *italics in original*.

31. Andrew Friedman, *Industry and Labour—Class Struggle at Work and Monopoly Capitalism* (London: Macmillan Press, 1977).

32. To cyber-feminists, however, the blurring of the human subject and the machine into what they call a 'cyborg' becomes a new starting point for fighting patriarchy and capitalism. That outlook is rather close to the hacker perspective.

33. Humberto Maturana & Francisco Varela, *Autopoiesis and Cognition—The Realization of the Living* (Dordrecht: Reidel, 1980), 82; hereafter cited in text.

34. "In a word, the real difference is not between the living and the machine, vitalism and mechanism, but between two states of the machine that are two states of the living as well. The machine taken in its structural unity, the living taken in its specific and even personal unity, are mass phenomena or molar aggregates; for this reason each points to the extrinsic existence of the other." Gilles Deleuze and Felix Guattari, *Anti-Oedipus—Capitalism & Schizophrenia* (London: Athlone Press, 2003), 286.

NOTES TO CHAPTER SIX

1. Michael Albert, *Parecon—Life After Capitalism—Participatory Economics* (New York: Verso, 2003).
2. Two books giving an overview of network science are Albert-László Barabási, *Linked—The New Science of Networks* (Cambridge Mass.: Perseus Publishing, 2002), Duncan Watts, *Six Degrees—The Science of a Connected Age* (New York: W.W. Norton & Company, 2003).
3. Alexander Galloway, *Protocol—How Control Exists After Decentralization* (Cambridge Mass.:MIT Press, 2004).
4. "Accumulation, where private property prevails, is the *concentration* of capital in the hands of the few, it is in general an inevitable consequence if capital is left to follow its natural course, and it is precisely through competition that the way is cleared for this natural disposition of capital." Karl Marx, *Economic and Philosophic Manuscripts of 1844* (USSR: Progress Publishers, 1981), 37, *italics in original*; hereafter cited in text as *1844*.
5. Thomas Malone & Robert Laubacher, "The Dawn of the E-Lance Economy" *Harvard Business Review* (September 1, 1998).
6. ed. Oliver Williamson and Sidney Winter, *The Nature of the Firm: Origins, Evolution, and Development* (New York: Oxford University Press, 1993).
7. Yochai Benkler, "Coase's Penguin, or, Linux and The Nature of the Firm", *The Yale Law Journal* vol.112 no.3 (December 2002), and *The Wealth of Networks—How Social Production Transforms Markets and Freedom*, (New Haven: Yale University Press, 2006).
8. Walter Powel, in *ed*. Barry Staw & Larry Cummings, *Research in Organizational Behavior* (London: Jai Press, 1990), 303.
9. A few hard-dies insist that the calculating power of computers have been the missing piece that finally can make a centralised, planned economy feasible:

   "Where the to be a revolution in any country in the world tomorrow, the possibility for an immediate transition to democratic and efficient planning using the Internet would put to rest the claims about the infeasibility of a socialist economy." Andy Pollack, in *ed*. Robert McChesney, Ellen Meiksins Wood & John Bellamy Foster, *Capitalism and the Information Age—The Political Economy of the Global Communication Revolution* (New York: Monthly Review Press, 1998), 220.

10. Kim Moody makes a valid point about the relation between small production sites and big corporations:

    "The irony here is that production systems have grown so large and complex over time that the giant facility of yesterday is not large enough to enclose more than a fraction of the overall process." Kim Moody, *Workers in a Lean World—Unions in the International Economy* (London: Verso, 1997), 151.

11. Alan Felstead, *The Corporate Paradox—Power and Control in the Business Franchise* (London: Routledge, 1993).
12. Bennett Harrison, *Lean and Mean—The Changing Landscape of Corporate Power in the Age of Flexibility* (New York: Guilford Press, 1997).
13. Cyril James, *State Capitalism & World Revolution* (Chicago: Charles H. Kerr Publishing Company, 1986).
14. Bob Jessop, *The Future of the Capitalist State* (Cambridge: Polity Press, 2002).
15. "At the roots of the crisis that induced *perestroika* and triggered nationalism was the incapacity of Soviet statism to ensure the transition to the new informational paradigm, in parallel to the process that was taking place in the rest of the world." Manuell Castells, *The End of Millennium*, vol.III (Oxford: Blackwell Publishers, 1999), 8.
16. Garrett Hardin, "The Tragedy of the Commons", *Science*, (December 1968).
17. Elinor Ostrom, *Governing the Commons: the Evolution of Institutions for Collective Action* (Cambridge: Cambridge University Press, 1990).
18. Self-managed collective use of commons is not an isolated event specific to pre-industrial times. New attempts are made in contemporary society when a community faces the depletion of resources on which it depends. For a collection of such examples, see David Fenny, Fikret Berkes, Bonnie McCay, and James Acheson "The Tragedy of the Commons: Twenty-two Years Later." in *ed.* John Baden and Douglas Noonan, *Managing the Commons* (London: Indiana University Press, 1998).
19. Lewis Mumford, *Technics and Human Development*, (New York: HBJ Book, 1967), 96.
20. Jean-Joseph Goux argues that with the post-modern turn of capitalism, Georges Bataille's thinking has become attractive to capital's apologetics. Jean-Joseph Goux, "General Economics and Postmodern Capitalism" Yale French Studies 78 (1990). Scott Shershow agrees with Goux but appeals for a rescuing of Bataille. Scott Cutler Shershow, "Of Sinking: Marxism and the 'General' Economy". Critical Inquiry vol 27, no 3 (spring 2001).
21. Georges Bataille, *The Accursed Share—An Essay on General Economy*, vol.I (New York: Zone Books, 1988).
22. Michael Heller, "The Tragedy of the Anticommons: Property in the Transition from Marx to Markets", *Harvard Law Review* (January 1998).
23. Marcel Mauss, *The Gift: Forms and Functions of Exchange in Archaic Societies* (London: Routledge, 1988).
24. Derrida declares that there can only be such a thing as a Gift if it is not thought of in terms of circulation and tit-for-tat exchange. Jacques Derrida, *Given Time. Counterfeit Money* (Chicago: University of Chicago Press, 1992).
25. In Peter Ekeh's presentation of social exchange theories, he writes that:

> "[. . .] social exchange processes yield for the larger society a moral code of behavior which acquires an independent existence outside the social exchange situation and which informs all social, economic, and political interpersonal relationships in society." Peter Ekeh, *Social Exchange Theory—The Two Traditions* (London: Heinemann, 1974), 58.

26. Igor Kopytoff "The Cultural Biography of Things: Commoditization as Process" in *ed.* Arjun Appadurai, *The Social Life of Things—Commodities in Cultural Perspective* (Cambridge: Cambridge University Press, 1986).
27. When Richard Barbrook wrote his article he set out to present an alternative to the cyber-libertarian, free market perspective that was then dominant on the Internet. The text was rhetorical and tongue-in-cheek and Barbrook has since modified the claims made in the article. Richard Barbrook, "The High-Tech Gift Economy", *First Monday* vol.3, no.12 (December 1998).

28. John Frow, *Time & Commodity Culture—Essays in Cultural Theory and Postmodernity* (Oxford: Clarendon Press, 1997), 207.
29. Peter Wayner, *Free for All—How Linux and the Free Software Movement Undercut the High-Tech Titans*, (New York: HarperBusiness 2000), 157, *my emphasis*.
30. Howard Rheingold coined the term 'virtual community'. Howard Rheingold, *The Virtual Community—Homesteading on the Electronic Frontier* (Cambridge, Mass.: MIT Press, 2000).
31. Robert Ellickson has demonstrated the pivotal role of norms rather than law in upholding social order. For norms to regulate social behavior, however, a few conditions have to be met:

> "To achieve order without law, people must have continuing relationships, reliable information about past behavior, and effective countervailing power" Robert Ellickson, *Order Without Law: How Neighbours Settle Disputes* (Cambridge, Mass.: Harvard University Press, 1991), 284.

32. Peter Ekeh, *Social Exchange Theory—The Two Traditions* (London: Heinemann, 1974), 205.
33. Jacob Strahilevitz "Charismatic Code, Social Norms, and the Emergence of Cooperation on the File-Swapping Networks", *Virginia Law Review* (May 2003). It doesn't occur to Strahilevitz that his idea could be reversed in order to explain the lack of reciprocity in the surrounding society. Uncharismatic Code conspires to hide from us the cooperative behaviour of our neighbours. Separated from our peers, our only source of security is in those structures which are upholding uncharismatic code. Virtual reality differs in that the means to write code is not monopolised by the state and capital. When peers are free to write code they choose to write it 'charismatically'.
34. Claude Lévi-Strauss makes this point quite clear in his study of archaic societies:

> "Goods are not only economic commodities, but vehicles and instruments for realities of another order, such as power, influence, sympathy, status, and emotion; and the skilful game of exchange [. . .] consists in a complex totality of conscious or unconscious manoeuvres in order to gain security and to guard oneself against risks brought about by alliances and by rivalries." Claude Lévi-Strauss, *The Elementary Structures of Kinship* (Boston: Beacon Press, 1969), 54.

35. In a study of the warez movement, Alf Rehn has documented the great length crackers go to in order to make their activity known to their peers. Mirroring the development in the copyright industry, some warez groups have even developed digital signatures to ensure that no-one fakes the credits announced in their releases. Alf Rehn, *Electronic Potlatch—A Study of New Technologies and Primitive Economic Behaviour* (Stockholm: KTH, 2001), 204.

NOTES TO CHAPTER SEVEN

1. Kostas Axelos, *Alienation, Praxis, and Techné in the Thought of Karl Marx* (Austin: University of Texas Press, 1976), 194.
2. Herbert Marcuse, *Eros and Civilization—A Philosophical Inquiry into Freud* (London: Routledge, 1998), 195, *italics in original*; hereafter cited in text as *Eros*.
3. Herbert Marcuse, "On the Philosophical Foundation of the Concept of Labor in Economics", *Telos*, 16 (summer 1973).
4. Georg Lukács, *Goethe and His Age* (London: Merlin, 1968).

5. Georg Lukács, *History and Class Consciousness* (Cambridge, Mass.: MIT Press, 2000), 140; hereafter cited in text as *history*.
6. Herbert Marcuse, *The Aesthetic Dimension: Toward a Critique of Marxist Aesthetics* (Boston: Beacon Press, 1978).
7. Eve Chiapello, "Evolution and Co-optation: The 'Artist Critique' of Management and Capitalism", *Third Text* vol.18, no.6 (2004).
8. Johan Huizinga, *Homo Ludens—A Study of the Play Element in Culture* (Boston: Beacon Press, 1955).
9. Roger Caillois, *Man, Play, and Games* (Urbana, Ill.: University of Illinois Press, 2001).
10. Gordon Burghardt, *The Genesis of Animal Play: Testing the Limits* (London: MIT Press, 2004).
11. Edward Thompson, "Patrician Society, Plebeian Culture", *Journal of Social History*, vol.7, no. 4 (summer 1974).
12. Francis Hearn, "Toward a Critical Theory of Play", *Telos* 30 (winter 1976–1977).
13. Max Horkheimer & Theodor Adorno, *Dialectic of Enlightenment* (London: Verso, 1997), 137.
14. André Gorz, *Reclaiming Work—Beyond the Wage Based Society* (Cambridge: Polity Press, 1999), Jeremy Rifkin, *The End of Work: The Decline of the Global Labor Force and the Dawn of the Post-Market Era* (New York: G.P. Putnam's sons, 1995), Jeremy Seabrook, *The Leisure Society* (Oxford: Basil Blackwell, 1988).
15. Quoted in Michael Perelman, *The Innovation of Capitalism—Classical Political Economy and the Secret History of Primitive Accumulation* (Durham: Duke University Press, 2000), p.46; hereafter cited in text.
16. Gustavo Esteva and Madhu Prakash have studied the coping strategies of the extremely poor in Third World countries. These people are forced to sustain themselves independently or partially independently of the circulation of commodities. The authors suggest that this provides a model for activists in the industrial world for cutting off ties with global circuits of capital. Gustavo Esteva & Madhu Prakash, *Grassroots Post-Modernism—Remaking the Soil of Cultures* (London: Zed Books), 1998.
17. Samuel Bowles and Herbert Gintis, *Schooling in Capitalist America—Educational Reform and the Contradictions of Economic Life* (London: Routledge & Kegan Paul Ltd., 1976).
18. Nicos Poulantzas, for instance, based his categorisation of the working class on the distinction in Marxist theory between productive and unproductive workers. It led him to exclude service workers, office clerks, and technicians, among others, from the working class. Nicos Poulantzas, *Classes in Contemporary Capitalism* (London: Verso, 1979).
19. Ernesto Laclau & Chantal Mouffe, *Hegemony and Socialist Strategy: Towards a Radical Democratic Politics* (London: Verso, 1985)
20. Judith Butler, Ernesto Laclau & Slavoj Zizek, *Contingency, Hegemony, Universality—Contemporary Dialogues on the Left* (London: Verso, 2000).
21. John Holloway, "Crisis, Fetishism, Class Composition" in *ed.* Werner Bonefeld, Richard Gunn & Kosmas Psychopedis, *Open Marxism*, vol.2 (London: Pluto Press, 1992).
22. Antonio Negri, *Revolution Retrieved—Writings on Marx, Keynes, Capitalist Crisis and New Social Subjects (1967–83)*, (London: Red Notes, 1988).
23. McKenzie Wark, *A Hacker Manifesto* (Cambridge Mass.: Harvard University Press, 2004).
24. Martin Jay, *Marxism and Totality: the Adventures of a Concept from Lukács to Habermas* (Cambridge: Polity Press, 1984).

25. Michel de Certeau, *The Practice of Everyday Life* (Los Angeles: University of California Press, 1984).
26. Frederick Brooks, *The Mythical Man-Month* (Reading, Mass.: Addison-Wesley, 1995), 7.
27. Gernot Böhme, "Technical Gadgetry: Technological Development in the Aesthetic Economy", *Thesis Eleven* 86 (August 2006).
28. Neil Gershenfeld, *FAB—The Coming Revolution on Your Desktop—From Personal Computers to Personal Fabrication* (New York: Basic Books, 2005).

NOTES TO SUMMARY

1. Theodor Adorno, "On the Fetish-Character in Music and the Regression of Listening" in *ed.*Andrew Arato and Eike Gebhardt, *The Essential Frankfurth School Reader* (New York: Continuum, 1998), 293.
2. http://news.bbc.co.uk/2/hi/asia-pacific/2960218.stm (accessed 2007-02-08).

Bibliography

Aglietta Michel. *A Theory of Capitalist Regulation*, London: NLB, 1979.

Albert, Michel. *Parecon—Life After Capitalism—Participatory Economics*, New York: Verso, 2003.

ed. Allen, Thad and Gabrielle Hecht. *Technologies of Power—Essays in Honour of Thomas Parke Huges and Agatha Chipley Huges*, Cambridge Mass.: The MIT Press, 2001.

Althusser, Louis. *Essays on Ideology*, London: Verso, 1984.

ed. Amin, Ash, *Post-Fordism: A Reader*, Oxford: Blackwell, 1994.

ed. Appadurai, Arjun. *The Social Life of Things—Commodities in Cultural Perspective*, Cambridge: Cambridge University Press, 1986.

ed. Appleby, Joyce and Terence Ball. *Thomas Jefferson—Political Writings*, New York: Cambridge University Press, 1999.

ed. Arato, Andrew and Eike Gebhardt, The Essential Frankfurt School Reader (New York: Continuum, 1998).

Axelos, Kostas. *Alienation, Praxis, and Techné in the Thought of Karl Marx*, Austin: University of Texas Press, 1976.

Babbage, Charles. *On the Economy of Machinery and Manufactures*, New York: Augustus M Kelley Publishers, 1971.

Baden, John, and Douglas Noonan. *Managing the Commons*, London: Indiana University Press, 1998.

ed. Balakrishnan, Gopal. *Debating Empire*, London: Verso, 2003.

Barabási, Albert-László. *Linked—The New Science of Networks*, Cambridge Mass.: Perseus Publishing, 2002.

Barbrook, Richard. *The Class of the New*, London: Mute, 2006.

Barnouw, Erik. *A Tower in Babel—A History of Broadcasting in the United States*, vol.I, New York: Oxford University Press, 1969.

Barry, Andrew. *Political Machines: Governing a Technological Society*, London: Athlone, 2001.

Barthes, Roland. *Mythologies*, New York: Hill and Wang, 1977.

——— *Image, Music, Text*, New York: Noonday Press, 1997.

Bataille, George. *The Accursed Share: An Essay on General Economy*, vol. I., New York: Zone Books, 1988.

Baudrillard, Jean. *The Mirror of Production*, St. Louis, MO: Telos Press, 1975.

——— *For a Critique of the Political Economy of the Sign*, St. Louis, MO: Telos Press, 1981.

Bauman, Zygmunt. *Work, Consumerism, and the New Poor*, Philadelphia, PA, Open University Press, 1998.

Baym, Nancy. *Tune In, Log On—Soaps, Fandom, and Online Community*, Thousand Oaks: Sage Publications, 2000.

Bell, Daniel. *The Coming of the Post-Industrial Society*, New York: Basic Books, 1973.

―――― *The Cultural Contradictions of Capitalism*, London: Heinemann, 1976.

Benjamin, Walter. *Illuminations*, New York: Schocken Books, 1969.

Benkler, Yochai. *The Wealth of Networks: How Social Production Transforms Markets and Freedom*, New Haven: Yale University Press, 2006.

Berggren, Christian, *Alternatives to Lean Production—Work Organisation in the Swedish Auto Industry*, New York: ILR Press, 1992.

Berners-Lee, Tim, and Mark Fischetti. *Weaving the Web—The Past, Present and Future of the World Wide Web*, London: Texere, 2000.

Bettig, Roland, *Copyrighting Culture—the Political Economy of Intellectual Property*, Boulder, CO: Westview Press, 1996.

Biegel, Stuart. *Beyond Our Control? Confronting the Limits of Our Legal System in the Age of Cyberspace*, Cambridge Mass., MIT Press, 2003.

Bijker, Wiebe. *Of Bicycles, Bakelites, and Bulbs—Towards a Theory of Sociotechnical Change*, Cambridge, Mass.: MIT Press, 1995.

Black, Edwin, *IBM and the Holocaust: The Strategic Alliance Between Nazi Germany and America's Most Powerful Corporation*, London: Little, Brown & co, 2001.

Bollier, David. *Silent Theft—The Private Plunder of Our Common Wealth*, London: Routledge, 2003.

ed. Bonefeld, Werner, and Richard Gunn and Kosmas Psychopedis. *Open Marxism*, vol.I, London: Pluto Press, 1992.

―――― *Open Marxism*, vol.II, London: Pluto Press, 1992.

ed. Bonefeld, Werner, and John Holloway. *Post-Fordism and Social Form—A Marxist Debate on the Post-Fordist State*, Basingstoke UK: Macmillan, 1991.

Bowles, Samuel, and Herbert Gintis. *Schooling in Capitalist America—Educational Reform and the Contradictions of Economic Life*, London: Routledge & Kegan Paul Ltd, 1976.

Brand, Stewart. *The Media Lab—Inventing the Future at M.I.T.*, Harmondsworth UK: Penguin, 1988.

Braverman, Harry. *Labor and Monopoly Capital*, New York: Monthly Review Press, 1998.

Brooks, Frederick, *The Mythical Man-Month*, Reading, Mass.: Addison-Wesley, 1995.

Boyle, James. *Shamans, Software, and Spleens—Law and the Construction of the Information Society*, London: Harvard University Press, 1996.

ed. Buck-Mors, Susan, and Julian Stallabrass and Leonidas Donskis. *Ground Zero Control—Technology and Utopia*, London: Black Dog Production, 1999.

Burghardt, Gordon. *The Genesis of Animal Play: Testing the Limits*, London: MIT Press, 2004.

Butler, Judith, and Ernesto Laclau and Slavoj Zizek. *Contingency, Hegemony, Universality—Contemporary Dialogues on the Left*, London: Verso, 2000.

Caffentzis, George. "On Africa and Self-Reproducing Automata", in *New Enclosures/Midnight Notes Collective*, Jamaica Plain, Ma.: Midnight Notes, 1990.

Caillois, Roger. *Man, Play, and Games* Urbana, Ill.: University of Illinois Press, 2001.

ed. Calabrese, Andrew, and Colin Sparks, *Toward a Political Economy of Culture—Capitalism and Communication in the Twenty-First Century*, Lanham, Md.: Rowman & Littlefield Publishing Group, 2004.

ed. Callari, Antonio, and Stephen Cullenberg and Carole Biewener, *Marxism in the Postmodern Age—Confronting the New World Order*, New York: Guilford Press, 1994.

Castells, Manuel. *The Rise of the Network Society*, vol. I, Oxford: Blackwell Publishers, 2000.

————, 2000, *The Power of Identity*, vol. II, Oxford: Blackwell Publishers, 2000.

———— 2000, *The End of Millennium*, vol. III, Oxford: Blackwell Publishers, 2000.

Certeau, Michel de. *The Practice of Everyday Life*, Los Angeles: University of California Press, 1984.

Cleaver, Harry. *Reading Capital Politically*, London: AK Press, 2000.

Commitee on Issues in the Transborder Flow of Scientific Data. *Bits of Power: Issues in Global Access to Scientific Data*, Washington: National Academy Press, 1997.

ed. Chant, Colin. *Sources for the Study of Science, Technology and Everyday Life 1870–1950—A Secondary Reader*, vol.II, London: Hodder & Stoughton, 1988.

Cohen, Gerhald. *Karl Marx's Theory of History—A Defence*, Oxford: Clarendon Press, 2000.

Collins, Hugh, *Marxism and Law*, Oxford: Clarendon Press, 1982.

ed. Comor, Edward. *The Global Political Economy of Communication—Hegemony, Telecommunication and the Information Economy*, St Martin's Press: New York, 1994.

Coombe, Rosemarry. *The Cultural Life of Intellectual Properties—Authorship, Appropriation, and the Law*, London: Duke University Press, 1998.

Costa, Mariarosa and Selma James. *The Power of Women and the Subversion of the Community*, Bristol UK: The Falling Wall Press, 1973.

Critical Art Ensemble. *Electronic Civil Disobedience—And Other Unpopular Ideas*, New York: Autonomedia, 1996.

Cross, Gary. *Time and Money—The Making of Consumer Culture*, London: Routledge, 1993.

Dahrendorf, Ralf. *Class and Class Conflict in Industrial Society*, London: Routledge, 1959.

ed. Daryl, Jennifer, and Fred Fejes. *The Ideology of the Information Age*, Norwood: ABLEX Publishing, 1987.

Davenport, Thomas, and John Beck. *The Attention Economy: Understanding the New Currency of Business*, Boston, Mass.: Harvard Business School Press, 2001.

ed. Davis, Jim, and Thomas Hirschl, and Michael Stack. *Cutting edge: technology, information capitalism and social revolution*, London: Verso, 1997.

Debora, Halbert. *Intellectual Property in the Information Age—The Politics of Expanding Ownership Rights*, Westpoint CT: Quorum Books, 1999.

Debord, Guy. *The Society of the Spectacle*, New York: Zone books, 1994.

Deleuze, Gilles, *Negotiations*, New York: Columbia University Press, 1995.

Deleuze, Gilles, and Felix Guattari. *A Thousand Plateaus—Capitalism and Schizophrenia*, London: Athlone Press, 1999.

———— *Anti-Oedipus—Capitalism & Schizophrenia*, London: Athlone Press, 2003.

Derrida, Jacques. *Given Time. Counterfeit Money*, Chicago: University of Chicago Press, 1992.

ed. DiBona, Chris, and Sam Ockman and Mark Stone. *Open Sources—Voices from the Open Source Revolution*, London: O'Reilly & Associates, 1999.

Drahos, Peter, and John Braithwaite. *Information Feudalism—Who Owns The Knowledge Economy*, London: Erthscan, 2002.

ed. Dreyfuss, Rochelle, and Diane Zimmerman and Harry First. *Expanding the boundaries of Intellectual Property—Innovation Policies for the Knowledge Society*, New York: Oxford University Press, 2001.

du Gay, Paul. *Consumption and Identity at Work*, London: Sage, 1995.

du Gay, Paul, and Michael Pryke. *Cultural Economy: Cultural Analysis and Commercial Life*, London: Sage, 2002.

Dyer-Witheford, Nick. *Cyber-Marx, Cycles and Circuits of Struggle in High-Technology Capitalism*, Chicago: University of Illinois Press, 1999.

Edelman, Bernard. *Ownership of the Image—Elements for a Marxist Theory of Law*, London: Routledge & Kegan Paul, 1979.

Edwards, Richard. *Contested Terrain*, London: Basic Books, 1979.

Ekeh, Peter. *Social Exchange Theory—The Two Traditions*, London: Heinemann, 1974.

Ellickson, Robert. *Order Without Law: How Neighbors Settle Disputes*, Cambridge, Mass.: Harvard University Press, 1991.

Essinger, James. *Jacquard's Web—How a Hand Loom Led to the Birth of the Information Age*, Oxford: Oxford University Press, 2004.

Esteva, Gustavo, and Madhu Suri Prakash. *Grassroots Post-Modernism—Remaking the Soil of Cultures*, London: Zed Books, 1998.

Ewen, Stuart. *Captains of Consciousness—Advertising and the Social Roots of the Consumer Culture*, New York : McGraw-Hill, 1977.

Featherstone, Mike. *Consumer Culture & Postmodernism*, London: Sage Publications, 1991.

Fehér, Ferenc, and Agnes Heller and György Márkus. *Dictatorship Over Needs*, Oxford: Basil Blackwell, 1983

Felstead, Alan. *The Corporate Paradox—Power and Control in the Business Franchise*, London: Routledge, 1993.

Felstead, Alan, and Nick Jewson. *In Work, at Home—Towards an Understanding of Homeworking*, London: Routledge, 2000.

Fiske, John. *Television Culture*, London: Routledge, 1987.

ed Fitzpatrick, Peter, and Alan Hunt, *Critical Legal Studies*, Kent: Basil Blackwell, 1990.

Florida, Richard. *The Rise of the Creative Class—And How it's Transforming Work, Leisure, Community & Everyday Life*, New York: Basic Books, 2002.

Fraad, Harriet, and Stephen Resnick and Richard Wolff. *Bringing it all Back Home—Class, Gender and Power in the Modern Household*, London: Pluto Press, 1994.

Francois Fortier: 2001, *Virtuality Check—Power Relations and Alternative Strategies in the Information Society*, London: Verso.

Friedman, Andrew. *Industry and Labour—Class Struggle at Work and Monopoly Capitalism*, London: Macmillan Press, 1982.

Frow, John: *Time & Commodity Culture—Essays in Cultural Theory and Postmodernity*, Oxford: Clarendon Press, 1997.

Fuller, Matthew. *Behind the Blip—Essays on the Culture of Software*, New York: Autonomedia, 2003.

Gaines, Jane. *Contested Culture—The Image, the Voice, and the Law*, Chapell Hill: The University of North Carolina Press, 1991.

Galbraith, John. *The Affluent society*, London: Hamilton, 1969.

Galloway, Alexander. *Protocol—How Control Exists After Decentralization*, Cambridge Mass.: MIT Press, 2004.

Garnham, Nicholas. *Capitalism and Communication*, London: Sage Publications, 1990.

ed Gay, Joshua. Free Software, Free Society: Selected Essays of Richard M. Stallman, Boston: GNU Press, 2002.

Gervers, Veronika. *Studies in Textile History—In Memory of Harold B. Burnham*, Toronto: Alger Press, 1977.

Gershenfeld, Neil. *FAB—The Coming Revolution on Your Desktop—From Personal Computers to Personal Fabrication*, New York: Basic Books, 2005.

Giddens, Anthony. *A Contemporary Critique of Historical Materialism*, London: Macmillan Press ltd, 1995.

Gillmore, Dan. *We the Media—Grassroots Journalism—By the People, For the People*, Cebastopol C.A.; O'Reilly, 2006.

Goldstein, Paul. *Copyright's Highway—The Law and Lore of Copyright from Gutenberg to the Celestial Jukebox*, New Yrok: Hill and Wang, 1994.

ed. Gordon, Wendy, and Richard Watt. *The Economics of Copyright—Developments in Research and Analysis*, Northampton, Mass.: Elgar, 2003.

Gouldner, Alvin. *The Two Marxism: Contradictions and Anomalies in the Development of Theory*, London: Macmillan, 1980.

Gorz, André. *Reclaiming Work—Beyond the Wage Based Society*, Cambridge: Polity Press, 1999.

Grant, Gail. *Understanding Digital Signatures—Establishing Trust over the Internet and Other Networks*, New York: McGraw-Hill, 1998.

Hafner, Katie, and John Markoff. *Cyberpunk—Outlaws and Hackers in the Computer Frontier*, London: Forth Estate, 1991.

Hagen, Ingunn, and Janet Wasko, *Consuming Audiences?—Production and Reception in Media Research*, Cresskill NJ: Hampton Press, 2000.

Hakken, David. Cyborgs @ *Cyberspace?—An Ethnographer Looks to the Future*, New York: Routledge, 1999.

ed. Hall, Stuart, and Dorothy Hobson and Andrew Lowe and Paul Willis. *Culture, Media, Language*, London: Routledge, 1996.

ed. Hanhardt, John. *Video Culture—A Critical Investigation*, New York: Virtual Studies Workshop Press, 1986.

Haraway, Donna. *Simians, Cyborgs and Women—The Reinvention of Nature*, London: Free Association Books, 1991.

Hardt, Michael, and Antonio Negri. *Empire*, Cambridge, Mass.: Harvard University Press, 2001.

—— *Multitude—War and Democracy in the Age of Empire*, New York: The Penguin Press, 2004.

Harrison, Bennett. *Lean and Mean—The Changing Landscape of Corporate Power in the Age of Flexibility*, New York: Guilford Press, 1997.

Harvey, David. *The Condition of Postmodernity*, Oxford: Blackwell Publishers, 1997.

—— *Spaces of Capital—Towards a Critical Geography*, Edinburgh: Edinburgh University Press, 2001.

Haug, Wolfgang. *Critique of Commodity Aesthetics: Appearance, Sexuality and Advertising in Capitalist Society*, Cambridge: Polity Press, 1986.

Hayes, Dennis. *Behind the Silicon Curtain—The Seduction of Work in a Lonely Era*, London: Free Association Books, 1989.

Heller, Agnes. *The Theory of Need in Marx*, New York: St. Martin's Publisher, 1976.

Hemmungs, Eva. *No Trespassing—Authorship, Intellectual Property Rights, and the Boundaries of Globalization*, Toronto: University of Toronto Press, 2004.

Himanen, Pekka. *The Hacker Ethic—The Spirit of the Information Age*, London: Secker & Warburg, 2001.

Hippel, Eric, *Democratising Innovation*, Cambridge Mass.: MIT Press, 2005.

Hirsch, Fred. *Social Limits to Growth*, London: Routledge, 1995.

Hobsbawm, Eric. *Bandits*, London: Ebenezer Baylis & Son, 1969.

ed. Hoekman, Bernard, and Michel Kostecki. *The Political Economy of The World Trading System*, Oxford: Oxford University Press, 1996.

Holland, John. *Hidden Order—How Adaptation Builds Complexity*, Reading, Mass.: Addison—Wesley, 1995.

Holloway, John. Change the World Without Taking Power, London: Pluto Press, 2005.

Horkheimer, Max, and Theodor Adorno. *Dialectic of Enlightenment*, London: Verso, 1997.

ed. Hugenholtz, Bernt. *Copyright and Electronic Commerce—Legal Aspects of Electronic Copyright Management*, London: Kluwer Law International Ltd., 2000.

Huizinga, Johan. *Homo Ludens—A Study of the Play Element in Culture*, Boston: Beacon Press, 1955.

Hyde, Lewis. *The Gift—Imagination and the Erotic Life of Property*, New York: Random House, 1983.

Illich, Ivan. *Tools for Conviviality*, London: Calder & Boyars ltd, 1973.

——— *The Right to Useful Unemployment and its Professional Enemies*, Ontario: Marion Boyars, 1978.

ed. Jain, Anil, and Ruud Bolle and Sarath Pankanti. *Biometrics—Personal Identification in Networked Society*, Boston, Mass.: Kluwer Academic Publishers, 1999.

James, Cyril. *State Capitalism & World Revolution*, Chicago: Charles H. Kerr Publishing Company, 1986.

Jameson, Frederic, *Postmodernism, or, the Cultural Logic of Late Capitalism*, London, Verso, 1991.

Jay Martin. *Marxism and Totality: the Adventures of a Concept from Lukács to Habermas*, Cambridge: Polity Press, 1984.

Jenkins, Henry. *Textual Poachers—Television Fans & Participatory Culture*, New York; Routledge, 1992.

Jessop, Bob. *The Future of the Capitalist State*, Cambridge: Polity Press, 2002.

Jhally, Sut. *The Codes of Advertising: Fetishism and the Political Economy of Meaning in the Consumer Society*, London: Frances Printer, 1987.

ed. Johnson, Benjamin, and Patrick Kavanagh and Kevin Mattson. *Steal this University—The Rise of the Corporate University and the Academic Labor Movement*, New York: Routledge, 2003.

Jordan, Tim. *Activism!—Direct Action, Hacktivism and the Future of Society*, London, Reaktion Books, 2002.

Jordan, Tim, and Paul Taylor. *Hacktivism and Cyberwars—Rebels With a Cause?*, New York: Routledge, 2004.

ed. Kabel, Jan, and Gerard Mom. *Intellectual Property and Information Law*, Hague: Kluwer Law International, 1998.

ed. Kahin, Brian, and Hal Varian. *Internet Publishing and Beyond* Cambridge, Mass.: MIT Press, 2000.

Katz, Claudio. *From Feudalism to Capitalism—Marxian Theories of Class Struggle and Social Change*, New York: Greenwood Press, 1989.

Kellner, Douglas. *Jean Baudrillard—From Marxism to Postmodernism and Beyond*, Cambridge: Polity Press, 1989.

Klemens, Ben. *Ma+h You Can't Use—Patents, Copyright, and Software*, Washington, D.C.: Brookings Institution Press, 2006.

Kline, Stephen, and Nick Dyer-Witheford and Greig De Peuter. *Digital Play—The Interaction of Technology, Culture, and Marketing*, London: McGill-Queen's University Press, 2003.

Kloppenburg, Jack. *First the Seed—The Political Economy of Plant Biotechnology*, 1492–2000, Cambridge: Cambridge University Press, 1988.

Kraft, Philip. *Programmers and Managers—The Routinization of Computer Programming in the United States*, New York: Springer-Verlag, 1977.

Kroker, Arthur, and Michael Weinstein. *Data Trash—The Theory of the Virtual Class*, Montreal: C Theory Books, 2001.

Kropotkin, Peter. *Fields, Factories and Workshops Tomorrow*, London: Freedom Press, 1985.

Laclau, Ernesto, and Chantal Mouffe. *Hegemony and Socialist Strategy: Towards a Radical Democratic Politics*, London: Verso, 1985.

Lash, Scott, and John Urry. *Economies of Signs & Space*, London: Sage Publications, 1994.

Lee, Martyn. *Consumer Culture Reborn—The Cultural Politics of Consumption*, London: Routledge, 1993.

Lehr, William, and Lorenzo Pupillo. *Cyber Policy and Economics in an Internet Age*, Cambridge MA.: Kluwer Academic Publishers. 2003.

Lessig, Lawrence. *Code and Other Laws of Cyberspace*, New York: Basic Books, 1999.
——— *The Future of Ideas—The Fate of Commons in a Connected World*, New York: Random House, 2001.
Lévi-Strauss, Claude, *The Elementary Structures of Kinship*, Boston: Beacon Press, 1969.
Levy, Steven. *Hackers—Heroes of the Computer Revolution*, New York: Delta, 1994.
Liu, Alan. *The Laws of Cool—Knowledge Work and the Culture of Information*, Chicago: The University of Chicago Press, 2004.
Lovell, Terry. *Pictures of Reality—Aesthetics, Politics, Pleasure*, London: British Film Institute, 1980.
Lukács, George. *Goethe and His Age*, London: Merlin, 1968.
——— *History and Class Consciousness*, Cambridge, Mass.: MIT Press, 2000.
ed. Lunenfeld, Peter. *The Digital Dialectic—New Essays on New Media*, Cambridge, Mass: MIT Press, 1999.
Lury, Celia. *Cultural Rights—Technology, Legality and Personality*, London: Routledge, 1993.
Lyon, David. *The Electronic Eye—the Rise of the Surveillance Society*, Oxford: Polity Press, 1994.
Machlup, Fritz. *Knowledge: Its Creation, Distribution and Economic Significance*, Princeton: Princeton University Press, 1984.
ed. MacKenzie, Donald, and Judy Wajcman, *The Social Shaping of Technology*, 2nd edition, Philadelphia, Pa: Open University Press, 1999.
MacLeod, Christine. *Inventing the Industrial Revolution—The English Patent System, 1660–1800*, Cambridge: Cambridge University Press, 1988.
ed. Makdisi, Saree, and Cesare Casarino and Rebecca Karl. *Marxism Beyond Marxism*, London: Routledge, 1996.
Makeen, Fouad. *Copyright in a Global Information Society, The Scope of Copyright Protection under International, US, UK and French Law*, Hague: Kluwer Law International, 2000.
Mallet, Serge. *The New Working Class*, Nottingham UK: Spokesman, 1975.
Mandel, Ernest. *Late Capitalism*, London: Thetford Press limited, 1978.
Marchand, Marie. *A French Success Story: The Minitel Saga*, Paris: Larousse, 1988.
Marcuse, Herbert. *One-Dimensional Man*, London: Lowe & Brydon Ltd, 1968.
——— *Counterrevolution and Revolt*, Boston: Beacon Press, 1972.
——— *The Aesthetic Dimension: Toward a Critique of Marxist Aesthetics*, Boston: Beacon Press, 1978.
——— *Eros and Civilization—A Philosophical Inquiry into Freud*, London: Routledge, 1998.
Markoff, John. *What the Dormouse Said: How the Sixties Counterculture Shaped the Personal Computer Industry*, New York: Viking, 2005.
Marx, Karl, *Economic and Philosophic Manuscripts of 1844*, USSR: Progress Publishers, 1981.
——— *Capital*, vol.I., London: Penguin Books, 1990.
——— *Capital*, vol.II., London: Penguin Books, 1992.
——— *Capital*, vol.III., London: Penguin Books, 1991.
——— *Grundrisse*, London: Penguin Books, 1993.
——— *The German Ideology*, London: Electric Book Co, 2001.
Maskus, Keith. *Intellectual Property Rights in the Global Economy*, Washington DC: Institute for International Economics, 2000.
Maslow, Abraham. *Motivation and Personality*, New York: Harper & Row Publishers, 1970.
Matthews, Duncan, *Globalising Intellectual Property Rights—The TRIPs Agreement*, London: Routledge, 2002.

Maturana, Humberto, and Francisco Varela. *Autopoiesis and Cognition—The Realization of the Living*, Dordrecht: Reidel, 1980.

Mauss, Marcel. *The Gift: Forms and Functions of Exchange in Archaic Societies*, London: Routledge, 1988.

May, Christopher. *Global Political Economy of Intellectual Property Rights—The New Enclosure?*, London. Routledge, 2000.

ed. McCaughey, Martha, and Michael Ayers. *Cyberactivism—Online Activism in Theory and Practice*, New York: Routledge, 2003.

ed. McChesney, Robert,, and Ellen Meiksins Wood & John Bellamy Foster. *Capitalism and the Information Age—The Political Economy of the Global Communication Revolution*, New York: Monthly Review Press, 1998.

Merrill, Stephen, and Richard Levin and Mark Myers. *A Patent System for the 21st Century*, Washington, D.C.: The National Academic Press, 2004.

Menn, Joseph. *All the Rave—The Rise and Fall of Shawn Fanning's Napster*, New York: Crown Business, 2003.

Mihevc, John. *The Market Tells Them So: The World Bank and Economic Fundamentalism in Africa*, New Jersey: ZED books, 1995.

Mill, John Stuart. *The Principles of Political Economy*, Kitchener, Ont.: Batoche, 2001.

ed. Mitchell, Clyde. *Social Networks in Urban Situations—Analyses of Personal Relationships in Central African Towns*, Manchester UK: Manchester University Press, 1969.

Mokyr, Joel. *The Lever of Riches: Technological Creativity and Economic Progress*, New York Oxford University Press, 1990.

Moody, Glyn. *Rebel Code—Linux and the Open Source Revolution*, London: Penguin Press, 2001.

Moody, Kim. *Workers in a Lean World—Unions in the International Economy*, London: Verso, 1997.

ed. Mosco, Vincent, and Janet Wasko. *The Political Economy of Information*, Madison, Wisc: University of Wisconsin Press, 1988.

Mosco, Vincent. *The Political Economy of Communication*, London: Sage Publications, 1996.

Mueller, Milton. *Ruling the Root—Internet Governance and the Taming of Cyberspace*, Cambridge Mass.: MIT Press, 2002.

Mumford, Lewis. *Technics and Human Development*, New York: HBJ Book, 1967.

——— The Future of Technics and Civilization, London: Freedom Press, 1986.

ed. Murphy, Timothy, and Abdul-Karim Mustapha. *The Philosophy of Antonio Negri—Resistance in Practice*, London: Pluto Press, 2005.

ed. Munzer, Stephen. *New Essays in Legal and Political Economy of Property*, Cambridge: Cambridge University Press, 2001.

ed Naples,.Nancy. *Community Activism and Feminist Politics—Organizing Across Race, Class, and Gender*, New York: Routledge, 1998.

National Research Council. *Computer Chips and Paper Clips—Technology and Women's Employment*, Washington: National Academy Press, 1987.

———. *Bits of Power: Issues in Global Access to Scientific Data*, Washington: National Academy Press, 1997.

———. *Digital Dilemma—Intellectual Property in the Information Age*, Washington DC: National Academy Press, 2000.

Naughton, John. *A Brief History of the Future: the Origins of the Internet*, London: Phoenix, 2000.

Negri, Antonio. *Revolution Retrieved—Writings on Marx, Keynes, Capitalist Crisis and New Social Subjects (1967–83)*, London: Red Notes, 1988.

———— *Marx Beyond Marx—Lessons in the Grundrisse*, New York, Autonomedia, 1991.

———— *Insurgencies—Constituent Power and the Modern State*, Minneapolis: University of Minnesota, 1999.

Nelkin, Dorothy. *Science as Intellectual Property*, New York: McMillan Publishing Company, 1984.

Newman, Nathan. *Net loss: Internet prophets, private profits, and the costs to community*, University Park, Pa.: Pennsylvania State University Press, 2002.

Noble, David. *Forces of Production—A Social History of Industrial Automation*, New York: Alfred A Knopf, 1984.

Noble, David. *Digital Diploma Mills: The Automation of Higher Education*, New York: Monthly Review Press, 2001.

Nolff, Markus. *PCT and Global Patent Procurement*, Hague: Kluwer Law International, 2001.

Novec, Alec. *The Economics of Feasible Socialism Revisited*, London: HarperCollins, 1991.

Offe, Claus. *Disorganized Capitalism—Contemporary Transformations of Work and Politics*, Cambridge: Polity Press 1985.

Ohmann, Richard. *Selling Culture—Magazines, Markets, and Class at the Turn of the Century*, New York: Verso, 1996.

Olstrom, Elinor. *Governing the Commons: The Evolution of Institutions for Collective Action*, Cambridge: Cambridge University Press, 1990.

ed. Oram, Andy. *Peer-to-Peer—Harnessing the Benefits of a Disruptive Technology*, Cambridge, Mass.: O'Reilly, 2001.

Pashukanis, Evgeny. *The General Theory of Law and Marxism*, New Brunswick, NJ: Transaction Publishers, 2002.

Patterson, Lyman. *Copyright in Historical Perspective*, Nashville: Vanderbilt University Press, 1968.

Perelman, Michael. *Class Warfare in the Information Age*, New York: St. Martin's Press, 1998.

———— *The Innovation of Capitalism—Classical Political Economy and the Secret History of Primitive Accumulation*, Durham: Duke University Press, 2000.

————, *Steal This Idea—Intellectual Property Rights and the Corporate Confiscations of Creativity*, New York: Palgrave, 2002.

Pertegás, Marta. *Cross-Border Enforcement of Patent Rights*, Oxford: Oxford University Press, 2002.

Plant, Sadie. *Zeros + Ones: Digital Women and the New Technoculture*, London: Fourth Estate, 1998.

Poster, Mark. *Foucault, Marxism and History: Mode of Production versus Mode of Information*, Cambridge: Polity Press, 1984.

———— *The Information Subject*, Amsterdam: G+B Arts International, 2000.

———— *What's the Matter With the Internet?*, Minneapolis: University of Minnesota Press, 2001.

Poulantzas, Nicos. *Classes in Contemporary Capitalism*, London: Verso, 1979.

ed. Rabinow, Paul. *The Foucault Reader*, London: Penguin Books, 1991.

Rand, Ayn. *Capitalism: The Unknown Ideal*, New York: New American Library, 1966.

Rehn, Alf. *Electronic Potlatch—A Study of New Technologies and Primitive Economic Behavior*, Stockholm: KTH, 2001.

Reich, Robert. *The Work of Nations—Preparing Ourselves for 21st-Century Capitalism*, London: Simon & Schuster, 1991.

Rheingold, Howard. *The Virtual Community—Homesteading on the Electronic Frontier*, (revised edition), Cambridge, Mass.: MIT Press, 2000.

230   Bibliography

———— *Smart Mobs—The Next Social Revolution*, Cambridge, Mass. Perseus Publishing, 2003.

Rifkin, Jeremy. *The End of Work: The Decline of the Global Labor Force and the Dawn of the Post-Market Era*, New York: G.P. Putnam's Sons, 1995.

———— *The Age of Access—How the Shift from Ownership to Access is Transforming Capitalism*, London: Penguin Books, 2000.

Robins, Kevin, and Frank Webster. *The Technical Fix—Education, Computers and Industry*, Basingstoke UK: Macmillan, 1989.

Rose, Nicolas. *Governing the soul—The Shaping of the Private Self*, New York: Routledge, 1990.

Ross, Andrew. *Strange Weather—Culture, Science, and Technology in the Age of Limits*, London: Verso, 1991.

———— *No-Collar—The Human Workplace and its Hidden Costs*, Philadelphia: Temple University Press, 2004.

Sahlins, Marshall. *Stone Age Economics*, Chicago: Aldine Publishing Company, 1972.

Sale, Kirkpatrick. *Rebels Against the Future—The Luddites and Their War on the Industrial Revolution—Lessons for the Computer Age*, Reading Mass.: Addison-Wesley Publishing Company, 1995.

Salus, Peter. *A Quarter Century of Unix*, Reading Mass.: Addison-Wesley, 1994.

Sassen, Saskia. *Losing Control?—Sovereignity in an Age of Globalization*, New York: Columbia University Press, 1996.

Schell, Bernadette, and John Dodge. *The Hacking of America—Who's Doing it, Why, and How*, London: Quorum Books, 2002.

Scherer, Frederic. *Industrial Market Structure and Economic Performance*, Chicago: Rand McNally & Co, 1970.

Scheuerman, William. *The Rule of Law Under Siege—Selected Essays of Franz L. Neuman and Otto Kirchheimer*, Berkeley: University of California Press, 1996.

Schumpeter, Joseph. *Capitalism, Socialism, and Democracy*, London: Cox & Wyman Ltd., 1976.

Scitovsky, Tibor. *The Joyless Economy—an Inquiry Into Human Satisfaction and Consumer Dissatisfaction*, Oxford: Oxford University Press, 1977.

Seabrook, Jeremy. *The Leisure Society*, Oxford: Basil Blackwell, 1988.

Sell, Susan. *Private Power, Public Law—The Globalization of Intellectual Property Rights*, Cambridge: Cambridge University Press, 2003.

Sennett, Richard. *The Corrosion of Character*, New York: Norton & Company, 1999.

Shapiro, Carl, and Hal Varian. *Information Rules—A Strategic Guide to the Network Economy*, London: McGraw-Hill, 1998.

Shiller, Dan. *Digital Capitalism: Networking the Global Market System*, London: MIT Press, 1999.

Shiva, Vandana. *Biopiracy: the plunder of nature and knowledge*, Boston: South End Press, 1997.

———— *Stolen Harvest: the Hijacking of the Global Food Supply*, Cambridge: South End Press, 2000.

Shy, Oz. *The Economics of Network Industries*, Cambridge: Cambridge University Press, 2001.

Siegel, Lenny, and John Markoff. *The High Cost of High Tech—The Dark Side of the Chip*, New York: Harper & Row, 1985.

ed. Slater, Phil. *Outlines of a Critique of Technology*, London: Humanities Press, 1980.

Smythe, Dallas. *Dependency Road: Communications, Capitalism, Consciousness, and Canada*, Norwood N.J.:Ablex, 1981.

Sobel, Richard. *White Collar Working Class—From Structure to Politics*, New York: Praeger, 1989.

Sohn-Rethel, Alfred. *Intellectual Labour and Manual Labour—A Critique of Epistemology*, London: MacMillian Press Ltd., 1978.

Spinello, Richard. *Regulating Cyberspace—The Policies and Technologies of Control*, Westport, Conn.: Quorum Books, 2002.

ed. Stamatoudi, Irini, and Paul Torremans. *Perspectives on Intellectual Property—Copyright in the New Digital Environment*, London: Sweet & Maxwell, 2000.

ed. Staw, Barry, and Larry. Cummings. *Research in Organizational Behavior—An Annual Series of Analytical Essays and Critical Reviews*, London: Jai Press, 1990.

Stefik, Mark. *Internet Dreams: Archetypes, Myths and Metaophores*, London: MIT Press, 1996.

—— *The Internet Edge—Social, Legal, and Technological Challenges for a Networked World*, Cambridge Mass.: MIT Press, 1999.

Sterling, Bruce. *The Hacker Crackdown—Law and Disorder on the Electronic Frontier*, London: Penguin, 1994.

ed. Sussman, Gerald, and John Lent. Global Productions—Labour in the Making of the 'Information Society', Cresskill NJ: Hampton Press, 1998.

Tapscott, Don, and David Ticoll, and Alex Lowy. *Digital Capitalism—Harnessing the Power of Business Webs*, London, Nicholas Brealey Publishing, 2001.

Taylor, Paul. *Hackers—Crime in the Digital Sublime*, London: Routledge, 1999

Terranova, Tiziana. *Network Culture: Politics for the Information Age*, London: Pluto Press, 2004.

Thurow, Lester. *The Future of Capitalism*, London: Nicholas Brealey Publishing Limited, 1996.

Toffler, Alvin. *The Third Wave*, New York: Bantam Books, 1981.

Torvalds, Linus, and David Diamond. *Just For Fun—The Story of an Accidental Revolutionary*, New York: HarperCollins Publisher, 2001.

Touraine, Alain. *Return of the Actor—Social Theory in Postindustrial Society*, Minneapolis: University of Minnesota Press, 1988.

ed. Trescott, Martha, *Dynamos and Virgins Revisited: Women and Technological Change in History*, London: The Scarecrow Press, 1979.

Vaidhyanathan, Siva. *Copyrights and Copywrongs—The Rise of Intellectual Property and How It Threatens Creativity*, New York: New York University Press, 2001.

Vaneigem, Raoul. *The Revolution of Everyday Life*, London: Left bank books, 1983.

Veblen, Thorstein. *The Theory of the Leisure Class*, London: Compton Printing, 1970.

ed. Virno, Paolo, and Michael Hardt. *Radical Thought in Italy*, Minneapolis: University of Minnesota Press, 1996.

Virno, Paolo. *A Grammar of the Multitude—For an Analysis of Contemporary Forms of Life*, New York: Semiotext, 2004.

Volosinov, Valentin. *Marxism and the Philosophy of Language*, New York: Seminar Press, 1973.

Wallace, James. *Overdrive—Bill Gates and the Race to Control Cyberspace*, New York: John Wiley & Sons, 1997.

Wark, McKenzie. *A Hacker Manifesto*, Cambridge Mass.: Harvard University Press, 2004.

Watt, Richard. *Copyright and Economic Theory—Friends or Foes*, Northampton MA: Edward Elgar Publishing, 2000

Watts, Duncan. *Six Degrees—The Science of a Connected Age*, New York: W.W. Norton & Company, 2003.

Wayner, Peter. *Free for All—How Linux and the Free Software Movement Undercut the High-Tech Titans*, New York: HarperBusiness, 2000.

Webster, Frank. *Theories of the Information Society*, 2nd edition, New York: Routledge, 2002.

ed. Webster, Frank, and Basil Dimitriou. *Manuel Castells—From the Informational City to the Information Age*, London: Sage, 2004.

ed. Wilkinson, Elizabeth, and L. Willoughby. *On the Aesthetic Education of Man—In a Series of Letters/Friedrich Schiller*, Oxford: Clarendon Press, 1982.

ed. Willcocks, Leslie, and Stephanie Lester. *Beyond the IT Productivity Paradox*, Chichester: Wiley, 1999.

Williams, Raymond. *Problems in Materialism and Culture*, London: Verso, 1980.

——— *Towards 2000*, London: Chatto & Windus, 1983.

ed. Williamson, Oliver, and Sidney Winter. *The Nature of the Firm: Origins, Evolution, and Development*: New York: Oxford University Press, 1993.

Winner, Langdon. *The Whale and the Reactor—A Search for Limits in an Age of High Technology*, Chicago: The University of Chicago Press, 1986.

Wolf, Naomi. *The Beauty Myth—How Images of Beauty Are Used Against Women*, London: Vintage, 1991.

Wolpert, Samuel. *Economics of Information*, New York: Van Nostrand Reinhold Company, 1986.

ed. Wood, Stephen. *The Degradation of Work?—Skill, Deskilling and the Labour Process*, London: Hutchinson, 1982.

ed. Woodmansee, Martha, and Peter Jaszi. *The Construction of Authorship—Textual Appropriation in Law and Literature*, London: Duke University Press, 1994.

Wright, Steve. *Storming Heaven—Class Composition and Struggle in Italian Autonomist Marxism*, London: Pluto Press, 2002.

Young, Robert, and Wendy Rohm. *Under the Radar—How Red Hat Changed the Software Business and Took Microsoft by Surprise*, Scottsdale, AZ: Coriolis, 1999.

ed. Zimbalist, Abrew. *Case Studies on the Labor Process*, New York: Monthly Review Press, 1979.

Zizek, Slavoj. *Organs Without Bodies—On Deleuze and Consequences*, New York: Routledge, 2004.

JOURNALS

Allen, Robert. "Collective invention." *Journal of Economic Behavior and Organization* (March 1983).

Aoki, Ketih. "Neocolonialism, Anticommons Property, and Biopiracy in the (Not-So-Brave) New World Order of International Intellectual Property Protection." *Indiana Journal of Global Legal Studies* 11 (1998).

Bakos, Yannis, and Erik Brynjolfsson, and Douglas Lichtman. "Shared Information Goods", *Journal of Law and Economics* (April 1999).

Barbrook, Richard. "The High-Tech Gift Economy." *First Monday*, vol.3, no.12 (December 1998).

Barry, David. "The Contestation of Code—A Preliminary Investigation into the Discourse of the Free/Libre and Open Source Movements." *Critical Discourse Studies* (April 2004).

Bassiouni, Cherif. "Universal Jurisdiction for International Crimes: Historical Perspectives and Contemporary Practice." *Virginia Journal of International Law*, vol.42, no.8 (2001).

Benkler, Yochai. "Coase's Penguin, or, Linux and The Nature of the Firm." *The Yale Law Journal*, vol.112, no.3, (December 2002).

Bettig, Roland. "The Enclosure of Cyberspace." *Critical Studies in Mass Communication* 14 (1997).

Bowing, Finn. "From the Mass Worker to the Multitude: A Theoretical Contextualisation of Hardt and Negri's Empire". *Capital & Class* 83 (2004).

Böhme, Gernot. "Technical Gadgetry: Technological Development in the Aesthetic Economy." *Thesis Eleven* 86, (August 2006).

Camara, Gilberto. "Open Source Software Production: Facts & Fiction." *Mute*, no 27, (2004).

Caruso, Denise. "The Legacy of Microsoft's Trial." *The New York Times*, (December 6, 1999).

Callinicos, Alex. "Sympathy for the Devil? John Holloway's Mephistophellan Marxism" Capital & Class 85 (spring 2005).

Chiapello, Eve. "Evolution and Co-optation: The 'Artist Critique' of Management and Capitalism." *Third Text*, vol.18, no.6 (2004).

Cohen, Amanda. "Surveying the Microsoft Antitrust Universe." *Berkeley Technology Law Journal* (2004).

Coombe, Rosemary. "Author/izing the Celebrity: Publicity Rights, Postmodern Politics, and Unauthorized Genders." *Cardozo Arts & Entertainment Law Journal*, no.10 (1992).

Dunford, Richard. "The Suppression of Technology." *Administrative Science Quarterly* vol.32, (1987).

Dibbell, Julian. "We Pledge Allegiance to the Penguin" Wired (November 2004).

Eaton-Salners, Alex. "DVD Copy Control Association v. Bunner: Freedom of Speech and Trade Secrets." *Berkeley Technology Law Journal* (2004).

Eisenberg, Rebecca. "Genes Patents and Product Development." *Science*, (August 1992).

Eisenberg, Rebecca. "Intellectual Property at the Public-Private Divide: The Case of Large-Scale cDNA, Sequencing", *University of Chicago Law School Roundtable* (1996).

Frow, John, "Information as a Gift Commodity." *New Left Review* 219 (September/October 1996).

Ghosh, Rishab, and Ruediger Glott and Bernhard Krieger and Gregorio Robles. "Free/Libre and Open Source Software: Survey and Study part IV." EU policy document (June 2002).

Ghosh, Rishab, and Vipul Prakash. *"The Orbiten Free Software Survey." First Monday* vol.5 no.7 (July 2000).

Gibson, Marcus, "Can Software Replace Hardware." *Ericsson Connexion* (June 1999).

Goettsch, Kerry. "SCO Group v. IBM: The Future of Open-Source Software." *University of Illinois Journal of Law, Technology & Policy* (fall 2003).

Goodman, Ellen. "Spectrum Rights in the Telecosm to Come." *San Diego Law Review* (February/March 2004).

Goux, Jean-Joseph and Kathryn Ascheim and Rhonda Garelick, "General Economics and Postmodern Capitalism" Yale French Studies 78 (1990).

Hardin, Garrett. "The Tragedy of the Commons." *Science*, (December 1968).

Hearn, Francis. "Toward a Critical Theory of Play." *Telos*, 30 (winter 1976–1977).

Heffran, Ira. "Copyleft: Licensing Collaborative Works in the Digital Age." *Stanford Law Review* (July 1997)

Heller, Michael. "The Tragedy of Anticommons: Property in the Transition from Marx to Markets." *Harvard Law Review* 61 (1998).

Hesse, Carla. "Enlightenment Epistemology and the Laws of Authorship in Revolutionary France 1777–1793." *Representations* 30 (1990).

Hobsbawm, Eric. "The Machine Breakers." *Past and Present*.1 (February 1952).

Jaszi, Peter. "On the Author Effect: Contemporary Copyright and Collective Creativity." *Cardozo Arts & Entertainment Law Journal* 10 (1992).

Joerges, Bernward. "Do Politics have Artefacts?" *Social Studies of Science*, vol.29, no. 3 (1999).

Krim, Jonathan. "Open-Source Fight Flares At Pentagon—Microsoft Lobbies Hard Against Free Software." *Washington Post*, (Thursday, May 23, 2002)

Kunstadt, Robert, and Scott Kieff and Robert Kramer. "Are Sports Moves Next in IP Law?" *National Law Journal*, (May 20, 1996).

Lawton, Graham. "The Great Giveaway", *New Scientist* 2328 (February 2002).

Lemley, Mark. "The Law and Economics of Internet Norms." *Chicago-Kent Law Review* (1998).

Liebowitz, Stan. "Copying and Indirect Appropriability: Photocopying of Journals." *Journal of Political Economy* 93 (1985).

Malone, Thomas, and Robert Laubacher. "The Dawn of the E-Lance Economy." *Harvard Business Review*, (September 1, 1998).

Marcuse, Herbert. "On the Philosophical Foundation of the Concept of Labor in Economics." *Telos* 16 (summer 1973).

May, Christopher. "The information Society as Mega-Machine—The Continuing Relevance of Lewis Mumford." *Information, Communication & Society*, vol.3 no.2 (2000).

McJohn, Stephen "The Paradoxes of Free Software" George Mason Law Review (fall 2000).

Merges, Robert. "Contracting Into Liability Rules: Intellectual Property Rights and Collective Rights Organizations." *California Law Review* (October 1996).

Meurer, Michael. "Too Many Markets or too Few? Copyright Policy Towards Shared Works." *Southern California Law Review* (July 2004).

Miles, Stephanie and Stephen Shankland "PIII debuts amid controversy". CNETNews. com (February 26, 1999).

Moglen, Eben. "Anarchism Triumphant: Free Software and the Death of Copyright." *First Monday* vol.4, no.8 (August 1999).

Nafus, Dawn, and James Leach, and Bernhard Krieger. "Free/Libre/Open Source Software: Policy Support", EU policy document, Cambridge, UK (March 2006).

Nuvolari, Alessandro. "Collective Invention during the British Industrial Revolution: The Case of the Cornish Pumping Engine." *Cambridge Journal of Economics* vol.28, no.3 (2004).

Perelman, Michael. "The Political Economy of Intellectual Property", *Monthly Review* (January 2003).

Ravicher, Daniel. "Facilitating Collaborative Software Development: The Enforceability of Mass-Market Public Software Licenses." *Virginia Journal of Law & Technology* (fall 2000).

Raymond, Eric. "The Cathedral and the Bazaar." *First Monday* vol.3, no.3 (March 1998a).

——— "Homesteading the Noosphere." *First Monday* vol.3, no.10 (October 1998b).

Samuelson, Pamela. "Regulation of Technologies to Protect Copyrighted Works." *Communication of the ATM* 39 (1996).

Sassen, Sakia. "The Internet and the Sovereign State: the Role and Impact of Cyberspace on National and Global Governance", *Indiana Journal of Global Legal Studies* 5 (1998).

Sayer, Andrew. "Postfordism in Question." *International Journal of Urban and Regional Research* 35 (1989).

Scott, Brendan. "Copyright in a Frictionless World: Toward a Rhetoric of Responsibility." *First Monday* vol.6, no.9 (September 2001).

Scott, Jason. *BBS the Documentary*, (2004).

Shershow, Scott Cutler "Of Sinking: Marxism and the 'General' Economy". Critical Inquiry vol 27 no 3 (spring 2001).

Stallabrass, Julian. "Empowering Technology: The Exploration of Cyberspace." *New Left Review* 211, (May/June 1995).

Stephen, McJohn. "The Paradoxes of Free Software." *George Mason Law Review* (fall 2000).

Strahilevitz, Jacob. "Charismatic Code, Social Norms, and the Emergence of Cooperation on the File-Swapping Networks." *Virginia Law Review* vol.89, no.3 (May 2003).

Terranova, Tiziana. "Free Labour: Producing Culture for the Digital Economy." *Social Texts* vol.18, no.2 (2000).

Sullivan, Andrew. "Counter Culture: Dot-Communist Manifesto." New York Times (Sunday 11, June 2000).

Thompson, Edward. "Patrician Society, Plebeian Culture." *Journal of Social History* vol.7, no.4 (summer 1974).

Travis, Hannibal. "Pirates of the Information Infrastructure: Blackstonian Copyright and the First Amendment." *Berkeley Technology Law Journal* vol.15, no.2 (spring 2000).

Winner, Langdon. "Do Artifacts Have Politics?" *Daedalus*, vol.109, no.1 (winter 1980).

Index